The
CORPSE
CAME BACK!

Secrets of that forgotten world AFTER the great disaster

Book 3 of a trilogy

Jonathan Gray

TEACH Services, Inc.
www.TEACHServices.com

World rights reserved. This book or any portion thereof may not be copied or reproduced in any form or manner whatever, except as provided by law, without the written permission of the publisher, except by a reviewer who may quote brief passages in a review.

The author assumes full responsibility for the accuracy of all facts and quotations as cited in this book. The opinions expressed in this book are the author's personal views and interpretation of the Bible and do not necessarily reflect those of TEACH Services, Inc.

Copyright © 2005 Jonathan Gray, All rights reserved
Copyright © 2008 TEACH Services, Inc.
ISBN-13: 978-1-57258-555-3
Library of Congress Control Number: 2008926066

Illustration Credits

If I failed to credit any illustrations reproduced in this book, I offer my apologies. Any sources omitted will be appropriately acknowledged in all future editions of this book.

Published by
TEACH Services, Inc.
www.TEACHServices.com

About the author

Jonathan Gray has travelled the world to gather data on ancient mysteries. A serious student of pre-history, he has investigated numerous archaeological sites, and has also penetrated some largely un-explored areas, including parts of the Amazon headwaters.
Between lecturing worldwide, the author has hosted newspaper columns and contributed to various magazines.

Other books by Jonathan Gray

Dead Men's Secrets
Sting of the Scorpion
The Ark Conspiracy
The Killing of Paradise Planet
Surprise Witness
Curse of the Hatana Gods
64 Secrets Ahead of Us
Bizarre Origin of Egypt's Ancient Gods
The Lost World of Giants
Discoveries: Questions Answered
Sinai's Exciting Secrets
Ark of the Covenant
The Discovery That's Toppling Evolution
UFO Aliens: The Deadly Secret
Jesus Christ: Fact or Fake?
The Da Vinci Fraud

CONTENTS

		Page
	PROLOGUE	7
1	Survival vessel lands – NERVOUS WAIT	9
2	The Flood recedes (a) – WHAT HAPPENED TO THE WATER?	20
3	The Flood recedes (b) – HURRICANE	34
4	Ararat: a new start – MOUNTAINS OF SURPRISE	45
5	Yes, it begins in Turkey – A SHOCKING DISCOVERY	56
6	Plant and animal distribution – THE MARSUPIAL MYSTERY	63
7	From Ararat: the first migration (a) – INTO THE UNKNOWN	71
8	From Ararat: the first migration (b) – ONE GLOBAL LANGUAGE	76
9	From Ararat: the first migration (c) – PYRAMID AND STONEHENGE MYSTERIES SOLVED	84
10	From Babel: the second migration (a) – THE NIMROD CONSPIRACY	92
11	From Babel: the second migration (b) – LANGUAGES AND THE DISPERSION	104
12	From Babel: the second migration (c) – THE MIGRATION BEGINS	114
13	From Babel: the second migration (d) – THE MAJOR CIVILISATIONS AFTER BABEL	125
14	From Babel: the second migration (e) – SKYSCRAPER TO STONE AGE	135
15	Racial history foretold – AN ASTONISHING PROPHECY COMES TRUE	144
16	Scattered races remember their origins – ROYAL FAMILIES TRACE BACK TO NOAH'S SON	149

		Page
17	The Ice Age – SHIVER ALL SUMMER	161
18	After-shocks continue (a) – HUMAN LIFE SPAN SLASHED	173
19	After-shocks continue (b) – THE MUMMY ROSE FROM THE SEA	183
20	The Flood "puddles" left behind – TRAPPED!	195
21	City folk become savages – SECRETS OF A LOST CITY	214
22	The nature "clocks" say 4,000 years– THE LOST SQUADRON	226
23	The human "clocks" say 4,000 years– PUBLISH – IF YOU DARE	236
24	Why the sea level is rising – A DEADLY PRACTICAL JOKE	245
25	Prophecies for Today WHAT'S COMING	264

EPILOGUE

SUMMARY

NOTES

INDEX

PROLOGUE

Forgotten World. That was a sub-title for *The Killing of Paradise Planet*, which is Book One of this series. An apt enough term for that Mother Civilisation that vanished so completely, we thought it never existed.

We saw stunning evidence of a once-global paradise, with a temperature-controlled climate, idyllic landscape and long-lived human giants... but a super culture ready to wipe itself out. The world BEFORE the Great Flood of 2345 BC.

In Book Two of this series, *Surprise Witness*, we saw the cosmic calamity that intervened, causing the world to wobble and ripping the crust of the earth to shreds. A Great Flood swept the whole planet. This cataclysm wiped the Mother Civilisation from the face of the earth. Not only were the antediluvian people buried, but their technological achievements were destroyed, including all forms of machinery and construction.

This is very relevant to us in this 21st century. To know where we're going, we have to know where we came from. What happens next is umbilically attached to where we've been.

The skeptic may shout himself hoarse. But this event happened. We saw evidence that is, one may boldly assert, more substantial than for any other event in history.

Now, in *The Corpse Came Back*! you will experience the action-packed, fascinating story of the settling down of the earth AFTER the Flood, and its effect upon human history.

Cities swallowed by the sea; the rapid birth of the Grand Canyon; the seaport that climbed a mountain range; the mummy that came up with a volcano; bells that ring under the sea... these are missing pieces of a puzzle that shatter our preconceptions of the history of man.

We shall see events unfolding in a pattern, and finally predictions coming true in an almost uncanny manner.

The Corpse Came Back! begins with the handful of refugees on board the survival vessel – the ship of Noah – and their journey into the unknown, new world.

Let's take a peek at this important little group...

1

Survival vessel lands -
NERVOUS WAIT

Nobody slept that night. Inside the vessel, four couples sat listening. Outside, the wind shrieked. Rain crashed. A mass hysteria had seized the once mocking crowd. Frantic banging. Concerted pushing on the door... "Please, oh please! Let us in!"

Sleep? How could they? Out there in the mob were neighbours, relatives...

Day 11: The storm continued unabated. The water level was rising, now, lifting that massive vessel from its protective earth ramparts. Soon, when the waters were in sufficient abundance that the ship could safely pass over the submerged landscape, it would be time to cut the cables.

The terror outside was mounting. The stampede to the heights was on. Those inside shuddered at the sound.

Day 16: Outside, all hell was raging. It was hard for those inside not to be affected by the screams of the drowning. And to think there was still a year ahead of them – each of those on board locked in with seven other people and thousands of animals.

Four married couples were set to go through this ordeal – the senior pair to manage and the other three to multiply when it was all over. They were to have an absolutely crucial place in human history. From their descendants all the nations of the earth would spring.

I think of that 'nobody' called Mrs Noah. (Her name was Naamah, says the Book of Jasher.) She must have been one of the greatest women who ever lived. She impacted the world's history forever. She was married to the man who was used to save the world's population from extinction. It is said that behind every great man is a wonderful woman. But she was more. Ultimately, she's your mother and mine.

For 40 days the Flood waters rose, covering the highest mountains. For a further 110 days, the tempest continued unabated.

"And the ark went upon the face of the waters."[1]
Violent land movements raged around the vessel. Sound travels through water faster than through air. The wild and incessant thundering must have been heard through the hull of the Ark. But inside this stronghold existed another world all its own. The Ark floundered on swirling currents, providing shelter for eight people and representative animal life.

ONBOARD FACILITIES

There are clues that the Ark was equipped with ingenious facilities for survival and perhaps comfort as well.

The Flood survivors preserved with them on board sufficient knowledge of the pre-Flood world, to give a rapid start to the new civilisations that would spring up "out of nowhere" soon after the Flood. Such cultures as Sumeria, Egypt and the Indus Valley would spring into existence fully developed, with no apparent transition from a primitive state, but with a fantastic ready-made high civilisation.[2]

Such almost "instant" civilisations are inexplicable, unless they inherited their culture basically from a prior civilisation - from the world that was wiped out in the Great Flood.

Thus in ancient ruins today we find evidence of quality carpets, metallic wallpaper, flush toilets, sewage, hot and cold water on tap, air conditioning, electricity, shipboard computers, and so on.

A thousand fascinating clues to this lost knowledge are catalogued in my book, *Dead Men's Secrets*.

One may be naturally curious, therefore, concerning the Ark.

It is unthinkable that, during the year-long semi-darkness of the Deluge, the top deck alone was bathed in daylight while the lower decks endured darkness. Ancient traditions assert that a light source powered by some form of electricity did indeed illuminate the Ark.[3]

One can only speculate regarding the supply of internal fresh air. Certainly the manufacture of oxygen was known in the immediate post-Flood era.

A well-preserved ancient document called the *Agastya Samshita*, now in the Prince's Library of Ujjain in India, contains information both on constructing an electric battery and on using this battery to 'split' water into two gases, hydrogen and oxygen.[4]

With such available technology, I see no problem in the provision of water supply, animal feeding chutes, waste disposal, computation of time, storage of records, or recreational facilities, to ensure at least bearable conditions on the long journey into the unknown.

The vessel, if sufficiently preserved and uncovered today, should exhibit a high standard of workmanship, with great intelligence and ingenuity in its construction and detail. Throughout, it should bear traces of the highest type of civilisation.

PRESERVED DOCUMENTS

One can be virtually certain that the voyagers took on board with them a range of scientific and historical information from the vanished world. In ages to come, some of these documents would still be preserved and treasured.

Later, one Assyrian king, Assurbanipal, founder of the great library of Nineveh, would refer to the great "inscriptions of the time before the Flood." He would leave to posterity a statement that he understood these writings and caused them to be translated. He wrote that he "loved to read the writings of the age before the Flood."

From books already old, later Egyptian scribes would continue to copy down information which they admitted was no longer understood by them.

In 1950, during preparations for an Oriental Archaeological Research Expedition to Mount Ararat, information surfaced concerning some ancient records alleged to be in the possession of a Masonic Order.

A Dr. Philip W. Gooch volunteered this tantalising news to Aaron J. Smith, American expedition leader. Gooch claimed that his Order held evidence that "a living witness... covered all the fine details of what went on during the Flood and after the Flood until her death in her 547th year."[5]

According to Gooch, she was the wife of Noah's son Japheth, "a student of Methuselah, under whom she was apprenticed, and who taught her all that had preceded the Flood. She was educated in all the history of the human race up to that time. Her book - she called it her diary...."

Gooch went on to say:

"Many of the problems confronting geologists today can easily be understood after one reads Amoela's diary. At her death, dying in the arms of her youngest son, Javan, her diary was placed in her mummified hands in a crystal quartz case, with tempered gold hinges and clasps, and was discovered by a high-ranking Mason in the latter part of the 19th century. The original and the translation are now in the possession of the Order."

It has been impossible to authenticate this claim, since Dr. Gooch died shortly thereafter, without having revealed the name or chapter of the Masonic Lodge.

THE NERVOUS WAIT

"And when the storm came to an end and terrible waterspouts ceased, I opened the windows and the light smote upon my face; I looked at the sea, tentatively observing, all humanity had turned to mud, and like seaweed the corpses floated.

"I sat down and wept, and the tears fell upon my face."[6]

After 150 days, the drogue (drag) stones suspended from the Ark's hull struck submerged ground. Apparently the waters had begun to recede.

At this point the Ark "came to rest".[7] It stayed in this position for 74 days. From this point Noah could watch the comings and goings of the waters in their tidal swells.

At the end of this time, a small piece of land appeared, the top of a submerged mountain. What excitement that day! The cheerful hope of deliverance was re-sparked.

The receding of the waters continued, exposing more shoreline by the day. It looked rocky and desolate, much as it is now.

Six weeks Noah waited, while more land was appearing. Now he decided to send out a raven. The purpose was to learn whether any other part of the earth were left dry by the water, and whether he might land and disembark safely. But the raven, finding the land still submerged, returned.

Once a week also, a dove was sent out. The second week it came back to him, covered in mud, and bringing a newly-sprouted olive leaf. But on the third occasion, the dove failed to return, a sign that there was at last enough dry land with some vegetal regrowth.

Noah understood the significance of that fresh olive leaf. Since the waters began receding, that leaf would have had as much as four months to sprout from an asexually propagated olive branch buried near the surface, before discovery by the dove.

But caution was required. Were there snags? Other dangers? A few more weeks elapsed...

DANGER POINT

Noah realised he could not moor at this point too much longer. The waters were decreasing. The current of run-off was becoming stronger. Soon the waters would become a raging torrent - no longer a sea but a rushing river, running off the mountains. Unless they acted quickly, they could be dragged over the landscape to the sea and that would be perilous.

Tomorrow would be Noah's birthday.[8] Tomorrow at high water slack, he would commit himself to driving the Ark aground to a safer spot. A day to remember. It would be his birthday and the time to begin a new world.

Next morning, he gave the order to cut the lines. The drogue stones that had anchored the Ark at her place of rest were now left behind on the submerged landscape, where they can still be found today.

GROUNDED

The Ark moved forward in the face of a cold wind, southeastward on the incoming current. They finally grounded high up in a semi-circle of small hills. These would protect the vessel from the tidal waves that rushed back and forth as the Flood subsided.

Noah looked out, "... and behold, the face of the ground was dry!"[9]

Noah was still hesitant to disembark. It would take time for the ground to dry at deeper levels and for remnants of vegetation to get re-established as food for the animals, when they should exit the Ark. Another couple of months, he figured.

Meanwhile the passengers waited aboard.

Just 377 days after they entered the survival vessel, the Noah family stepped out. The Flood waters had covered the earth for just over a year.

SUMMARY OF ARK'S LOG BOOK

		Month	Day
Day 1	The Flood begins	2	17
		3	1
Day 40	Maximum water height reached	3	27
		4	1
		5	1
		6	1
		7	1
Day 150	Abatement of water begins	7	17
		8	1
		9	1
Day 224	First land seen	10	1
		11	1
Day 264	Raven sent out	11	11
Day 271	Dove sent out	11	18
Day 278	Dove sent out: olive leaf	11	25
Day 285	Dove sent out: no return	12	2
Day 314	On dry ground	1	1
		2	1
Day 370	Leave the Ark	2	27

Add 7 days at the beginning, during which they embarked.

WHAT THEY SAW

The eight human survivors left their shelter to enter a world of intensely red sunsets and blue and green moons - optical effects from the volcanic dust. Ironic, perhaps. In part, the Deluge began because of violent bloodshed.[10] It ended with blood-red sunsets.

Just months before, the Ark door had closed on a world of almost perfect beauty. Now, as the door slid back, they recoiled from the desolation that met their gaze.

"Their eyes searched for the plains and the hills, the rivers and lakes. The truth was terrible; the destruction was awful."[11]

Stones, ledges and jagged rocks covered the ground. There was virtually no vegetation. Hills had disappeared without trace; plains had given way to broken mountain ranges. Gashed and torn, the surface was desolate. All the luxuriant forests were gone. Green meadows and flowering trees were washed away or buried.

Here and there clumps of growth had begun to re-establish, but the rich antedeluvian world was largely plowed under, out of sight. The soil that remained was leached and relatively infertile. It would take centuries to rebuild enough soil to carpet large areas.

The place was a wreck! And before plant cover would become re-established, erosion of unbelievable magnitude would occur on the planet.

And the climate? The air wasn't just cooler. It was miserable, freezing and wet. Clouds obscured the sky, and drifting very low, hung as a fog. The smoke of the volcanoes caused darkness, not complete, but intense. This condition would prevail for decades, and only very gradually would the dust subside and the water vapours condense.

In this eerie night which reigned over the earth even during the day, the sun, in a sense, no longer existed. But this ruined world was lit up at intervals by frightful conflagrations, revealing the full horror of the situation.

However, all was not bleak. Despite the destruction of the old world, a Divine Artist had reshaped countless scenes of beauty to refresh the new population. Waterfalls, dramatic landscapes, sunken valleys and caves, pinnacles, rainbows and wild sunsets - all these by-products of the Deluge were things of stark beauty.

Creation still hadn't lost its grandeur. Even when torn and twisted, heaved, tossed and stood on end, its beauty still holds us spellbound!

THE PLAN IN THE DELUGE

The destruction was accomplished in such a way as to prepare a more suitable home for a degenerating human race. The first world had provided an environment too rich and bounteous for a fallen humanity. So it was refitted. Riches were hidden away beneath the surface and an impoverished and stubborn soil must now be worked under strenuous climatic conditions. This was more fitting: men could resist evil influences best while earning bread by hard sweat.

Exploration would confirm the change

Years would pass before the full impact of the Deluge became clear. Exploring parties would discover that the tilting of the earth's axis had brought a sudden change in the relation of the earth to the sun, and thereby created climatic zones.

Terrific extremes of heat and cold were a new environmental factor. (Such extremes have probably contributed to the stunted, asymmetrical and "degenerated" appearance of our modern flora and fauna, compared to that found in fossil form.)

Even the new continental areas were vastly different. Twelve months of total geological upset had changed the planet.

Arctic lands, for example, were denuded, the detachable mantle washed away leaving a barren stone surface. This effect, as with many that today are attributed to ice, was caused not by ice but by onrushing water.

RAINBOW

The Noahs wasted no time in constructing an altar to express gratitude for divine protection during the year-long Deluge.

They were aware that for twelve perilous months their tiny speck on a raging global tempest had not been deserted. Throughout this ordeal, "God remembered Noah, and the beasts, and all the cattle that were with him in the ark."[12] To each survivor, the ever-watchful care of a Supreme Being for His creatures in that Ark amid such dangers stood out distinctly.

Now they received assurance that the earth would never again be destroyed with such a Flood.

The same Creator who had communicated the instructions for building the Ark, now gave this promise.

A rainbow arching over the slopes became a beautiful and striking token of this promise.

The rainbow, due to the sun's rays striking water droplets in the sky, was a totally new phenomenon. Before the Deluge, the sky had been filled with invisible water vapour which could not refract and separate the visible light spectrum. But since the Flood, clouds of minute water droplets are able to produce the beautiful rainbow.

Certainly the survivors would have welcomed this sight whenever they saw it from then on.

As the human family thereafter spread out over the earth, the memory of the rainbow as a NEW phenomenon was told and retold.

In Hawaii it was related that the waters destroyed all of mankind except Nu-u, his family and the food, plants and animals in his specially built great canoe. When Nu-u came out upon the land after the water had subsided, Kane the great god left the **rainbow** behind him as a token of his forgiveness.

In far away Lithuania, the story was similar.

Yes, and even in the Americas.

The old Chibchas of Bogota, high up in the mountains of Colombia, have a myth that when Bochicha appeared, to end the Deluge, he was seated on a **rainbow**.

Harold Wilkins reports:

"But what is even more remarkable is the insistence in the Genesis story of the Bible, the Babylonian legend on the Gilgamesh tablets from Nineveh, and in the traditions of very ancient date, current in Peru of the Incas, that, after the Great Catastrophe, something was seen in earth's skies that was not there before: the **Rainbow**!"[13]

In fact, myths "in North, South and Central America all make a great point that **rainbows** were not seen in our skies before the time of the Great Flood."[14]

The old Mayans preserved this memory in the *Book of Chilam Balam of Chumayel*.

EIGHT SURVIVORS

The memory that there had been just eight human survivors would also come to be retained in various parts of the world. Although we noted this in our first book, it will bear repeating.

- *Mexico:* An old myth of the Toltecs says all the world drowned, except 8 men. These escaped in a floating house called "tlapitlipetlocalli". The Toltecs, on their rolls, painted it as a small boat with an awning on top, and 8 heads peering out.
- *Australia (the Aborigines):* A rainbow serpent came down when a great flood was supernaturally sent because of man's wickedness, and told 8 people to climb on board its back so that it could save them from this flood.

- *Hawaii:* When Kane decided to destroy the earth which man's wickedness had spoiled, he allowed Nu-u, the Righteous Man, to escape by building a great canoe with a house on it. He was told to take on board his wife, 6 other people (total 8) and all the animals he wanted, to await the great flood.
- *India:* Manu, the father of the human race, was instructed to build a ship and take in seven others (total 8), plus all the different seeds. The waters reached the mountains.
- *China:* Curiously, the ancient character for "ship" (still printed in Chinese books and papers) is composed of the pictures for "boat" and "8 mouths", suggesting that the first ship was a boat carrying eight persons.[15]

From a study of the Chinese ideographic system of relaying written information, it is clear that there were thought to be eight survivors within both words for the Ark and the Flood itself.

And I am told that the Chinese "lucky" number is 8. (Because 8 people survived in the Ark?)

THE NAME "NOAH"

The name of the Flood survivor crops up in the traditions of widely separated peoples. This is remarkable, when you consider the ultimate language differences between peoples, and the extreme local distortions which developed in Flood legends. Yet the same name survived virtually unchanged in such widely separated places as:
- Hawaii (where he was called Nu-u)
- The Sudan (Nuh)
- The Amazon region (Noa)
- Phrygia (Noe)
- Africa (Noh and Hiagnoh – among the Hottentots)
- India (Ma-nu).
- *China:* The Chinese ancestor Nu-Wah survived the destruction of the world by a flood and accomplished the reconstruction. There followed legendary heroes sometimes referred to as the Three Sovereigns (Noah's three sons?). After these came the Three Dynasties, Hsia, Shang and Chou (held by scholars to initiate the historical period).

- **Venezuela:** In the Sierra Parima between Brazil and Venezuela, there is reported to be a dead city called Ma Noe, signifying "the waters of Noah."
  "The waters of Noah". Now that raises a question. If the water was so high over all the land, and now it's not... then whatever happened to all that water? Where has it gone?
  Would you like to know? Let's find out.

2

The Flood recedes (a) -
WHAT HAPPENED TO THE WATER?

"So what did you find?" asked Rebecca, dishing out the potatoes as she spoke. "Oops, I'll wipe that off your jacket."

"It's still too early," sighed Ham. "Dad and I went down the valley about fourteen miles. The water's dropping quite fast. But it will be a while before we can build and cultivate down there. The tide keeps surging back."

"Anyway," quipped Japheth, "you girls seem quite cozy here inside the Ark. Why ever do you want to move?"

"You're kidding!" laughed Helene. "You guys are out most of the day."

* * * * * * *

Certainly in these bleak weather conditions, the Ark furnished safe living quarters. For a time at least, it must have been used for sheltering the domestic variety of animals, as well.

And even after the four couples moved down the valley to build their first house in the new world, the old Ark probably furnished a ready supply of stored seed and other requirements.

Meanwhile, the planet was gradually shedding its water to lower levels.

And how that occurred is quite interesting. To understand this event, perhaps we should backtrack a little to the Flood year itself...

WATER BEGINS TO RECEDE

All the water that had previously been in the underground basins or in the vapour canopy now lay over the earth's surface.

From the 150th day[1] the waters began to recede, perhaps at a rate of 20 feet per day. This would continue for the best part of a year, before the earth was pronounced "dry".

Throughout this subsidence period, tidal waves continued to sweep back and forth. "And the waters returned from off the earth continually",[2] or, as a literal translation of Genesis would render, "they subsided going and coming."

This tidal action would explain the laying down of successive strata, alternately burying land organisms and aquatic forms of plants and animals, ultimately to fossilise them.

WHERE DID ALL WATER GO?

Genesis implies that some of the water was re-absorbed by the atmosphere: "And God made a wind to pass over the earth, and the waters assuaged."[3]

However, other mighty forces were at work.

Neither the total amount of water, nor the total amount of soil or rock needed to change, just their relative positions.

So where did all the water go?

It is suggested by some scientists who acknowledge the Deluge, that the continents were raised and the ocean beds lowered, to drain off the Flood waters.

Evolutionists also have embraced the idea of land rising and sinking under the sea, in order to build up sediments. They speculate that it happened many times over billions of years, however.

Sounds fine. But there's a problem for both ideas.

Thin sediment on ocean bed

When exploration of the ocean floor became possible, it was found that ocean floor sediments were much thinner than those on the continents. This was not expected.

That's the problem.

You see, if the oceans and continents were of equal age and in permanent positions, the sedimentation rates and distributions should be similar for each.

You can see how this hurts the evolutionist's strata formation theory.

Ocean sediments have not been found comparable to the "older" continental sediment profiles. If continents were uplifted ocean floor, then the sediment profile of the oceans should be comparable to those "older" sediments on land.[4] Not so, however. And that's quite embarrassing.

But back to the Great Flood.

If continents and oceans are fixed and existed during the Flood as they are now, then we also have a problem.

During the Flood, thicker sediments should have been deposited in the ocean basins - because they're lower. But the opposite is true. Flood sediments on the continents average 10,000 feet deep. But there's only a fraction as much on the ocean floor.

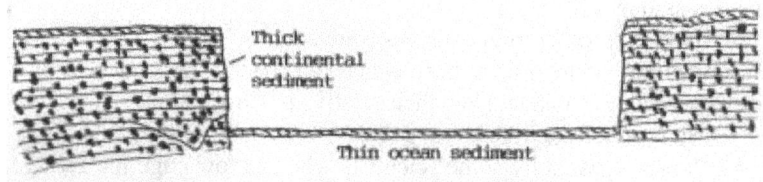

However, there's a solution. If the ocean basins were formed AFTER the major load of continental sediments had been deposited, then the thinner and younger ocean sediments can be explained. I say "younger" ocean sediments, because they match the "younger" top layers of sediments on the continents, but not the lower, "older" continental strata.

Originally no big ocean bed between the continents

On a globe of the earth, take a careful look at the coastlines of Western Africa and Europe, as well as those of South and North America. Notice how the land masses look like a giant jigsaw puzzle that has been pulled apart?

This is more than an interesting idea. Here's why:

1. Fossil bones found on Africa's west coast match the fossil bones found on the east coast of South America.

2. Sedimentary strata also match along the lines of fit.
3. Mountain ranges from one continent match surprisingly well with the mountain ranges on the other.

Map: David W. Unfred

All the continents can be fitted together in this manner - not along their coastlines (which would leave gaps between) but along their coastal shelves.

Around each continent, the continental shelves vary in width out from the shore, but when you put the shelves together, they fit almost perfectly.

Another point. Two geologists, A. Du Toit of South Africa and S. Carey of Australia, saw evidences that indicated a common ice cap had covered portions of South America, Africa, India and Australia.[5] These areas today are separated by thousands of miles of ocean.

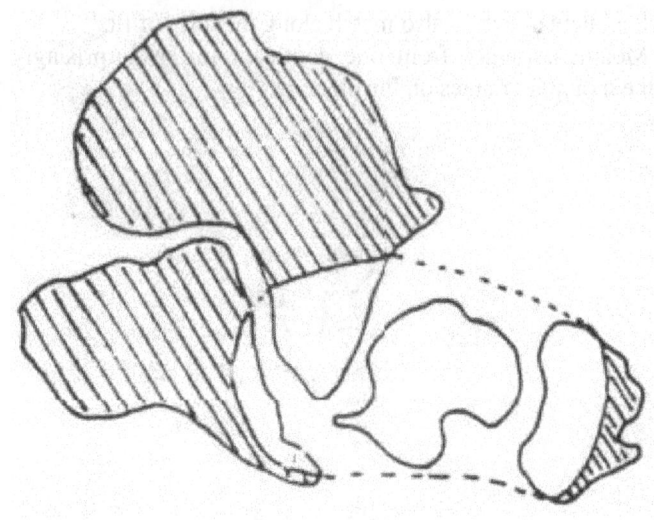

The unshaded and encircled area represents regions of South America, Africa, Antarctica and Australia thought to have been once covered by a common ice sheet. Map: after David W. Unfred

This seems to make sense only if the continents were at one time joined. And if they were once joined, the continents must also have become separated.

CONTINENTAL SPLIT

In 1912, a German meteorologist, Alfred Wegener, made the bold assertion that the continents must have been joined. For fifty years, most scientists rejected the idea.

The reason for rejection most commonly given was that the theory failed to provide an acceptable mechanism to move continents. However, it was also a fact that those in control of the scientific media could not accept challenges to popular and cherished theories on which many academic reputations rested.

So naturally everybody "knew" that continental drift was wrong. Any scientist who was unwise enough to argue for displacement of continents was cold-shouldered by referees and editors and became the butt for snide comments.[6]

Such is the history of "scientific objectivity". The scientific community prejudice and ridicule continued for decades.

But, eventually faced with the need to explain how Antarctica could once have been tropical, the scientific world at large adopted the concept that continents have moved. Evolutionists, of course, say it has taken 200 million years for the continents to drift apart. They speak of slowly moving tectonic plates.

Plate tectonics theory

It is speculated that the earth's crust is composed of fairly rigid plates which move horizontally. They ride on convection currents acting as a conveyor belt. Continental plates "float", carried along by the moving ocean floor, cyclically colliding, joining and separating.

It is assumed that new ocean floor is being extruded up from the mantle through oceanic ridge-rift systems. New ocean floor spreads out from both sides of these underwater ridges and pushes the older crust laterally further away. When it collides with a continental plate, the heavier oceanic crust descends into a trench and dives beneath the continental plate. This process is termed subduction.

Serious doubts concerning tectonic plates

Plate tectonics have attained widespread popularity and, therefore, are taught with varying degrees of certainty as scientific fact. However, more recently, major problems have emerged with the tectonic plate theory. What it predicts fails to reconcile with newly discovered geological data concerning the ocean floor.

a. No evidence of massive subduction

In the African plate "ocean floor spreading zone" there is no trench system available to swallow "older" crust. Neither does geological evidence for massive oceanic subduction exist in the Peru-Chile trench.[7] The Antarctic plate is bounded on all sides by "spreading" zones. Again, according to the theory, an area of oceanic crust no less than the size of the continent would have to be subducted. No sign of such a massive subduction exists. Where the plate boundaries meet, there are no trenches available to "swallow" the older oceanic crust.[8]

Theoretical diagrams of ocean floor spreading and subduction may appear convincing. However, when plate tectonic principles are applied on a global scale, the geologic evidences are lacking. The absence of massive subduction mitigates against continental dispersion based on plate tectonics.[9]

b. **No evidence that friction can do it**
At a scientific symposium in Tasmania, one geophysicist pointed out another problem:
"...we cannot prove that friction between mantle and crust - how else can thermal convection be converted into direction motion? - is sufficient to drive crustal plates, large and small."[10]

c. **Map reconstructions do not fit all areas**
Another problem is this. Geometric patterns of continental fit used by plate tectonists suffer from a major inadequacy: reconstructions are made of relatively small areas without reference to effects on surrounding areas. So other spots (when maps are correctly drawn) are thrown out of alignment.

Did the earth's radius expand?

The failure of plate tectonic models to reconcile theory and geological data has revived interest among some scientists in an expanding earth. The theory is respectable, but not widely publicised.

Pascual Jordan, a Professor of Physics at the University of Hamburg, shows from a vast amount of physical and geological evidence that both the earth and the moon appear to have undergone considerable expansion in the past.

Jordan and other scientists calculate that the earth's radius is about 25 percent bigger today than it was in the past. This means that the earth's surface area has increased by a colossal 56 percent.[11]

Concerning the pattern of global fracture zones, geologist V. Oppenheim states:

"This pattern... would suggest that expansion of the Earth's crust has taken place."[12]

Vast amounts of thermal energy could achieve such expansion. Expansion of the underlying magma could result in the earth's crust literally cracking apart like the shell of an overheated egg.

It is claimed that **extension** and **rifting** are the predominant features of the earth's surface.[13] Might that tell us something?

The question should now be raised: Could continental separation be the result of expansion of the earth's interior?[14]

A motor for such an expansion[15] would be a change in the density of the inner core, a change in the gravitational constant. Expansion does **not** require additional "mass", but a weakening in the electric force within atoms, causing an expansion of individual atoms, and thus of the earth itself.

An expanding earth - whether we like it or not - would solve the problems raised by continental drift.

a. **The problem of 'gaps'**

On correctly projected reconstructions using the earth radius of modern dimensions, small 'gaps' occur between the continental jigsaw bits. These gaps disappear on smaller radius earth projections.[16]

On this point, geologist J. Stocklin, declares:

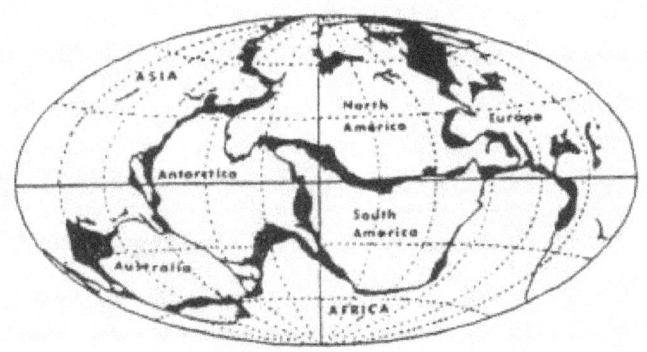

Reduction of the earth's radius by 60 to 70 percent results in an ancient world dominated by land possibly separated by narrow seas. Reconstruction after I. Kirillow, 1958, in Expanding Earth Symposium, 1983, p.22 (David Unfred)

"Palaeomagnetic data for the late Palaeozoic and earliest Mesozoic, if applied to an Earth of present size, require a wide Tethyan oceanic separation between India and Eurasia; if applied to an Earth of smaller size, no such separation is required. The geology of the Himalaya fails to indicate a Tethys Ocean of Paleozoic-earliest Mesozoic age and in this respect supports the theory of Earth expansion."[17]

The October-November, 2000 issue of *Nexus* magazine came out with an article supporting earth expansion.
Geologist James Maxlow produced spherical models of the ancient Earth by progressively removing sea-floor crust parallel to the mid-ocean ridges and re-fitting the crust along each mid-ocean ridge at a reduced Earth radius. At the end of this exercise, "all continents were refitted together, like a spherical jigsaw puzzle, at about 62% of the present Earth radius, or about 3,540 kilometres."[18] He concludes that the original radius was about 3,200 kilometres – roughly 50% the size of the present radius.
Oceans were represented by a network of continental seas.

Outdated scientific opinion

"Acceptance of Earth expansion as a viable tectonic process is currently envisaged by researchers from many countries to be thwarted by major obstacles which supposedly outnumber the evidence in favour," notes the writer.

He points out, however, that "These opinions are based on outdated research carried out during the 1950s to 1970s, well before the advent of modern global tectonics, computer technology, global data-gathering capabilities and multi-media communication. Unfortunately, these same outdated opinions are being carried through to recent literature without proper scientific investigation, regardless of advances made in Earth expansion."

James Maxlow states, however, that "Mathematical studies based on modelling research demonstrate that the Earth is indeed expanding" but that the "mean density of the Earth has remained constant, or near constant, since creation, and, of importance to life on Earth, the surface gravity has been steadily increasing with time. The surface gravity during the dinosaur era, for instance, is calculated to be approximately half the present value, hence dinosaurs were bigger, longer and heavier than they could ever be on Earth today."

He argues that "Readily available geophysical and geological data plotted on each of the models demonstrates that the ancient equator, determined from the ancient pole positions, agrees in principle with plate tectonic locations using palaemagnetic and climatic data. Ancient polar ice-caps, limestone reefs, coal deposits, vegetation patterns, and marine and terrestrial life-forms all coincide with the ancient equator and pole positions throughout Earth history. This coincidence is an impossibility on an Earth of constant radius.

"This modern geological and geophysical data can now be used to accurately quantify Earth expansion, making the evidence for expansion very favourable."

Ancient polar regions

Ancient magnetic poles, when plotted on expanding Earth models, cluster as diametrically opposed north and south poles. These pole locations show that the ancient North Pole was located in Mongolia to northern China, prior to moving north to its present location after the continents split. The ancient South Pole was located in western central Africa prior to the split.

Antarctica once ice free

This, of course, agrees with what we have been saying all along. For example, in *Dead Men's Secrets*, pages 5, 92 and 168, we indicate that high post-Flood civilisations inhabited Antarctica. They probably came to an end when the continents suddenly split and Antarctica was shifted to its present position.

b.   The problem of thinner and "younger" oceanic sediment

If the oceans were, in fact, created after the major load of continental sediments had been deposited (this depositing having occurred during the Flood), the thinner and "younger" oceanic sediments can be explained. The ocean basins would have formed in between the continents as the earth expanded.

Continental split was "recent"

The continental splitting, I suggest, was triggered during the initial stages of the Great Flood and continued in its aftermath.

Yes, I know. Someone will object that such large areas could not be moved over such a short time. Surely mantle convection to move continents and subduct so much oceanic rock would require unrealistically high temperatures and energy input.

A valid objection indeed - if mantle convection (as in the plate tectonics theory) were the mechanism. However, this cannot have been the agency. We have already noted the lack of evidence for such a mechanism.

Rather, the earth expanded in such a way that the viscous forces were not involved. The expansion of the earth caused by an expansion of each individual atom due to a change in the electric force is a possibility. And this would avoid the viscosity problem.[19]

That the continents separated "recently" is shown by the lack of great erosion at the lines of fit. There is not the erosion that one would expect after millions of years of separation.

Furthermore, we noted the comparatively thin sediment on the ocean floor (not hundreds of millions of years' worth). And one cannot rely on the ocean floor replacement idea which is part of the plate tectonics theory, to explain this away. It is a theory in trouble, as we have noted.

Another point. The study of the ocean floor confirms that the land masses have been RIPPED APART – suddenly, violently.

Whether the cause of this earth expansion was naturalistic or miraculous is not the point. Several global tectonic events are described in Scripture and they are now evidenced in the earth to be a fact.

A "recent" separation of the continents is further documented in the racial memory of various nations. This will be seen in Chapter 18.

Forget about plates and "collision features"

If the earth has expanded, then what have been assumed by the plate tectonics theory to be plates colliding, are really polygons formed as a result of tensional (pull-apart) stress, with their boundaries being zones of vertical rising of magma.

These "primary polygons" are thousands of miles across.[20]

The edges of the large primary polygons could well represent rupture of the entire mantle down to the fluid core. These primary polygons are broken into smaller polygon basins and swells hundreds of miles across. The smaller polygons are the result of shallower tension (pull-apart) adjustments in the mantle.[21] The basins may result from a lag in rising as the earth expands, and the swells from tectonic pressure.

The polygonal pattern dominates the earth's surface.

Rickard makes this observation: "The preponderance of near 120° intersections suggests that, as in the case of polygonal systems in other materials, - e.g. mud, permafrost, and basalts, etc. - these polygons were formed in tensional stress field."[22]

What are mistakenly identified as *collision features*, could well be a diapiric rise of the mantle. This rise exhibits gravity spreading at the surface. This results in ultramatic belts, basement horsts, fanned lineations and gravity nappes.[23]

Okay, so much for the assumed "plates" and "collision features".

But now let's get back to the Flood - and that question, WHERE DID ALL THE FLOOD WATER GO?

On a smaller earth today's water volume would cover today's mountains

If the earth was once 60 to 70 percent of present radius, the present volume of oceanic water would completely cover the smaller earth with an average depth of 7 to 10 kilometres (4½ to 6¼ miles).[24]

I am not suggesting that the pre-Flood mountains were as high as those today.

But the profile of modern global sediment does suggest a former earth radius, when covered by Flood waters, of approximately 60 percent of the present earth radius.[25]

Earth expansion provides "run-off" areas

The evidence leads one to conclude that the ocean basins have formed since the Flood. Here is how it may have occurred:

The silica-rich granitic continental platforms would expand at about half the rate of the magnesium-rich (and silica-poor) basaltic mantle. Though both were expanding, the interior of the earth would expand at twice the rate of the continental cover.[26]

After most of the Flood sediments had been deposited, the expansion of the earth's radius opened up deep rifts or "expansion cracks". Water rushed off the continental platform to fill these.

The continental split at this time would have been rapid at first, though partial. For a considerable time the earth's radius continued to expand. The continental separation may well have involved several rapid-movement stages - the final stage occurring several centuries later.

Although the rift movement has all but ceased now, it is still measurable. The famous open rifts in Iceland are still widening at an average rate of 5mm per year.

Land swells and buckles

Violent land movements were taking place throughout the continental land platforms.

The result was a massive buckling, folding and distorting of the newly laid strata in nearly every region of the world.

This was gradual. Although largely completed during the Flood year, it would continue on a lesser scale for centuries to come.

Rifts open

As we noted, between the continental "swells" appeared tension rifts - enormous areas which remained lower in relation to the rising "swells".

A writer in the *Reader's Digest* has noted:

"Every ocean bed has long, narrow chasms where the bottom falls away AS THOUGH SOME TITANIC FORCE HAD SUCKED THE CRUST INWARD TOWARD THE EARTH'S CORE."[27]

The evidence prompted Dr. K.K. Landes, Head of the Geology Department at Michigan University, to say:

"Can we, as seekers after truth, shut our eyes any longer to the obvious fact that large areas of sea floor have sunk vertical distances measured in miles?"[28]

It is more likely that these enormous rifts resulted not from surface depressions, but rather from a lag in rising as the earth expanded.

Water rushes off

We have noted also that the waters rushed off the continental areas to fill the gigantic new tension rifts.

Psalm 104 in the Old Testament provides additional insights regarding events during those 7 months in which the waters are said to have receded from the land:

1. The waters of the Flood-judgment enveloped the whole earth, even to the extent of covering the pre-Flood mountains.[29]
2. The Flood waters began to abate only after divine intervention; the waters receded rapidly once God gave the command.[30]
3. The Flood waters flowed over the mountains and into the valleys (tension rifts) as they receded off the continents.[31]
4. The suggestion is then given that a geological boundary exists, so that the Flood waters collected in the ocean basins can never again cover the continental land masses.[32]

New land barriers were formed, limiting their extent.

The rising water level in the newly opened basins would stabilise ultimately, to form shore lines around the planet.

The edges of today's continental shelves mark the true boundaries between continental blocks and ocean basins.

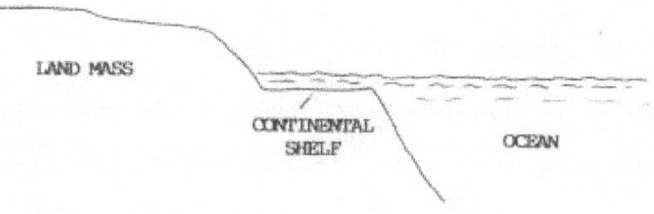

I have always been fascinated by such bizarre features of nature as archways, ancient beaches on hills, hanging valleys, mesas, dry canyons, and so on.

How long did it take these to form? Is there any connection between these and the events we are discussing?

Indeed, there is. As we shall now see...

3

The Flood recedes (b) -

HURRICANE

"Great Scott! What's that!"

"Looks like a waterfall."

The submarine slowly descended, its nose toward the cliff... down... down... down.

The watchers within gasped in awe... 400... 900... 1100... 1500... 1900 feet.

"What a whopper!" exclaimed the light technician. "Your cuppa's getting cold," yelled a crewmate.

"Forget THAT," shouted the technician, peering into the cliff. "THIS is the sight of a lifetime. Jenny would love this. She's crazy about waterfalls."

Off the coast of Tasmania, these scientists from the Australian Navy research laboratories had discovered a deep-sea "waterfall" 12 times higher than Niagara Palls and 6 times higher than Victoria Falls. The "waterfall" is 1,970 feet (600 metres) high.[1]

It appears that toward the end of the Flood year, as great ocean basins opened up, before all the water poured off the continental platform, large areas now 6,000 feet below sea level were, for a time, free of water cover. [2]

Meanwhile, the enormous run-off of water rapidly eroded great gorges in the soft, exposed sediment.

Some of these canyons were themselves soon submerged by the progressive influx of waters running off the continent.

This would explain the submarine canyons which exist in great numbers around every continent of the world.

These are strikingly similar to canyons on land. They must have been formed above the ocean - before they were drowned. The same is true of drowned waterfalls.

THE FIERCE WIND

Upon the mountains and hills rising from this vast turbid sea, dead bodies were strewn everywhere.

Genesis speaks of a tremendous wind that passed over the earth as the waters were abating.

The new temperature differentials being established (cooler near the poles and intensely hotter near the equator) would soon generate a great complex of atmospheric motions.

There is evidence that winds beyond anything known today were indeed whipped up.

In Alaska, for example, thousands of bodies of animals were torn to pieces, limb from limb, and violently mixed with trees and other Flood debris. A suddenly lowered temperature then froze the muck before the carcasses could decompose much more.

In some places, these violent winds even swept away mountain tops, piling up rocks, earth and trees above the bodies of the dead.

Such terrific winds would revive huge, violent waves on the universal ocean. With a boundless sea of water and a sudden great air movement from the poles to the equator, unimpeded by frictional resistance from land surfaces, the potential wave size during this period must have been enormous.

The force of such huge waves driven by this wind had a tremendous effect in moulding the earth's soft surface.

At first, the wind-driven water levelled heights. As the continental area arose, its high points appearing above the stormy sea were buffeted by these wind-driven waves.

The soft land - entire ranges, in fact - would suffer incredibly from erosion during those weeks of Flood abatement. What would normally require thousands of years occurred largely in just a few weeks.

There must have been some new mountains with their soft strata, which were reduced to mere hogbacks in just weeks. Such eroded ranges can be seen today with their talus extending out to a considerable distance on both sides.

Later, after the soil dried out, huge quantities were carried in terrific dust storms.

Within mere days, arches, deep clefts and rocky pinnacles were sand-blasted into shape. "Eons" of erosion were accomplished "overnight".

Bizarre "city" that the wind built

Come with me now to a bizarre landscape that has not its like on this earth. This is the Tassili sandstone plateau in the central Sahara.

The sand-laden wind, blowing after the Great Flood, carved this plateau into a huge labyrinth of "streets" and "buildings" in which, without a guide, you could be lost forever.

There are some ravines here up to 2,000 feet deep. But most of the area is cut by narrow canyons from 65 to 200 feet in depth.

The canyons run through the plateau like the streets of a large city, with "apartment houses" between them. The urban image is enhanced by a thick network of cracks that give the impression of masonry. There are "blind alleys", intersections - and even bridges arching over the "streets".

Between the steep cliff walls, some of the lanes are so narrow, you can hardly squeeze through.

Other parts of the plateau reveal caves and corridors. And just as in a town you can enter a large building from one street, walk through it, and then emerge in a totally different street, so is it with these "buildings". You can pass through corridors several hundred feet long (either upright, or having to crawl) and find yourself in the next "street".

In areas, several dozen narrow canyons run parallel, each separated by rock slabs just a few feet wide but over 150 feet high. The wind has drilled numerous holes in these rock walls.

Elsewhere you may enter a wide, open "plaza" in which rock needles are placed standing 100 feet high.

And in other spots, forests of mushrooms 10 to 15 feet high are standing.

What formed these streets, buildings, needles and mushrooms? Just the abrasive action of sand blown by the wind. The biggest sand grains, which also have the largest abrasive surface, are heavier, so are not carried as high as the smaller grains. For this reason, the stronger erosion is lower down and the lower levels of the pillars are eroded away faster. Hence the mushroom shape.

Formation of sand wastes did not require long ages

The sandy oceans of dunes, the endless wastes of gravel in which so much has been worn down, even levelled - one might expect to have been formed over millions of years.

It was, in fact, accomplished within a few months or years.

The power of these fierce post-Flood wind storms bombarding the soft Flood deposits is beyond calculation.

Then, in time, vegetation took hold and families moved in to live. Later, as the lakes dried up, the region reverted to desert. And all of this within recorded history.

Junior World Encyclopedia

The power of wind

Do you really understand what wind can do?

How wind can work on land unprotected by vegetation was vividly demonstrated in the dustbowl regions of the western United States during the early 1930s. Mountains of sand were actually moved over **hundreds** of miles. **Single** dust storms raised sand and clay up to two stories high, covering buildings.

The vast and splendid city of Nineveh, capital of the Assyrian Empire, was a London or Tokyo of the ancient world. And yet, only 200 years after its fall, the site was unrecognisable, so completely had winds from the desert covered it.

MORE HEAVY RAIN

Toward the close of the Flood, more torrential rain began to fall.

The earth movements caused increasing friction within the earth's crust, with a corresponding increase of volcanism. Many new volcanoes were now being exposed by the receding waters. The result was more dust and clouds.

Vast inland "puddles" of stranded water - future inland seas - added to the copious atmospheric wet.

The Flood water temperature was still at near subtropic levels; the sudden lowering of the air temperature generated a build up of thick clouds.

A sky thus darkened with clouds shed rain and snow continuously.

ALLUVIAL PLAINS, CANYONS AND MESAS

Just think of the enormous volume of water rushing on with ever-increasing speed toward the new, lower levels, as the new seabed was being formed and new high continental areas were being born.

The eroding, transporting and stratifying force of such masses of water in motion, is beyond calculation.

Try to imagine what would happen today if the base of the Pacific Ocean were to be lifted and its water poured out over the American and Australian continents in one great splash! Could anything withstand the force? Mountains would be levelled, valleys filled up, and rocks, boulders, gravel and sand, hurled in layers over hundreds of miles. Changes would take place that would normally require millions of years.

Now notice. The central region of the United States is one large alluvial flat - the Great Plains. The deposits are of a magnitude far beyond that of present sedimentation. Only waters of a global magnitude can account for such deposits. Marine plateau covers 250,000 square miles of Utah, Arizona, Colorado and New Mexico.

It appears that the sediments were all laid down fairly rapidly and continuously. Then, **while the sediments were STILL SOFT** and the river run-offs were carrying enormous discharges, *canyon downcutting ensued rapidly*.

Remember, these waters were rushing on toward the newly-created basins, over the soft, churned-up debris of a world that had been soaked for a year.

Volumes of water, laden with rocks, gravel and debris, rushing over newly-deposited, still unconsolidated soft ground, but confined to rush out through narrow channels because of rising mountains, could easily scoop out a Grand Canyon and build up great deltas measuring hundreds of miles, in a matter of days and weeks. It would not need fantastic millions of years.

As the water rushed off, it gouged out river systems, canyons and valleys, leaving scars everywhere.

Well known in the U.S.A. are **mesas**, such as those between Cheyenne and Denver. These were once left as islands during the last of the retreating waters.

On the almost horizontal drainage plains, in the line of this **old drainage channel**, one notices a mass of rocks in the middle of the channel. Still visible on either side of these rocks are wide and deep depressions where the increased speed of the water swirled around them.

Similar phenomena occur all over the world.

Today, **raised shore lines** and **river terraces**, found worldwide, tell the same story of RETREATING WATER.

All over the world are evidences of **former high water levels** in the rivers and lakes. **Every inland lake** exhibits ancient beaches high on the surrounding hills.

Likewise, **every river** reveals old river terraces high above the present flood plains. Furthermore, most large stream valleys are deeply filled with alluvium.

Rivers today universally occur in valleys too large for the present stream. To put it another way, practically every river is now an "underfit stream", far too small to have produced its own canyon or valley or the extensive alluvium beds through which it flows.

Present day rates of erosion and deposition fail to account for this. But these ancient deposits are consistent with a tectonically induced **retreat of the waters** after the Great Flood, when great swollen rivers plunged rapidly toward the sea.

Furthermore, the rainfall of the early post-Flood centuries must have been much greater than it is now.

DRY CANYONS AND FALLS

In some parts of the world are picturesque "scabland" areas, which contain vast **hanging valleys, dry canyons, dry waterfalls, rock-rimmed basins** and other bizarre features. The Columbia Plateau is an example. Wilpena Pound in South Australia is another.

Such features are clearly **not being formed** anywhere at the present time.

Studies by Bretz and others confirm these to be catastrophic in origin. And a sudden vast flood is seen as the only agency that could create such forms.

POWER OF WATER

The carrying power of water multiplies with speed. For example, a stream can carry:
- at 10 m.p.h.: a stone of 5 tons;
- at 15 m.p.h.: a stone of 55 tons;
- at 25 m.p.h.: a stone of 320 tons.

Here are some examples of what water can do:
- Kanad Creek, Southern Utah: In July 1883, a **two day** flood cut the creek bed down 40 feet. Later floods increased the depth to 60 feet for a distance of 15 miles.
- A flood in Kanad Canyon cut a channel 50 feet deep and 260 feet wide in less than **8 hours**!
- Providence Canyon, near Lumpkin, Georgia: Since white settlement, water on old Indian trails has eroded canyons 200 feet deep, 300 feet wide and half a mile long.
- In China, gorges hundreds of feet deep have been cut by a single, short flood.

Now imagine the vast quantities of sediment eroded and transported when rain poured for weeks all over the world without ceasing!

CONTINUING WIND STORMS

Now link this with the power of hurricane force winds!

It may help us to visualise this, if we recall a modern wind storm.

In 1980, the Mount St. Helens eruption caused a hurricane velocity wind of 100 miles per hour (160 kilometres per hour). Aided by this wind, a mud flow cut a **140 feet deep canyon** in ONE DAY!

Engineers Canyon, 200 feet wide, was formed, with a tiny stream flowing through it. The stream did not slowly form the canyon; the canyon formed the stream.

This wind formed in just ONE DAY a **minutely layered strata deposit**, which an evolutionist would expect to take millions of years.

Successive layers of rock strata were formed by the hurricane blasts. Over 600 feet of deposits, minutely layered, formed in just 6 years. Erosion has exposed a cliff in the deposits and revealed the strata.

Last century, when Darwin visited South America and saw the Canyon of the Santa Cruz (700 feet wide and 200 feet deep) with only a small river flowing through it, he could only imagine that this river had cut the canyon. If so, he theorised, it must have taken millions of years. So was born his theory of "geological gradualism".

How wrong could he have been?

Winds hasten deserts

There must have been large areas where pre-Flood plant life lay covered beneath hundreds, or even thousands, of feet of earth, sand, volcanic ash or lava.

Such areas must have remained barren for years, perhaps even centuries, before grass, weeds or small shrubbery gained a foothold over the barren, devastated surface. And more centuries were required for reforestation.

But soil unprotected by vegetation is extremely unstable. In some areas, the results of erosion hastened the formation of deserts as the inland lakes dried up.

SEA LEVEL STABILISES

Once the major run-off from the newly exposed land was over, the sea level stabilised.

But there is evidence that it stood at this time about 20 feet higher than at present.

In many places all over the world, there is a "shoreline" 18 to 20 feet above today's sea level.

At the Cape of Good Hope, South Africa, shoreline caves and beaches are seen at a uniform height of 20 feet above the sea.

This phenomenon appears around the Atlantic - along the southwest African coast, the coast of Brazil, the coast from the Gulf of Mexico to New York, as well as on many islands of the Atlantic. The shoreline of beaches, terraces and caves is of the same altitude above the sea. St. Helena Island (Napoleon's place of exile), provides one such example of now dusty sea caves with water-worn pebbles, 20 feet above the surf.

In the Atlantic, Indian and Pacific Oceans, many islands reveal this higher shoreline of uniform height. In Samoa, islands spread across 200 miles show a shoreline uniformly 20 feet above the sea.

The same is seen in Europe. And along the coast of eastern Australia this raised shoreline extends for at least 1,000 miles.

Local exceptions don't disprove the rule.

Let's face it. Upthrusting forces, warping the earth, could not have formed a uniform water line over hundreds of miles. This would be seen, however, if the sea level had since dropped.

SEA LEVEL DROPS FURTHER

Between the present shoreline and the 20 foot line on the same beaches, there are no intermediate surf lines. This shows that the further drop in water level was not gradual. It was sudden... abrupt. And it occurred all over the world.

P.H. Kuenen of Leyden University, referring to R.A. Daly's discoveries in this matter, states:

"In thirty-odd years following Daly's first paper many further instances have been recorded by a number of investigators the world over, so that this recent shift is now well established."[3]

Daly (of Harvard), as well as Kuenen and others, place the occurrence at 3,000 to 4,000 years ago.

From ancient historical documents, I believe that we can set the time of this drop in sea level at around 300 to 340 years after the Great Flood, that is, very close to 2000 BC. (4,000 years ago). I have arrived at this date independently from Daly and Kuenen - and for a different reason.

Moreover, there is reason to believe that the sea level dropped not 20 feet (to today's level), but some 500 feet lower than it is today, before gradually rising again to its present level. (We shall touch on this further in Chapter 23.)

Apparently, many centuries were required for the crust of the earth to readjust from the stresses of the Deluge period. (See Chapters 18 and 19.) One repercussion was this further sudden dropping of the sea level.

Since then, of course, the melting of ice (which formed soon after the Flood), as well as the draining into the oceans of trapped water from inland basins, has caused the oceans to slowly recover to present levels.

Well, considering all this, just how were people coping? Let's go back to the valley in Turkey where, after the Flood, things got moving again. We shall begin to trace the story from there.

4

Ararat: a new start -

MOUNTAINS OF SURPRISE

"Goodbye, Naamah, my dear."

Tears ran down the old man's cheeks. With a sniffle he breathed, "I'll ever love you."

One of the little party tossed a handful of petals onto the coffin and they slowly turned away. Noah lingered at the grave site, recalling the days spent with his beloved. She was somewhat older than he. A more loyal wife he could never have found.

In the world now gone, she had supported him at every turn – in his appeals to the people, and yes, in the building of the Ark. She had endured hostility and ridicule with him. She was the only believing female of her generation aboard the survival vessel. And those young women who became his sons' wives – their faith was in no small measure due to her prayers.

With him she had stepped into the Ark and left nearly everything behind. And she had faced this new world with him, sharing its harshness and heartache with courage. Yes, she was a woman of spiritual strength. He would miss her deeply.

Her grave would never be neglected. It was in the garden beside the house, surrounded by Naamah's favourite rose bushes. The marker clearly indicated this as HER resting place.

INSCRIPTIONS AND RUINS

Ararat, in eastern Turkey, was the stepping-stone between the old world and the new post-Flood world.

The names of many, if not most, towns, villages and landmarks of the Ararat region, stem from words or phrases connected with some aspect of the Flood, the landing, or the lives or deaths of family members after the Great Flood.

One of the first this century to draw attention to this was Colonel Alexander Koor, of the White Russian army.

Koor drew several maps of the region. On them he circled various locations with the words:
THIS AREA SHOULD BE SEARCHED.

There are perhaps 50 or more archaeological sites in the Ararat region which have never been investigated - ruins of ancient villages, towns, buildings, tombs and caves.

A few persons have taken up the challenge. Up in this wild mountain area, one amateur archaeologist was led by his Kurdish guide to a boundary marker which bore a very ancient inscription. Pictorially it showed mountains in the vicinity, which can be identified clearly today. And it portrayed the Ark as resting near them. You will find a picture of this rock and its inscription in my book *The Ark Conspiracy*.

THE FIRST CIVILISATION

Until early in the twentieth century, when driven out by the Turks, the Armenians dwelt in this area. The Armenians trace their ancestry to Hiak, the "Son of Targom [Togarmah], a grandson of Noah."[1] They claimed to have inhabited the Ararat region since that time.

If the Ararat mountains were, as the book of Genesis insists, the landing place of the Ark after the world Flood, then this is the very place where the first civilisation, and therefore the earliest archaeological sites, should be found.

ARCHAEOLOGICAL SITES

The few searches undertaken in this area have yielded incredible surprises.
* In 1969, on a small hill called Korhan, two Americans, Cumming and Hewitt, discovered a magnificent shrine with walls ten feet thick, a 30 foot high altar, an ancient cemetery with inscribed tombstones, a 5 foot diameter grinding mill, and other buildings. So remote is the area that even the mountain folk seldom venture there; no outsider would even consider it.

* In 1967, the remains of Altin Tepe were found. Its walls were over 30 feet thick. Blocks of granite weighing 40 tons were skilfully raised to a height of 200 feet (20 stories) and then fitted together. The luxury here was "unreal". Furniture was decorated with gold and silver; bronze bed and table legs were carved into animal feet. Rulers and compasses were used in executing elaborate drawings for frescoes.

* Significantly, it is in the vicinity of Ararat that we find the first known indications of cities built according to specific plans.

EARLIEST SITE OF METAL WORKING
- JUST A FEW MILES FROM NOAH'S HOME!

It was from the mountains of Ararat that the news went out to this world concerning the discovery of remains that matched the dimensions of the biblical Ark of Noah. Subsequent excavations led to an announcement by Turkish authorities that the ancient survival vessel had been found.

My teams were involved in follow-up expeditions to the first 25 expeditions led by the recognised discoverer, Ron Wyatt.

One of the most exciting discoveries at the site of the alleged Noah's Ark was the large amount of metal found in the remains of the wreck.

Further down the valley, near the village of Kazan, Wyatt discovered a most ancient ruined house, with walls three feet thick, now partially buried in alluvial silt. One wall, now recorded on video tape, was inscribed with the sequence of the Flood events. Beside the house were two grave sites. From the markers it could not be misunderstood as to who was buried here.

And a nearby wall was inscribed with pictures of the sequence of Flood events.

I have explored that valley, known as the Valley of Eight, a number of times. With my own eyes I have seen some of the remains, coated with patina. There is no doubt that it all happened exactly as the book of Genesis says.

Just across the dirt road (to the south of the ruined house with the grave sites) is the village of Kazan, in which a large number of giant anchor stones from a large ship can be seen. Out of place in this mountain region... unless?

Behind the complex of fences, house and grave markers (to the north) is a very ancient stone altar located upon a ridge between two hills.

On the north side of that ridge of hills is the Araxes River – and across the river is the site of Medzamor. Here, within a few miles of Noah's home, is what has been termed "one of" the oldest, if not "THE" OLDEST metallurgical factory site IN THE WORLD!

Analyses of copper found there showed **14 different alloys**, including tin, lead, antimony and zinc.

The centre was sophisticated. Clay pipes were found inserted into the furnaces, as well as phosphorus brickettes, used in the smelting of cassiterite to obtain tin.

Here vases and objects made of all the common metals have been found. Fourteen varieties of bronze were smelted for different purposes. Medzamor also produced metallic paints ceramics and glass. And the Medzamor craftsmen wore mouth-filters and gloves, as do modern craftsmen. The factory is believed to have had more than 200 furnaces.

Medzamor was the industrial centre of this early post-Flood period. Ore was brought in and the finished products distributed to all other areas.

Several pairs of steel tweezers have been unearthed here. The steel used in the tweezers was of an exceptionally high grade. The tweezers were like eyebrow tweezers, that enable chemists and watchmakers to handle micro-objects which they cannot manipulate by hand. The manipulation of such micro-objects implies the use of microscopic lenses.

A 3 storey astronomical observatory was erected nearby.

SOPHISTICATED FROM THE START

Archaeological sites are excavated to discover the **sequence** of materials; those found directly above virgin soil with nothing below them represent the earliest occupation level.

At Medzamor, **the earliest phase** yielded bronze slag.

This discovery continues to puzzle archaeologists. Why? Because it has been assumed (from the evolutionary theory) that man progressed very slowly through various stages of knowledge – firstly the discovery of fire, then the invention of the wheel, then cultivating crops and domesticating animals, and then, much later, the knowledge of metals and metallurgy.

But here is evidence that man appeared "on the scene" from the start with tremendous technological knowledge, producing an alloy (bronze) which requires tin and sometimes includes zinc for increased hardness.

French journalist Jean Vidal reported in *Science et Vie* of July, 1969:

"Medzamor was founded by the wise men of earlier civilizations. They possessed knowledge they had acquired during a remote age unknown to us that deserves to be called scientific and industrial."

How few people today have heard of this early post-Flood complex!

Manganese

We mentioned GLASS. "Glass making also flourished at Metsamor, as indicated by six types of metallurgical material, including zinc and **manganese**, alloyed in different ways to make different colours."[2]

Interestingly, ballast samples from the "hull" of the Ark formation on Cudi Dagi have been tested showed over 85% **manganese**!

The findings at Medzamor show that a procedure undoubtedly taught by the Flood survivors was continued here.

Earliest rivets

In our investigation of the Ark site, we also noted the use of very large rivets in the structure.

It seems reasonable to expect that Noah and his sons would also have passed the usage of rivets on to their descendants. And that is exactly what the evidence shows.

At Amiranis-Gora, north of the area of the Ark, a cemetery revealed pottery with "knobs along the top of the shoulder.... [that] seem to imitate rivets."[3]

But lest there be any doubt, another very puzzling group of artefacts came to light in 1974 and 1975.

A Turkish antiquities dealer brought the objects to the Adana (Turkey) Museum, giving first one and then another explanation of their origin. It is known for certain that he did obtain them in the region and that they date to very near the third or early 2nd millennia BC. Among the artefacts are numerous copper knives, swords, chisels and axes. One interesting feature is that two of the swords are almost 36 inches long, "...which would have been difficult to wield with one hand".[4]

But the feature that interests us now is the fact that these have been dated to **very early** times by the archaeologists, and the craftsmen used **RIVETS** to attach the handle! In fact, on all of the knives **rivets** were used.

NAKHICHEVAN FOUNDED BY NOAH?

The Ararat Plain, or Araxes Valley, is about 80 to 90 miles long. It begins a little west of Ararat and extends through present-day Iran into the old U.S.S.R. This valley appears to be the general area through which Noah's family expanded, and since the Ark (the region of Noah's home) is in the vicinity of the western portion of this plain, the general direction of expansion would naturally have been to the east.

Near the eastern end of this valley is a town called Nakhichevan. Numerous Armenian traditions ascribe the founding of Nakhichevan to Noah. While Noah and his wife most likely continued to maintain their home at Kazan, "the place of eight", until their death, nevertheless it does seem logical that as the patriarch of the family, Noah would have travelled with his younger family members as they explored the region in search of suitable areas to establish new settlements, then returning to his own home. Therefore, the traditions that state that he founded Nakhichevan could be based on actual fact.

Another evidence which gives credence to the idea of Noah's family expanding eastward along the Araxes River is the fact that **the other very early metallurgical centre was at Nakhichevan!**[5] There is no doubt that the immediate descendants of Noah would be those who had the earliest knowledge of metallurgy and employed it from the beginning.

BUT WHERE ARE ALL THE EARLY METAL OBJECTS?

It is often assumed that because metal objects are not found at early sites, that the people who lived there didn't have metals. But metals were a precious commodity for a very long time, and some are valuable even today.

When people moved, they left their pottery behind because it was easy to make a new batch after they reached their new location and it was too bulky to take with them on long journeys.

But metal implements would be considered very valuable and would therefore be carried along when people moved. The metal could also be reshaped into new items. Therefore the absence of metal objects in early abandoned sites is to be expected. Even in 586 BC, when Nebuchadnezzar conquered Jerusalem, he collected all the metal objects as spoils of war.[6]

IT ALL BEGAN AGAIN IN TURKEY

After the Great Flood, mankind began in this region. Noah's descendants were born there. Their advanced knowledge came from Noah and his sons, who carried it from the pre-Flood world. And from this region, mankind spread across the face of the earth.

Evidence indicates that this Araxes Valley is the "original home from which this culture subsequently expanded in all directions."[7]

Ararat sits in a most unique position on the globe, only hundreds of miles from the very centre of the world's geographical land masses.

There are no geographical barriers to hinder migration from Ararat to any land around. The usual barriers – mountain chains, oceans or deserts – are absent. Dispersion in any direction could take place easily.

No place on earth is so uniquely suited as a starting place from which to replenish the earth.

Could it be coincidence that Noah's Ark landed so near to the centre of the world's land mass in the ideal location from which the earliest migration could occur?

CIVILISATION BEGAN IN MOUNTAIN AREAS

Something else of significance. After the Great Flood, civilisations developed FIRST in the **mountain areas**.

"Summarising the work of many eminent authorities on the subject, R.J. Braidwood and B. Howe[8] concluded that genetic studies confirm the archaeological finds and leave no doubt that **agriculture** began exactly where Thinking Man had emerged... in the Near East. There is no doubt by now that agriculture spread all over the world from the Near Eastern arc of **mountains and highlands**."[9]

In every instance, the plants and cereals basic to human survival and advancement and a variety of fruit bearing shrubs and trees kept coming out of the Near East and spread from there to Europe and other parts of the world. One might mention our familiar apples, pears, olives, figs, almonds, pistachios and walnuts, for example.

"It was as though the Near East were some kind of genetic-botanic laboratory, guided by an unseen hand, producing every so often a newly domesticated plant.

"The scholars who have studied the origins of the grapevine have concluded that its cultivation began in the mountains around northern Mesopotamia and in Syria and Palestine... No wonder. The Old Testament tells us that Noah 'planted a vineyard' (and even got drunk on its wine) after his ark rested on Mount Ararat as the waters of the Deluge receded. The Bible, like the scholars, thus places the start of vine cultivation in the mountains of northern Mesopotamia."[10]

(I shall make a slight correction to Sitchen's statement. The Bible does not state that the Ark landed on Mount Ararat, but *upon the mountains* of Ararat – a range of mountains, Genesis 8:4. The difference is important, for one wishing to view any surviving remains of the Ark.)

This area possesses a "special fertility"[11] which is indicative of the special provisions God made for the first family in re-establishing life on this planet. I just couldn't believe the size of the cabbages at a roadside vegetable stand in this area! Several times bigger, I still believe, than cabbages I have seen anywhere in the world.

PLANT FOODS CAME FROM SEEDS BROUGHT ON THE ARK

Noah took on board the survival vessel plant life as food for both people and animals.[12]

And when they left the Ark, they began to sow the seeds that would produce food. And archaeological evidence fits this scenario perfectly.

"Paleo-botany had provided evidence illuminating the earliest stages of the cultivation of emmer and einkorn wheat and two-row barley, with subsequent mutations resulting in improved strains; but still **the problem of the ultimate geographical sources** of the wild grains found in the earliest excavated settlements **awaits solution,…**"[13]

"Even more important than the different varieties of timber available for building were the species of edible plants. Of these of course the most important are the cereals, but also the most problematic because of **the unsolved questions of their origins**."[14]

The unsolved questions are only in the minds of researchers who neglect to take into account the Great Flood – and the world that preceded it.

EARLIEST GRAINS ALREADY HIGHLY SPECIALISED

Something else. Scholars are unable to explain how the EARLIEST grains were already uniform and highly specialised. As Sitchen elaborates:

"There is no explanation for this botanogenetic miracle, unless the process was not one of natural selection but of artificial manipulation.

"Spelt, a hard-grained type of wheat, ... is the product of 'an unusual mixture of botanic genes,' neither a development from one genetic source nor a mutation of one source. It is definitely the result of mixing the genes of several plants.

"Modern scholars have no answers to these puzzles, nor to the general question of why the mountainous semicircle in the ancient Near East became a continuous source of new varieties of cereals, plants, trees, fruits, vegetables, and domesticated animals."[15]

I shall now give you the facts that solve this mystery.

HELP FROM NOAH?

The ancient *Gilgamesh Epic* and the 3,400 year old *Book of Jasher* both tell us that pilgrimages were made to the house of Noah to learn the ancient wisdom.

It seems reasonable to conclude that Noah and his aids were constantly cultivating and refining strains of plants to help the dispersing population cope with the greatly reduced capacity of the new, impoverished world.

PLANTS FROM THIS CENTRE

It was in Anatolia (Turkey) that many plants were "re-born" – planted there by Noah and his family from pre-Flood seeds. And from there carried to the various parts of the world.

"Anatolia is situated at the meeting of three principle zones of distribution of plants: these are the so-called Euro-Siberian zone (Europe, Russia and Siberia), the Irano-Turanian zone (the steppes of central Asia, Iran and central Anatolia) and the Mediterranean zone... Recent work has shown **a large percentage of plants** which are endemic, that is, **confined to Turkey**: this is particularly true of the Taurus ranges, where the Irano-Turanian and the Mediterranean zones meet."[16]

This last statement is particularly exciting. It tells us that in the general region of south central Turkey – the Noah's Ark region – there is a large number of plants that are found ONLY there!

This suggests that some of the original plants Noah brought from the pre-Flood world never made it past the region of the Ark and Babel. When the time came that the groups left the area, it looks like they took with them only the major grains and staple plant foods, leaving behind a variety of plants whose beginnings were in the pre-Flood world.

NOAH'S FRUITS STILL GROW IN THE COLD CLIMATE

Apples, plums, apricots, peaches and mulberries are common in the eastern highlands. They thrive in spite of the severe winters.

Noah planted grapes.[17] Vineyards are usually found in warm climates, certainly not in regions with winters as dreadfully cold as is eastern Turkey. Yet the vine is at home here... even today.

"IN THE MOUNTAINS"

Scholars who ignore the Flood of Noah find themselves facing this dilemma: Why did agriculture first appear not in the fertile and easily cultivated plains and valleys, but **in the mountains** skirting the low-lying plains?

Why, one asks, would farmers avoid the plains and confine their sowing and reaping to the more difficult mountainous terrain?

You may have guessed the answer by now. But I shall hint at it by asking another question: Could it be that the low-lying lands were, at the time when agriculture began, **uninhabitable**? It seems plausible that the low-lying areas were not yet dry enough following the Great Flood.

It would be many years before the valleys and plains would dry off sufficiently so that the people could come down from the mountains and settle the low-lying plains of Mesopotamia.

And do you know, we actually have an answer in Sumerian texts. They state that cultivation, first undertaken in the hill country, was possible by keeping the floodwater at bay, but was ultimately extended to the lowlands.

You see, the Great Flood holds the key to this mystery. Believe the record of the world Flood and of the survivors landing in the mountains of Ararat,[18] and the mystery evaporates.

* * * * * * *

But the scholarly world remains in shock. Why? That's coming up next.

5

Yes, It begins in Turkey -

A SHOCKING DISCOVERY

The hairs on Jack's neck were bristling. Professor Jack Bell was sitting in on a conversation that was, to put it mildly, getting overheated.

"You idiot," snapped Rodriguez. "South America's where it all started. The oldest cities and - "

"You know nothing," cut in Downes. "Any fool knows civilisation began in Egypt."

"Go back to school, Downes," mocked Laske. "Sumeria had it first."

"Rubbish!" shrieked Moonie. "It's Africa, I tell you!"

Bell was now squirming. He scratched the hairs on his neck, the ones that flowed down from his grey beard. This was painful... these "experts" all shouting each other down. He'd heard enough.

"Hey, you guys, cap it, will you!" he shouted.

The others glared at him.

"You are all so very wrong. There's vital evidence you're ignoring. All of you. Don't you know?"

"Okay, four eyes, spill your guts." A ripple of derision was heard. Bell ignored it.

"Civilisation began in TURKEY."

"TURKEY!" spluttered Downes. "You've flipped, man!"

Scientific smugness was so routine, these days, that Bell had expected some such response. He would field that remark, then get on with his evidence. Good evidence.

He had it organised. And he'd let them have it.

FIRST PLANT DOMESTICATION

We touched on this in the previous chapter - that cultivation of cereals began in TURKEY. But let's go into this a little further.

Today's advances in science are breaking new ground. Take einkorn wheat, for example. DNA fingerprinting of plants is determining the likeliest location for the first switching of einkorn wheat from its wild form to its domesticated form.

In the mid 1990s, a group of European scientists assembled specimens of ancient einkorn that had been collected from archaeological sites stretching from Iran to the Balkans. They also assembled specimens of modern einkorn that still grow wild. The scientists included Manfred Heun from the University of Norway, Falf Schafer-Pregl and Francesco Salamini from the Max Planck Institute of Cologne, and others.

From extensive DNA profiling of all the specimens, a clear finding emerged: That the earliest domestication of einkorn had occurred not in Iran, Iraq, Syria or Israel, but in eastern Turkey.[1] The closest match to the earliest domesticated einkorn was found to be *Triticum monococum*, subspecies *boeoticum*, a wild strain which still grows in the Taurus mountains of eastern Turkey.

But even decades before these findings, plant specialist M. Hopf showed that other staples such as barley, lentils, chick peas, rye and broad beans, all originated in environs of Turkey and northern Mesopotamia.

Furthermore, it was from this same region that Europe derived all of its subsequent plant cultivation knowledge, over a period of some 4,000 years.[2]

FIRST WOVEN TEXTILES

And the world's earliest known scrap of textile? This was found at Cayonu in south-eastern Turkey. Cayonu is in the upper reaches of the Tigris River, in the same Taurus foothills that saw the first cultivation of einkorn.

This piece of textile was found in the early 1990s by archaeologists from Istanbul University and the University of Chicago. It had ended its days as a piece of rag to enable someone to get a better grip on a handle.

FIRST ANIMAL DOMESTICATION

It is again in the environs of Turkey that we find the earliest evidence of animal domestication. At Zawi Chemi, just south of

Turkey's border with Iraq, comes the first evidence of wild sheep, goat and red deer suddenly giving way to the herding of young domesticated animals.[3]

Likewise, the best available evidence concerning cattle domestication suggests that when it does occur, it is again in the Turkey/Anatolia region.[4]

Even back in the late 1980s, the eminent Colin Renfrew (Professor of archaeology at Cambridge University) was recognising the signs:

> "There can be little doubt that the principal plant domesticates and some of the animals too came... from Anatolia [Turkey]."[5]

THE FIRST POTTERY

From plant and animal domestication, we turn to pottery.

One should bear in mind that from radio-carbon dating alone, with its vagaries, it is impossible to be exactly sure where the first true pottery artefacts were made.

But Beldibi in south-west Turkey is a leading contender.[6]

This is certainly consistent with the trend for Turkey to have been a major source of innovation.

THE FIRST METALLURGY

We have already spoken of the first metallurgical factory site in the world - Medzamor. And now comes the discovery of one of the earliest known examples of the use of metallurgy, likewise in Turkey. Here at Asikli, a 50 foot high mound on the western side of Turkey's Konya plain, to the south-east of Aksaray, a woman's grave has yielded jewellery.[7]

EARLIEST TOWN PLANNING

At the same Asikli site, some 400 houses have been excavated.

Constructed of baked mud-bricks and meticulously-shaped blocks of local volcanic stone, the town was laid out with roadways in an organised street plan. This appears to be another world first – again, in Turkey.

SKEPTICAL REACTIONS

The findings of scientists involved in these discoveries have been greeted more with skepticism than any enthusiastic acceptance. Mesopotamia and Egypt "have to" be the cradle of civilisation. To accept Turkey as the origin of such things, goes against traditional thinking. Turkey should have hardly any civilisation at all at that early time.

LANGUAGES CAME OUT OF TURKEY

And then came another bombshell. The news that broke on December 1, 2003, left segments of the scientific world in shock.

The roots of our language had also been traced... to Turkey!

As said the *New Zealand Herald* on that day:

"Auckland University researchers have stunned academics around the world by tracing the origins of the English language to Turkish farmers.

"Using a novel approach to develop an Indo-European language tree, the researchers say they have evidence the roots of the English language go back about 9,000 years to Turkey.

"Associate Professor Russell Gray and PhD student Quentin Atkinson published their research in the British journal *Nature*...

"Gray was encouraged that his research had been supported in the United States by Stanford University's eminent geneticist Luigi Luca Cavalli-Sforza...

"Gray and Atkinson had analysed thousands of words from 87 languages (past and present) to find out when the various branches of the Indo-European family tree started diverging.

"We looked at words from different languages that were clearly related and grouped them in sets.

"Gray said a simple example was that five was *cinq* in French and *cinque* in Italian.

"We built matrices of all our information, gleaned from the Internet and every obscure etymological dictionary we could find.

"The researchers then used sophisticated computer programs to do the analysis and build language trees.

"The length of the resulting branches and their various offshoots showed when each language diverged from its predecessors and developed a separate identity.

"Gray said Hittite (an extinct Anatolian language) was the first major language group to branch from the Indo-European trunk.

"Over subsequent millennia the same trunk sprouted Tocharian, Armenian, Greek, Albanian, Iranian, Indic, Slavic, Baltic, Germanic, French/Iberian, Italic and Celtic language groups.

"Gray said the findings had wider implications than just language development. Languages, like genes, provided vital clues about human history, he said.

"A Marsden Fund grant from the government and a James Cook Fellowship from the Royal Society of New Zealand helped pay for the research, which included the equivalent of three solid years of computer time." [8]

The time factor for language development will be addressed in Chapter 11. What is worth noting here is the origin of the language tree in the territory now occupied by TURKEY.

TURKEY - THE CRADLE OF CIVILISATION

So it is in Turkey that we find the first cultivation of plants and true cereals.

It is in Turkey that we find the first domestication of animals.

It is in Turkey that we find the first woven textiles.

It is in Turkey that we find the first pottery.

It is in Turkey that we find both the world's first metallurgical factory and the first known use of metallurgy.

It is in Turkey that we find the first known indications of cities built according to specific plans.

And it is in Turkey that we find the origins of our language.

Isn't this just what the book of Genesis has been trying to tell us, all along, that Noah's survival vessel landed "upon the mountains of Ararat?"[8] And Ararat is IN TURKEY! There should be no more quibbling about this. The replanting of world civilisation after the Great Flood, was in Turkey!

Still, when I first raised this question, a scholar named Ed, for whom I have some respect, emailed me this comment:

"First civilization in Turkey? What is your definition of civilization? Already 14,000 years ago our ancestors used the stars to sail the Atlantic ocean. Such astronomical science didn't come from Turkey, instead it must have come from Morocco/Algiers. The beautiful 30,000 year old art in the caves of southern France is still being rated as some of the best in the world. Was that not civilization?"

Absolutely correct, Edo. They were civilised. So how could human civilisation - in fact, all human activity –after the Great Disaster, be replanted in Turkey as late as 2344 BC, and still be the **FIRST**?

This throws up another hot potato: our *dating* systems. For example, the script found in the caves of Rochebertier, France, is traditionally claimed to be 12,000 years old. But this resembles and in some cases is identical to that of Tartessus (known to be 2500 to 2000 BC).

So I ask you. Are we to believe that a script, once developed, would remain relatively unchanged for 10,000 years? History shows that this does not happen. So what do the two scripts really demonstrate? Just this – that these cultures must have been of the same period.

The same is true of Paleolithic antler bones found at Le Mas d'Azil and La Madelaine. These are inscribed with signs identical to Pheonician script from about 2000 BC.

And painted pebbles from Le Mas d'Azil are marked with signs and symbols that were once predominant throughout the Mediterranean – again, between 3000 and 2000 BC.

Don't be taken in by wild dating claims, of 30,000 BC, and such like. Orthodox science has made an enormous error of interpretation. This cannot remain permanently ignored or suppressed from the public. In Book 1 of this series, *The Killing of Paradise Planet* (chapters 14 to 16), I exposed the scandal of the radiometric dating cover-up. And you will find more hard facts on dating in the present work, chapters 22 and 23.

I repeat: the replanting of global civilisation began in Turkey.

* * * * * * *

Okay, you ask, but what about all the wild animals? ... Australian marsupials, for example. How do we account for the dispersion of animals to far-away Australia? Kangaroos are found only there - nowhere else. And how could the frail, timid platypus have migrated to Australia all the way from Turkey?

The evolution theory says they evolved there. And if that's so, then you can toss out almost everything we have so far discussed. So let's see...

6

Plant and animal distribution -

THE MARSUPIAL MYSTERY

MYSTERY! It lures, tantalises and begs us to seek a solution. Rutherford Platt thought he'd stumbled upon such a mystery. For lack of imagination, I'll call it the SAXIFRAGE MYSTERY. Platt was so intrigued that he put pen to paper and sent off his problem to *Scientific American*. Here was his riddle:

"How does one account for the existence of precisely the same peculiar plant at two points thousands of miles apart, separated by oceans and continents?"[1]

The saxifrage is just one example, of course. The same species of other plants have been found in spots widely separated and remote from each other, but not in between.

PLANT DISTRIBUTION

Now that's something to get people scratching their heads. But, of course, if you've already read Book 2 of this series *Surprise Witness*, you may have answers like these:

Could it be that the seed was scattered at the time of the Great Flood? Or that in these two spots the seed was not buried too deep by Flood sediment?

Around the world, numerous living trees and shrubs grow today above rock layers containing fossils of the same type of tree or shrub.

Now isn't this just what one would expect? Propagules which were buried at the right surface depth during the Flood would have re-sprouted as the waters abated.

(Of course, plants we know today can also be found as fossils in areas that they no longer inhabit today. This is simply evidence of localised extinction since the Flood.)

ANIMAL DISTRIBUTION

But **not so** with the animals of the world.

I shall first explain the difference between FOSSILS and SUB-FOSSILS.

FOSSIL animals are found in strata formed during the Great Flood. SUB-FOSSILS are found in superficial deposits laid down more recently.

By and large, NOWHERE ON EARTH is there a connection between fossil animals (as distinct from sub-fossils) and the living ones inhabiting the same region.

This is no help to the evolution theory. The evidence is consistent with a Flood wipeout, followed by **a totally new animal distribution pattern**.

There is a common belief that Australia's unique fauna must have evolved there. So an evolutionist may ask questions like these:

Question: **Surely marsupials must be an isolated evolutionary development of Australia, since their fossils are found nowhere else?**

That's a reasonable question. And it deserves an answer.

(By the way, marsupials, if you didn't know, are those type of mammals whose female has a pouch to carry her young. In placental animals, the foetus is nourished in an organ within the uterus.)

Now here is something that most people don't know about.

The peculiar animals of South America, New Zealand and Australia are found in those SAME regions **locally** in the RECENT "sub-fossil" deposits (that is, the superficial post-Flood deposits).

But did you know, on the **other continents**, they also occur in GENUINE FOSSIL FORM – in strata laid down by the Flood.

"Marsupial fossils - of a 12 foot kangaroo, for instance – have been discovered also in Europe and in North and South America."[2] In Australia, they are found **only** in RECENT upper strata, such as the Pleistocene (post-Flood).

I have received a report that in January, 1984, the *Cairo Times* broke the news that archaeologists working at Fayum near the Siwa Oasis uncovered kangaroo and other marsupial fossils.[3]

Late in 2003, it was announced that a fossil marsupial had been dug out of a quarry in China. Scientists claimed their find proves marsupials evolved in Asia.[4]

For that matter, marsupial fossils have now been found on **every** continent - yes, even Antarctica.

The marsupials possibly lived in Asia and along the Malay Peninsula for only a short time, on their journey to Australia. Since animals leave fossil remains only under rare and special conditions[5], the lack of fossil evidence for marsupials in southern Asia cannot be used as proof that they have never been in that area.

So much for FOSSIL marsupials. As for LIVING marsupials, A. Franklin Shull, Professor of Zoology at the University of Michigan, suggested a possible solution to the problem of why marsupials are today found for the most part only in Australia:

"The marsupials spread over the world, in all directions. They could not go far to the north before striking impossible climate, but the path south was open all the way to the tips of Africa and South America and through Australia... The placental mammals proved to be superior to the marsupials in the struggle for existence and drove the marsupials out... that is, forced them southward. Australia was then connected by land with Asia, so that it could receive the fugitives... Behind them the true mammals were coming; but before the latter reached Australia, that continent was separated from Asia, and the primitive types to the south were protected from further competition."[6]

The presence today of living marsupials in North and South America forbids the idea that the marsupials are an isolated evolutionary development of Australia.

Question: **But how could the frail, timid platypus have migrated to Southern Australia from Ararat?**

Perhaps a discovery announced in the press in 1993 may throw some light on this question:

"Australian palaeontologist Michael Archer has found another definite fossil platypus tooth in South America, making three in all. The teeth are almost identical to fossil platypus teeth found in Australia.

"He says, 'This should shatter our warm conviction that the platypus was uniquely Australian.'

"Today's platypuses, which have no teeth, are far inferior to earlier platypuses in other ways, too, Dr Archer notes. He is quoted as saying it has 'changed from a highly robust animal with good sets of teeth' into what is effectively 'an extremely degenerate small mammal'."[7]

So you can be sure that, like other animals, the platypus was originally a large, robust creature, well able to survive and migrate long distances.

Again, evidence shows not evolution, but the reverse - devolution.

More examples of dispersion
Let's take a quick look at some other examples of dispersion:
- The tapir, structurally distinctive and unique, occurs only on **opposite** sides of the globe - in Central and South America and in southeast Asia. When you think about it, the Ararat region (being central to both) is a logical dispersion point.
- Large, flightless birds of New Zealand, Madagascar and elsewhere probably dispersed to these remote areas soon after the Deluge. Their isolation protected them, until predators arrived in modern times.

The urge to disperse and replenish the earth was written into the instincts of animals. The tendency in most animals is to spread in all directions.

The gradual migration from Ararat took place as a relay race over successive generations. Along the route, only those environments that were suitable became permanent homes for particular groups. Some groups even became extinct.

In fact, animal migration is still taking place. And it can occur RAPIDLY. When Krakatoa erupted, there was total destruction of life there. Thirty-eight years later, 573 "species" of animals were back on the island!

Some mammals and reptiles are able to swim wide stretches of salt water. Did you know that crocodiles have been known to cross 558 miles of open ocean? Even reindeer have been captured by ships far from land. Snakes, polar bears and hippopotami are some other long swimmers.

And once they were in a new environment, adaptive changes could occur rapidly.

Post-Flood fossils

Most of the fossil-bearing layers of the earth were set down during the Flood. In exceptional circumstances a few may have been formed before that event. But we do know that some have been formed by localised catastrophe since the Deluge.

There are some localities where the deeper Flood strata are topped with post-Flood fossils in superficial layers above them. And some such post-Flood remains are as much as 50 feet below the surface.

WHAT ABOUT THE TIME FACTOR?

The question will surely be asked, Since we have so many varieties of animals and plants today, how on earth could these have developed from the ones that left the Ark?

Isn't 4,500 years just too short a time?

On the Galapagos Islands, for example, there are 13 species of finches. It is usually speculated that for these to develop from an original pair of finches must have taken from one million to five million years.

Well, let's see.

This is a good time to draw attention to a fact of genetics that has a bearing on this question.

PROGRAMMED FOR VARIATION

The laws of genetics have shown us that each basic type, whether dog, butterfly or human, has programmed into it the capacity for variation. This ensures survival in different environments.

The Yarrow is an example of the marvellous adaptability which lies within the hereditary complex of many plant kinds:
- medium height races along the coast
- tall races inland
- low, mat-forming races on the mountain tops.

Yet, with all this variety within the basic type, there is never any doubt that a new race of yarrow is still a yarrow.

It is true, you see, that an organism's DNA programme (inbuilt set of instructions) imposes limits:
- variations within the basic type, yes,
                    BUT
- capacity to turn into a different basic type of organism, no!

Take dogs, for example. From an original pair have come wolves, dingoes, coyotes, and so on.

In the varieties that appear, *no new genetic information* is introduced. Each new variety is more *specialised* than the original parent, and thus carries less information – and consequently has less potential for further selection. (Thus, in dogs, you can't breed Great Danes from Chihuahuas.)

So no matter how many variations take place within a "kind", kangaroos are still kangaroos, dogs are still dogs and finches are still finches.

A long-legged sheep may mutate into a short-legged sheep – but never into a deer. A white moth species may change into a grey moth – but never will it become a spider. Scientific breeders can produce seedless grapefruit, white turkeys, cattle without horns – but all within the limits of the original type.

There are LIMITS to change, you see. These limits are set by the amount of information that was originally present, from which to select.

HOW LONG FOR VARIATIONS TO OCCUR?

Now for the time factor.

The important point to remember is this.

All these life forms **don't have to spend time evolving new features. They only have to select from the genetic information they already possess**.

And this does NOT take long!

That's the clue.

Sweet peas can be frilled, plain, scented, scentless, red, white or blue – but they are still sweet peas. Did you know that of the 500 types of sweet pea we have, all have developed from a single type since the year 1700?

Well, that's artificial selection, I hear someone say. That is quick, simply because man is deliberately acting on each generation.

All right. Then let's observe natural selection at work on its own.

Darwin's finches are usually hailed as an example of evolution. So that is a good place for us to start. Did you know that an experimental study was done on these finches?[8]

Finches native to one island were placed on other isolated islands in the Galapagos that had no finches – and they were studied for their ability to adapt to the various ecological niches.

It was discovered that after 17 years each island had finches that were unique to that particular island. This was an adaptive process that evolutionists predicted would take 40 million years.

The intensive study of the Galapagos finches undertaken by Princeton zoology professor Peter Grant produced surprising results. He found that during years of drought, as finches depleted the small-seed supply, the finches that survived were those with larger, deeper beaks which could get at the remaining large seeds. This shifted the population in that direction.

Grant was amazed at the *observed* rate of change in the population. At this *observed* rate, he estimates, it would take only 1,200 years to transform the medium ground finch into the cactus finch, for example. Or only 200 years to convert it into the more similar large ground finch.[9]

Geneticist Dr Eugene Dunkley of Oxford University gave this assessment of the findings:

"Clearly, adaptation in the natural world is based on principles and mechanisms not proposed by evolutionists, and these mechanisms must be inherent throughout all living organisms."[10]

You see, *no new genes are being produced* by mutation. It is simply the selection of what is already there. This fails to qualify as evidence for real, uphill (macro) evolution.

Rather, it is evidence that "downhill" adaptation into several varieties can easily occur *in just a few centuries* – not requiring millions of years.

Dr Dunkley puts it this way, that "all organisms would have needed an inherent ability to rapidly adapt to the altered [post-Flood] environments. This would require specific created mechanisms for survival and precludes the possibility of random mutational changes (neo-Darwinistic evolution) as the means for variety of life on this planet."[11]

According to this geneticist, the evidence points to original genetic pre-programming, for survival, and not random mutations.

Bear in mind, also, that after the Flood, with
- residual catastrophes occurring as the earth was settling down and drying out (see Chapters 18 and 19), and with
- changing climate (Chapter 20), and
- rapid migration into new, empty niches,

selection pressure would have been much more intense.

Evidently, the time factor since the Great Flood is quite adequate.

* * * * * * *

In this chapter, we have briefly surveyed the dispersion of animal and plant life after the Deluge.

Now we embark on an even more interesting topic – the launching out into the unknown by the first bands of adventurous humans.

7

From Ararat:
The first migration (a) -

INTO THE UNKNOWN

"I love you," said Helene. "I love you so much. I want a son who'll be just like you."

Shem snuggled close to his wife. "Let's have a little one soon, my sweet."

"Hear that rain outside?" she whispered. "It scares me. If anything should happen to you..."

"Nothing to worry about, angel. The rainbow is a promise it will never happen again."

"I know. But I can't help it. Everything's so different now..."

"By this time next cycle, you'll have it."

"Not **IT**, Shemmy," she giggled. "He's going to be a **PERSON**! Then there'll be nine of us."

* * * * * * *

SPEED OF POPULATION GROWTH

After the Flood, Noah and his family became the total world population. Those eight people must have felt a deep sense of being alone. Surely they had a great longing for children. That they started to fulfil that longing right away is indicated by the fact that the first recorded post-Flood birth was in the year after they came out of the Ark.[1]

Several factors would have favoured a rapid population growth:

1. The Table of Nations in Genesis 10 suggests that **large families** must have been normal. Sixteen sons are listed for Noah's 3 sons. Since each boy had a wife, Noah's 3 sons must also have had about an equal number of daughters for a total of, say, 32

children, or just under 11 per couple. Eleven sons are listed for Canaan and 13 for Joktan. How many daughters they had, is of course, unknown. From these examples it seems reasonable to suggest that the average family had at least 10 children.

2. **Longevity** also favoured rapid population increase.[2] Given the facts of the book of Genesis, it would not be unreasonable to suggest a low mortality for at least the first 200 years after the Flood. These factors would favour rapid population growth. Also, according to Genesis 10, the time span from the birth of one generation to the next (not the length of life) averaged 30 or so years, or about three generations per hundred years.

At ten children per family per generation, what would have been the population in 100 years after the Flood? In 200 years after the Flood?

With three couples to start (Noah's three sons Ham, Shem and Japheth, with their wives), each couple having ten children, and having their first child at 30, the following would have been the result:

Generation	Yrs after Flood	Population
3 begins	60	800
4 begins	90	4,000
5 begins	120	20,000
8 begins	210	2,500,000

On this result, the yearly average population growth would have been a little over 5.5 percent.

A modern example

An example of rapid population growth (mainly from births) from Canadian history, may be of some interest.

"In the conquered province of Quebec, the people multiplied with astonishing celerity. In 1760, their numbers were approximately 60,000, and in 1790, 160,000, an increase in one generation of about 166 percent, about 5 percent annually. The birth rate after the conquest seems to have been higher than before it; in 1770 it had reached the astronomical figure of 65 per 100. After all, there was land and food for all."[3]

The conquest spoken of was the British conquest of Canada in 1759 and 1760.

The increase mentioned was wholly or mostly due to births. After 1759 there was very little immigration for quite a few years.

A COMMON CIVILISED ORIGIN

Despite misleading speculations by some people, real archaeological evidence almost invariably points to the origin of true civilisation as having occurred in the Middle East several thousand years ago. The evidence comes from agriculture, animal domestication, metallurgy, pottery, writing, urbanization and language.

And something else. The reality of all **verified** history - not theories, but verified FACTS - depicts man AT HIS BEST in the beginning.[4]

However far we go back, for example, into the history of Egypt, there is no indication of any early period of savagery or barbarism there. This applies to all cultures.

And, as we saw in Chapter 4, the traceable footsteps come from the Middle East mountains. This should not surprise us, if the Genesis record is true history.

TWO HUMAN DISPERSALS

An interesting claim is made in the Bible: that there were TWO DISPERSALS after the Deluge.

1. "And the whole earth was of one language, and of one speech."[5] This was the initial rapid dispersal FROM ARARAT, with one language over the whole world, during which was undertaken a geographical survey of the globe. Over "the whole earth".
2. Later, a language disturbance at BABEL resulted in the inhabitants being scattered "abroad upon the face of all the earth."[6] This was a widespread, though more limited dispersal.

Clues in ancient writing

Place names can give valuable clues for events in ancient history.

Nelson Glueck observed that the most ancient geographical names are faithfully reflected in modern designations. For example, Eriha is the word Jericho; Beisan is old Beth-shan, and so on. When an explorer or archaeologist is searching for an ancient site it is crucial for him to pay attention to the modern place names in the area he is searching.[7]

We can follow the path of Alexander the Great as he conquered the East by observing the place names that still exist all the way from Macedonia to India. These **place names capture moments of history** 2,300 years ago.

Place names go back further still.

There is abundant evidence that before the Phoenicians and Egyptians travelled the world, certain key names and words had already been taken throughout the world.

Although these names and words have undergone change, they can still be recognised. They are found in the native names of rivers and mountains, of volcanoes, waterfalls, lakes, islands, regions, towns and cities. They are found in tribal names, in mythological and deified names, and the names for animals, birds, fish, flowers, trees, foods and parts of the body.

These KEY WORDS, blended into many combinations in many languages, can be identified in TWO DISTINCT GROUPS.

Long term studies by Irish etymologist John Philip Cohane have established that there were anciently TWO MAJOR DISPERSALS of people from the Middle East.

Each group took with it an already established group of root words.

He says:

"If one puts a charted overlay containing only the first group of names on top of a map of the world and then puts on top of that another charted overlay containing only the second group of names, the most logical conclusion is that, in prehistoric times, instead of one there were two dispersions from the Mediterranean."[8]

Words of the first group are found in all parts of the world.

The FIRST dispersal covered the "whole world" in a very short time.

The SECOND was heavily concentrated in a limited area of the world: the Mediterranean area, Africa and parts of Asia, "petering out along the eastern coast of the Americas in one direction (and) in Japan, the Philippines, Australia and New Zealand in the other direction."[9]

Thus **two old dispersions** of people have been identified and recorded.

We shall now follow in the footsteps of the **first migration wave** - which includes those who re-mapped the world after the Great Flood.

8

The first migration (b) -
ONE GLOBAL LANGUAGE

That afternoon in 2002, as Gary Vey of *ViewZone* magazine trudged out of the dry canyon, it was blistering hot.

But he was excited. He had just located some ancient petroglyphs.

The remote canyons of the Pergatoire River nestle in the Comanche National Grassland, just south of La Junta, Colorado.

The river is fed by winter snow in the higher Rocky Mountains. But when Gary went in again in 2002, the river was almost dry.

It was time now to re-examine the petroglyphs. Photos had already been taken in the mid-1990s by William McGlone after he had carefully enhanced the petroglyphs with aluminium powder.

There was something special about these particular petroglyphics.

The ancient alphabetic symbols were virtually identical to those found in the Har Karkom region of the Negev desert of Israel, in South Australia, in Yemen, in Chile (South America), and in the British Isles!

The Colorado inscriptions. Photo: Gary Vey

Large, house-sized chunks of rock rested near the shore of the river. They had once provided an ideal blackboard. The stone surface was typically flat, and the ancient writers had pecked alphabetic symbols into the stone. Pecking with a sharp object would have originally exposed the bright underlying layer of fresh stone, in contrast to the dark outer surface. This made petroglyphs an excellent and permanent medium for writing.

Today the petroglyphs have a layer of dark patina, or varnish, which makes them the same black colour as the surface of the stone. This is evidence of their extreme antiquity. But it also makes them difficult to photograph.

Often these older petroglyphs will be found underneath more recent Amerindian carvings. They are distinguished by their "pecked" construction. Most American Indian petroglyphs are, by contrast, scraped into the surface of the stone.

After numerous attempts at deciphering, translations were eventually made with success through an old Hebrew dialect. This was achieved by concentrating on words containing one, two or three consonants.

The Colorado alphabet contains basic, distinct geometric shapes, 22 in all, and with some variations.

It is in the "cursive" style, where individual letters are combined and are read from right to left, from top to bottom.

This same ancient alphabet has now been found on six continents. Vey has termed it "The First Tongue".

Israel's Negev desert has been explored by Dr. James Harris, of BYU. He documented the "old Negev" script in the desert during the Harvard expedition in 1994. A superb job was done in identifying some of the grammar and structure of the petroglyphs.

In Australia, another team examined and depicted similar petroglyphs. And translations of that material proved that it originated with the same root culture and ascribed to the same rules of grammar and symbols.

"Translations and grammar," asserts Vey, "suggest a global human culture thrived in antiquity."

As this chapter was being prepared, Vey had led four expeditions to document this ancient alphabet. He had found and translated ancient script in North America, Yemen, Israel and Australia.

SAME ORIGINAL CULTURE, SAME RELIGION

The content of the translations, although not complete, suggests a common culture and religious belief system.

Although not enough translation was yet completed to determine the specific message, the multiple references to "breed" and "pedigree," as well as references to fleeing from "poisonous powder" (dust) and "painful light" are quite interesting.

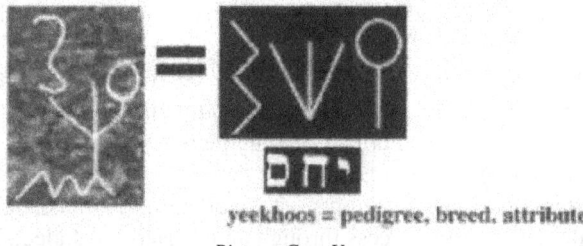

yeekhoos = pedigree, breed, attribute

Picture: Gary Vey

Such references would be most pertinent in those early turbulent centuries which followed the Flood.

In Colorado's Pergatoire Canyon, two common petroglyphs represent the names of deity - "EL" and "YAH". "EL" represents the abstract form of deity - that which cannot be comprehended by man, while "YAH" is the Creator. Both concepts represent a single deity - One God - but recognise the aspects of "knowable" and "unknowable" deity.

avad=lost illi=overhead tsel=protection

Notice the Lamed+Yod on the far left, arranged as an "arm," protecting "overhead."

Picture: Gary Vey

A successful translation has been made of the entire top row, reading, "YARE HA EL", or "PRAISE THE LORD".

This indicates a religious belief akin to that of the later Hebrews. It hints at an original faith inherited from Father Noah... and reflected in the Bible.

THE GLOBAL SURVEYORS

In this early period, surveyors likewise left their traces all over the world. They employed a larger variety of symbols.

The Flood survivors, you see, found themselves on a changed and damaged planet.

One resource was of particular concern. Pre-Flood scientists had unlocked a secret. They had discovered our spinning planet to be a giant generator, its land masses crisscrossed with energy lines. These magnetic currents they had harnessed. But now all trace of the power network was gone.

Within centuries the rapidly expanding population sent out exploratory expeditions. Soon almost every corner of the world was visited by a group of men who came with a particular task to accomplish.

They were charged with relocating those energy springs and constructing a grid pattern to harness them.[1]

Messages on stone

These early surveyors left their traces on every continent. A single system of signs was used. They used 241 special sequences of particular geometric signs and symbols. In their repetition and locations, the symbols had meaning and purpose. They left these guide signs on stone to mark the way for others who would follow them.

Research by English archaeologist S.F. Hood and by others indicates that this single system of signs originating in the Middle East was spread over a wide area in a very short time. There are striking parallels in symbols in Europe, Asia, Africa, America and Australia.

An Australian example is Chambers Gorge, in the grid zone surrounding Wilpena Pound. This ancient river valley contains two cliff walls facing each other, absolutely covered in writing. Deeply etched, ancient rock carvings, some of them strangely familiar, and yet not an Aboriginal motif amongst them.

Light-box tracings from infrared photographs reveal the clarity and precision of the various 'written entries' on the cliff face.

Many of the highly stylised glyphs are remarkably similar to that of early Sanskrit, Easter Island and early Chinese. There are even figures that remind one of early Egyptian or Phoenician craft.

The suggestion is of a mother tongue belonging to a one-time world culture.

Another incredible site, likewise in South Australia, is Red Gorge. It is now a dry river bed with twin cliff faces of blood-red stone that has weathered in huge blocks.

Here, as elsewhere, the circle within a circle with a straight line through it, appears to be the signature of those who came to this power grid intersection point when the earth was young. The same symbol is found at other key grid vortexes around the world.

Before the Aborigines

The archaeological reports from the 1930s make it clear that the Aboriginal people of the time had no knowledge of the carvings, and insisted they were made long before their people came.[2]

To Antarctica

Maps from this ancient period[3] show that the world was mapped before, during and after the Ice Age. This included the rivers and fjords of Antarctica BEFORE the ice sheet formed.

The evolutionary view speculates that ice has covered Antarctica for a million years. This has to be wrong!

Several ancient traditions indicate that Antarctica was once inhabited.

Australian Aborigines call Antarctica a "land of the gods" which became covered at an early time with "cool water and quartz crystals" (ice and snow).

Polynesians declared that before Antarctica became covered with ice, several nations peopled it.

If Antarctica was once of sufficient interest for surveyors to carefully map its ice-free coastline, mountains and rivers, surely one may assume that people lived there and engaged in commerce.

During the International Geophysical Year, American scientists fished up from the bed of the Antarctic Ocean specimens of a muddy sediment which showed that in comparatively "recent" times Antarctic rivers had borne down to the sea the alluvial products of an ice-free land.

Serge Hutin mentions a report in 1961 that one of the American stations in Antarctica found beneath an enormous accumulation of ice the remains of a very old stone pavement.[4]

Pacific region

Legends of New Zealand, Hawaii and the New Hebrides talk about fair-complexioned people who preceded the Polynesians.

There can be no doubt about this. There were **two** migrations. But those people of the first migration have been all but forgotten.

They travelled and mapped the world.

ONE ORIGINAL LANGUAGE

The fact that the whole world once spoke the same language survives in the racial memory of many people.

A fragmentary Sumerian tablet copied by the Oxford cuneiformist Oliver Gurney speaks of a time when "the whole universe" spoke "in one tongue."

The epic tale *Enmerker and the Lord of Araita*, published by Professor S.N. Kramer, of the University of Pennsylvania, records that all mankind spoke one and the same language until Enki, the Sumerian god of wisdom, confounded their speech.

The idea that there was a time when all men spoke the same language is found also in ancient Egyptian and Indian writings.

Even the *Popul Vuh*, a book of the Central American Maya records that "those who gazed at the rising of the sun [the ancestors who formerly lived eastward of the Americas]... had but one language... before going west."

And the book of Genesis records that "all the earth was of one language, and of one speech."[5]

Yes, one language... and a unified alphabet.

WHAT THE ALPHABET TELLS US

Man's great sophistication in very early times, widespread travel, and interaction with distant lands and peoples, is seen in a study of the alphabet.

We have all been lulled with the story that writing began with cruder forms of speech recorded as pictograms and that the alphabet was a relatively recent discovery made many thousands of years later.

Wrong! There is now good evidence that most of the alphabetic signs are older than hieroglyphics. The alphabet was not derived from hieroglyphics or pictograms.[6]

For the alphabet, there is no trace of any sequence of simple to complex, as required by the evolution theory.

In the most ancient times, both Egypt and China had an alphabet, but chose not to develop their communication system by this means.

It is well known that many ancient peoples used their alphabet as a system of numerals. But there was more to it. There seem to be connections between the alphabet and the calendar, in which the forms and arrangement of the letters owe something to astromony.

Gustavus Seyffarth, an expert on the decipherment of Egyptian hieroglyphics, also translated Phoenician, Chinese, Chaldean, Greek and Roman myths which clearly relate the formulation of the alphabet to the zodiac.[7] The zodiac, you may realise, is simply the visible pathway taken by the sun or moon against the background of the starry sky.

Vowels in some ancient alphabets represent the position of planets among the houses of the lunar zodiac (the **consonants**) *at a critical point in human history*. We should note, in passing, that this is in no way connected with astrology. Nor was there such a necessary connection in the very ancient world.

It appears that the alphabet was derived from an original 28 to 30 lunar signs (representing the days of the month - and the location of the moon against the starry sky on each day). Indeed, there are startling correspondences between the lunar and the alphabetical signs.[8] It seems that each letter of the alphabet represents the daily halting place of the moon in relation to a nearby constellation.[9]

The alphabet must have had great antiquity, wide diffusion and some powerful cohesive principle outside itself in order to hold the signs in established order despite time, geography and circumstances.

Related lunar lists in both hemispheres reflect an ancient global network of mariners.

David Kelley collated and compared on both sides of the Pacific the day-names and animals used to represent the days of the lunar month, or the lunar zodiac. His results show no possibility of separate inventions, but point to the lunar zodiac as the common source of the more than 200 similar phonetic alphabets, with due allowance for considerable borrowing of the forms and values of the letters.[10]

So what do words and symbols tell us? They speak of an ancient sophistication. They tell us of ancient travel patterns, showing that ancient travellers left their calling cards all over the world. These were in the form of place names and symbols, which can be traced back to their sources in the Middle East.

But the surveyors had more on their minds than just mapping the earth.

Have you ever wondered about that spectacular circle of stones in Britain, known as Stonehenge? Speculations about its purpose have raged for years. I think we now have the answer...

9

The first migration (c) -

PYRAMID AND STONEHENGE MYSTERIES SOLVED

The ancient world surveyors had more on their minds than the earth's energy grid.
The calendar had to be re-calculated. The ancient calendars, you see, had the *year at 360 days long*.
It is from this number that is obtained the division of a circle, and the earth being divided into 360 degrees.
The ancient **Chinese** calendar was a 12-month year of 30 days each.
Babylonian records likewise show a year of 12 months of 30 days each. The old star maps had the sun moving through a path divided into 36 sections, each 10 days long.
The earliest **Romans** also had a year of 360 days. Plutarch, in his life of Numa, declared that in the time of Romulus the year was composed of twelve 30 day months.
The **Mayan** year (called a "tun") was of 360 days.
The *Aryabhatiya*, an ancient **Indian** work on mathematics and astronomy, says: "A year consists of 12 months. A month consists of 30 days. A day consists of 60 nadis. A nadi consists of 60 vinadikas."
The original **Egyptian** year was likewise 360 days long, according to the *Ebers Papyrus*.

A LONGER YEAR

But later, every nation changed its calendar.
It has been discovered in a number of ancient sources that there were four 9-day weeks to each lunar month – giving a month of 36 days. This special 9-day phase has been found, for example, in ancient Chinese, Greek, Babylonian and Roman sources. Of course, these lunar computations did not fit with a year of 360 days. So the

calendars were altered to a 10-month year. We can see in this an attempt to arrange the "new" year to fit the "old" 360-day year.

The people in the Gilbert Islands, the Marquesis Islands and also the Chams of Indonesia were found with a calendar of 10 months.

And we are familiar with a calendar change in which five days were added, and an extra day every fourth year.

This rearrangement of the calendars in antiquity has long been a puzzle to scholars. Why did all those ancient nations change their calendars from years of 360 days to 365 ¼ days?

Evidence of evolving knowledge... or of something else?

My neighbour Rob Payne thought he had come up with the answer. "Oh, I can explain that," he said. "The ancients first proposed a rough system of yearly count, and later, when their mathematical knowledge increased, they refined it."

Nice try, Rob.

Except we've now discovered that those ancient peoples were already excellent astronomers and mathematicians - yes, even when they created the 360 day calendar.

For example, the Maya have left us some of their calculations. They computed the synodal period of the moon as 29.5209 days, as accurately as we can calculate today with our sophisticated equipment. Their degree of accuracy would surely not have been less for the year.

Furthermore, would so many cultures in such widely scattered regions of the world all have made the very same mistake for the length of the year, and then all rectify it in the same way?

There is good reason to believe that the Great Pyramid of Egypt was built within a few hundred years after the Flood. The Great Pyramid accurately stands in the centre of the land surface of the earth as it now exists and must have existed at the time the pyramid was built.

It could be called a huge planet marker, a giant survey post. It marks both the longitude and latitude at which there is more land and less sea than at any other meridian on earth. Evidently the builders were well acquainted with the exact amount of land on the surface of the earth, as well as its geographical distribution.. This suggests that results of the global survey were already in.

It would explain why the **new length of the year** was also incorporated into the measurements of the Great Pyramid.

The external features, dimensions and units of this pyramid together give precisely and accurately every essential value of the earth's present motions and orbit.

For example, intentionally or by accident, the circuit distance around its base, measured direct from corner to corner, is 36,524.22 primitive inches. This is exactly 100 times 365.2422 - the value in days of our solar year.

This is so astonishing, we must take off our hats to those early post-Flood scientists. They were ahead of us in many ways. There was no rough count; it was precise to the ten thousandth of a decimal point.

What really happened

A tablet discovered at Tanus in the Nile Delta in 1866 reveals that in the ninth year of Ptolemy Euergetes (c. 237 BC), the priests at Canopus decreed that it was "necessary to harmonise the calendar according to the present arrangement of the world."

The reason the ancients gave for the re-calculated calendars was **not** that they were in error, nor that they had improved on more primitive techniques. It was that there was a "changed order of things."

And with each passing century, the calendar misalignment had become more pronounced.

The nations that sprang up after the Flood with a ready-made culture, inherited their knowledge basically from the world that was wiped out at the Deluge. They continued where Noah left off. They inherited, along with everything else, the antedeluvian (pre-Flood) calendar.

Was there, at the time of the Deluge, a change not only in the planet's axis, but **a change in its orbit**, which in turn caused the lengthened year?

It does bring to mind that curious biblical reference to the Creator, who was believed to "move the earth out of her place."[1]

It would certainly clear up a lot of mystery about Stonehenge, for example.

To re-calculate the earth's position (among other things)

The precision of Stonehenge is astonishing.

Consider the heel stone. This heavy boulder had to be set in a hole in the ground exactly in the right position. If placed too high, it would need to be taken out and the hole deepened. If too low, it would once more have to be shifted. Even if it had been dropped into precisely the right position, its 35 ton weight might well have made it settle lower. Nobody could know for sure how much it would eventually settle.

Such accuracy applied to every stone that was positioned.

Some of the fallen stones were re-erected in 1958. Extremely powerful cranes were used. Yet, even with this modern equipment, it proved impossible to align or set them up as accurately as had the ancient builders!

Gerald Hawkins, on the basis of computer syntheses of a great many measurements at Stonehenge, suggests that Stonehenge was, in fact, a computer for measuring all the relationships between earth, the sun and the moon.[2]

The heel stone and the trilithons and the shadows cast by the pillars all played an intricate role.

Experts have long puzzled over the 56 Aubrey holes. Hawkins suggests they could have functioned as a computer, this way:

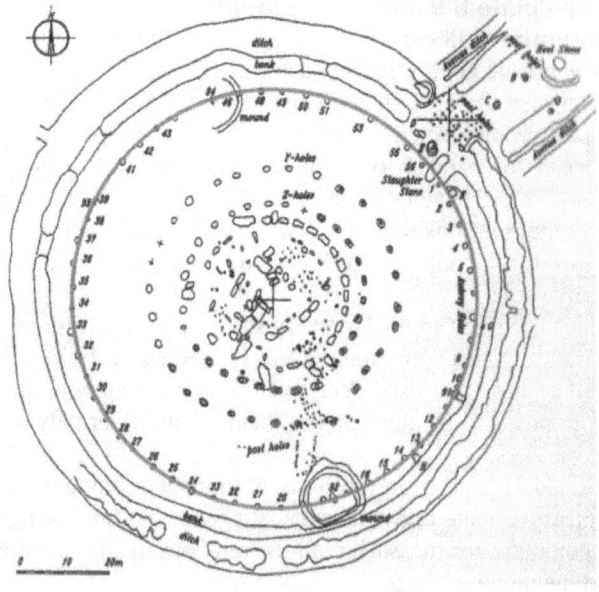

If one stone was moved around the circle by one hole each year, then all the extremes of the seasonal moon and eclipses of the sun and moon at the solstices and equinoxes, could have been foreseen. If six stones, spaced 9,9,10,9,9,10 Aubrey holes apart, were used, each of them moved one hole counterclockwise each year, amazing powers of prediction could result.

With 6 stones (3 white, 3 black), the Aubrey hole computer could have predicted - precisely - every important moon event for hundreds of years.

The terrestrial axis is currently inclined at 23½ degrees. The early Greek philosophers viewed this tilt as an "irregular condition," and not something that had been fixed since the beginning. Anaxagoras wrote:

"In the beginning the stars moved in the sky as in a revolving dome, so that the celestial pole which is always visible was vertically overhead; but subsequently the pole took its inclined position."

The Northern Hemisphere sun moves from a maximum position of $+23½°$ northward in summer to a $-23½°$ extreme southern declination in winter. The moon does a reverse move - north in winter, south in summer. The moon also has a more complicated relative motion than the sun; it has TWO northern and TWO southern maxima. In an 18.61 year cycle, it varies so that its far north and south declinations move from $29°$ to $19°$ to $29°$ again. This difference is due to the combined effects of the earth's tilt and precession of orbit.

The Stonehenge complex was precisely aligned to EVERY ONE of these movements. With the 18.61 - year cycle, the only way to attain accuracy with whole numbers is by the sequence 19-19-18, which, added together, make 56 - *the number of Aubrey holes!*

Amazing but true. Stonehenge is a brilliantly designed and constructed astronomical device, WHICH COULD CALCULATE EVERY POSITION of the sun and moon.

And why all this?

The Great Flood, we should consider, had a great deal to do with the construction of this and other precise stone structures. It appears that Stonehenge was built to determine the new orbital position and thus the new length of the year, as well as the new axial position of the earth, following the catastrophe.

If indeed the earth had been jolted abruptly from its original orbit, such a jolt would also have severely affected the moon. If the moon was on the side away from the sun when it happened, a change of our orbit away from the sun would have brought the moon closer to earth. The original shorter-year calendar (360 days) suggests that the earth was slightly closer to the sun. The original ancient lunar month was 36 days, which implies that the moon orbited the earth at a greater distance. The jolting of earth would have reversed this - the earth now being further from the sun would make a longer year; and the moon in orbit nearer to earth, a shorter month.

The truth is that revised ancient calendars reflect this change.

Stonehenge and its counterparts were built, one may reasonably conclude, to re-evaluate the length of the year and the lunar month.

Similar stone computers covered the whole of Britain and western France. They formed, possibly, a huge complex, with Stonehenge as the central unit, against which the findings of all the others were correlated.

And after their purpose had been accomplished there was no further need for them, and they were left.

That answers another question that has puzzled scholars. Why, after the final phase of Stonehenge was completed, was the site abandoned for many centuries - until the Druids began to use it as a gathering place?

The answer makes perfect sense. It was built to perform certain specific functions. Its purpose was accomplished. It was needed no more.

Degrees in a circle changed

The re-evaluation of the length of the year and the lunar month would ultimately lead to a revision of the ancient calendars. This was not accomplished overnight.

It is apparently from the original 360 day year that we still use a 360 degree circle. Interestingly, when the Chinese changed their year reckoning from 360 days to 365¼ days, they also altered their divisions of the circle. Instead of 360 degrees as formerly, they now calculated it into divisions of degrees.

Interestingly, as I was about to complete this chapter, a young lady emailed me concerning a television programme she had just seen.

"It mentioned a stone in England, at a place called Ilkley, with a carving on it similar to a swastika," she reported.

"They said that the carving was very ancient - and that only three such carvings existed in the world. I think one was in Italy.

"The point they made was that geographically the three locations create an exact equilateral triangle."

When you consider it, the fact of three stone carvings similar to each other, which are located to create an exact equilateral triangle, does make a lot of sense.

You see, after the Great Flood, when the surface of the earth was so much altered, so was the earth's orbit. This naturally affected the length of the year.

So surveying parties went all over the planet, to re-map the world and to re-calculate earth's relationship to the sun, moon and other objects in the sky. Triangulation of reference points, using three locations on earth would have been a part of this procedure.

Stonehenge and other sites served a common purpose. The three special stones the lady mentioned were very likely positioned as part of this mapping process. And new calendars would be an eventual result.

Originally, the swastika represented the cycle of the sun's perceived movement in the heavens.

But, as we know, in the mid-20th century, it came to represent something more sinister!

****

Yes, the first great migration was peaceful and successful. But the second would be a shocking disaster!

And talking about surprises... What was the body doing under the floor? Stay tuned. That's coming up next.

10

From Babel:
The second dispersal (a) -

THE NIMROD CONSPIRACY

Ahead of the dust cloud, twenty-two wild riders galloped in through the gates.

"Wiped out heaps more today," shouted the one behind the leader. "But they're spreading fast."

The first rider, a dark man of noble bearing, who looked to be the leader, slid down from his mount. He raised his arms to lift off the headband. Towering from it were two crescent horns. Bull's horns.

The roar of the villagers swelled to fever pitch. And was that music to his ears! He pushed through them and disappeared inside. Such adoration... how he loved it! Soon he'd have them eating out of his hand.

The earth had been devastated and the population almost wiped out. Since the disaster, the climate had become unstable, vegetation struggling. Food was hard earned. Men and wild beasts competed for survival. Nimrod's hour had come.

* * * * * * *

We cannot even imagine what the world was like around the Ark's landing place when the animal kingdom was reintroduced to the earth. It must have been terrifying at times, especially after the animals had grown in numbers. As families grew, it would have been necessary to build their homes in groups where they could protect themselves and their domesticated flocks and herds from the rapidly increasing numbers of predatory animals.

The wild animals were multiplying faster than the people. Predators such as lions and tigers, for example, reproduce in litters, having six or more young at a time, with very short gestation periods, compared to people and domesticated animals like cattle, sheep and goats, who generally produce only one or two offspring at a time with much longer gestation periods.

NEED FOR PROTECTION

It would be extremely important for families to remain together for mutual protection and that of their flocks and herds.

Ancient sites in Turkey have revealed large stone walls which, in the absence of any evidence of invaders, could only have been for protection from the wild animals. Also many ancient homes have been found which had no doorway but were entered through the roof by ladders which also could have been for this purpose.

The Asikli site (described in Chapter 5) is a good example. Here, entry and exit to the dwellings was via holes in the roof.

In various ancient sites, some houses were built side by side almost as one single unit, with doors entering a central courtyard with a single exit to the outside.

Also many buried their dead below a stone slab under the floor of their houses; this could very well have been to protect them from being dug up and eaten by animals. Man has long recognised the necessity of preventing animals from acquiring a taste for human flesh. A good example of this is the "man-eating tigers" of which we hear occasionally.

At Asikli, the dead were buried beneath the rooms' floors. They were interred complete with their jewellery. One woman has been found adorned with necklaces of beads, semi-precious stones and copper. (This is one of the very earliest known examples in the world of the use of metallurgy.)

The rapid growth of the predators must have made life very dangerous for the first, straggling populations. The situation was still the same 800 years later when the Israelites were entering their promised land:

"I will not drive them [the Hivite, the Hittite and the Canaanite] out from before thee in one year, **lest the land become desolate, and the BEASTS OF THE FIELD MULTIPLY AGAINST THEE.**"[1]

NIMROD THE HUNTER

"And Cush begat Nimrod: he began to be a mighty one in the earth. He was a mighty hunter before the Lord: wherefore it is said, Even as Nimrod the mighty hunter before the Lord."[2]

Nimrod was a grandson of Ham, ancestor of the coloured races. It was these very people who were destined to undertake the pioneering task of opening up the world, subduing it, and rendering it habitable. All the earliest civilisations of note would be founded and carried to their highest technical proficiency by Hamitic people.

Evidently, Nimrod established himself as the great "protector" of the people as he hunted down and killed the fierce, marauding animals. And this would have given him great influence and power among the people. It was he who **gathered** the people together and **organised** them to fight the wild and ferocious beasts.

There is a great deal of evidence of animals in the region which are no longer found there (hippopotami, elephants, cave bear, hyaena, and so on). Their fossils are not pre-Flood; they were post-Flood animals.

Nimrod emancipated the people after the Flood from their fear of the wild animals. His prestige grew. He became the leader in secular affairs. He was ambitious. So it was that Nimrod built a city of houses and surrounded this city with a high wall and gathered the people therein. Thus the people were protected and Nimrod was able to rule over them.

PAGANISM IS BORN

If Nimrod had simply delivered the people from the fear of wild beasts, that would have been fine. But not content with this, he now set out to deliver them from their awe of the Creator.

Nimrod wanted to be the "shining star" – the supreme one. And we shall explain how this was accomplished.

One early type of idol found all through the area is the "mother goddess of fertility". After the Flood, first and foremost in importance among the people would have been procreation – having children, as well as rapid growth in supply of animals and crops. Also, there is early evidence of nature worship, such as of the sun and moon.

Everything was dependent on the sun for life. The moon was perhaps looked upon as pertaining to the seasons for planting, etc.

Interestingly, the early pantheons of "gods" consisted of EIGHT – the same number of people who came through the Great Flood and founded the new world. To these eight "gods" were assigned separate attributes of the true God. But things expanded from there. Thus the concept of ancestor worship entered the new pagan religious system.

In fact, some of the very concepts that originated with Nimrod have remained through the ages and their influence can be found in almost every religion of today.

HOW COULD THE PEOPLE TURN FROM THE ORIGINAL FAITH SO QUICKLY?

The evidence available on this subject indicates to us that Nimrod was the person who developed the concept of the sun god – and, in fact, claimed to be the god, himself.

How could this happen?

Let's reflect back to their situation. Mankind was "beginning again", so to speak.

So long as the people remained around Noah in the Araxes Valley, they were exposed to the knowledge of the true God. But life was hard. Before the Flood, when mankind had first been placed upon this earth, it was perfect. Now, after the disastrous Flood, the entire face of the earth was harsh and rugged. Plants had to be cultivated, animals had to be bred and cared for. Everything had to be re-established under the harshest of conditions.

Hearing and re-hearing the story of the Flood and the wickedness of mankind which had brought about the Flood, it appears that in time, the majority of the people wanted to get away from Noah and his God, and "make **US** a name".

It appears that they also wanted a "new god", or religion, or at least accepted it quite readily. Noah's God couldn't be seen. The people decided they wanted something **visible**, even if only in a stone statue or in the physical presence of the sun.

Of course, the Creator (Noah's God) had "ruined" the world – first with a destructive world Flood, and now, for hundreds of years, the climate resulting from that cataclysm was wet, cold and largely sunless. This aftermath of the Flood would persist for centuries.

But the sun – now, **that** was warm and cheery – why couldn't that be their god? After all, it gave LIFE to everything, didn't it? And so SUN WORSHIP began to take root.

So it was that Nimrod – and later powerful leaders – could get the people to do **anything** they wanted by convincing them that they (the leaders) were, as it were, "god in the flesh", or at least the god's chosen representative on earth. And that they MUST obey this "god" (or "god's representative").

TIME TO MOVE OUT

There had already been a First Dispersion. And in Chapter 8 we noted two features of that earlier dispersion, which was from the Ararat region of what is today Turkey:
1. A global survey was undertaken.
2. Some colonies were established here and there for the exploitation of resources. Some of these small colonies would eventually grow into cities.

But most of the population remained clustered around the Middle East "cradle".

Now Nimrod's group decided to get out of Noah's valley – the Araxes valley - and set up somewhere else.

"FROM THE EAST"

This is where we come upon an ancient biblical narrative which tells of the exodus of a group of people from the area first settled by Noah and his descendants after the Flood. "…as they journeyed **from the east**, they found a plain in the land of Shinar: and they dwelt there"[3]

From experience in field research, I have discovered the biblical writings time and again to be a credible authority. So let's note this statement carefully. It says that the people who left the area of Noah's Ark travelled **to the west**. Common sense adds the additional information that they travelled along a river – a water supply for the people as well as their flocks and herds would have been an absolute necessity.

It seems that the migrants began their journey at the beginning of one of the mountain streams that was a tributary of the Euphrates River near the area of the Ark, and followed it to the west until they came **to a plain**.

Topographical and flight maps of the region show where the Euphrates River exits the mountainous region – roughly a 250 mile journey from the region of the Ark. And there, where the mountains end, one finds a tremendous plain!

Another route which they could have taken would have brought them to the same plain but by an easier and more direct path. This second route would have taken them in a south-west direction for about 140 miles until they reached the west side of Lake Van. From there, they would have travelled along a river about 50 miles through a mountain pass, to exit onto the vast plain. Here they could travel west until they reached the Euphrates.

These are the only two natural east-west routes across Anatolia. Which route they took, we may never know. However, both would have brought the group to the same general area.

Put yourself in their place. Once they found this massive plain, would they have travelled further, if that region already contained all the natural resources that they would have needed, which it did? (We shall discuss these resources later.)

Could this be the biblical "plain in the land of Shinar" where they settled? On the map, you will see the location of Ararat (the Ark region, top right hand corner) and in the map centre is a black dot, which marks the spot where the mountains end and the plain begins. Could this be where Babel was located?

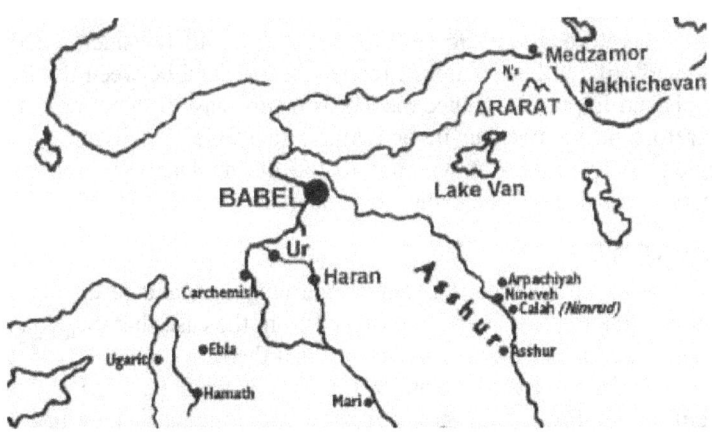

"A PLAIN IN THE LAND OF SHINAR"

The term "land of Shinar" has been interpreted to mean only the area far to the south of the Turkish plains – the area of Babylon. But, in fact, we have no firm evidence of the boundaries of this "land of Shinar".

Akkadian cuneiform texts mention "Shanhara" as being in northern Mesopotamia, west of Nineveh, the same mountainous region that is today called "Singar". The Amarna Letters (Egyptian) also mention a land called "Shanhar" which is also in northern Syria. These examples are in the same general region as our suggested site.

In fact, the name may still be reflected, even today, in a road sign for a town we discovered very close to here. In Turkish, "C" is pronounced "Ch". This town in southern Turkey is on the edge of the giant plain which we were discussing earlier – and our Turkish helper told us it is pronounced "**Shinar**" ("**Chinar**")!

The next biblical mention of Shinar occurs at a much later date:

"And the Lord gave Jehoiakim king of Judah into his hand, with part of the vessels of the house of God: which he carried into the land of Shinar to the house of his god".[4]

Since this above passage refers to the Babylon of Nebuchadnezzar's time, we know where it is located, which is far south of this region.

Therefore, there are several possibilities to consider: perhaps "Shinar", like "Mesopotamia", referred to the land between the Rivers Tigris and Euphrates. Since the Tigris begins east of our site, it would therefore be included in it; or perhaps in Daniel 1:2 it refers to the region (Babylonia) that was dominated during Daniel's time by the people (Chaldeans) who came from the more northerly region.

THE TOWER

"And the whole earth was of one language, and of one speech. And it came to pass, as they journeyed from the east, that they found a plain in the land of Shinar; and they dwelt there.

"And they said one to another, Go to, let us make brick, and burn them thoroughly. And they had brick for stone, and slime had they for mortar. And they said, Go to, let us build us a city and a tower, whose top may reach unto heaven: and let us make us a name, lest we be scattered abroad upon the face of the whole earth."[5]

BAKED BRICKS AND "SLIME"

"And they said one to another, Go to, let us make brick and burn them thoroughly. And they had brick for stone, and slime had they for mortar."[6]

They built the city and tower of Babel with baked brick and used "slime" for mortar. In 1995, when I first explored the region and examined a very large tell, I took samples of the baked brick and the mortar. The very black mortar consisted of a mixture of sand and tar (bitumen/asphalt) which hardens when dried.

Since this is a petroleum product, we must enquire: Did this area have a supply? The 1985 *Encyclopaedia Brittanica* states that the only oil fields in Turkey are in Ramana (west of this site) and Gaziantep (east of this site), both less than 100 miles away. The latest revision of the flight map shows oil wells in the immediate area, and the pipeline between Gaziantep and Ramana follows directly under the region. In our 1995 expedition, we saw working oil derricks in the immediate vicinity.

The presence of oil here, about 4,000 years after the time of Babel, indicates that an ample supply of bitumen most likely could have been obtained by the builders of this infamous city and tower. In fact, it may have been a major reason for selecting the area.

"LET'S BUILD US A CITY AND MAKE US A NAME"

"And they said, Go to, let us build us a city and a tower, whose top may reach unto heaven; and let us make us a name, lest we be scattered abroad upon the face of the whole earth"[7]

The command had been given to Noah's family: "Be fruitful, and multiply, and replenish the earth".[8] Yet, in the passage concerning Babel we learn that when the time came that the mass of people set out from the Ararat region, they all congregated together to build ONE city in order to AVOID being scattered "upon the face of the whole earth".

They also wanted to "make US a name". Evidences of ancient history all point to the fact that these earliest of people had, for the most part, rejected the sovereignty of their Creator.

Yes, the people wanted their OWN name, and they received it, as we shall later see. But it wasn't what they had in mind.

ADVANCED KNOWLEDGE

"And the Lord said, Behold the people is one, and they have all one language; and this they begin to do: and now nothing will be restrained from them, which they have imagined to do."[9] The implication is that the people at Babel possessed tremendous knowledge. I dare say that the ziggurats and cities at Babylon and Ur in lower Mesopotamia reflect nothing of what these people were capable of. Even the pyramids of Egypt, which are even today a great engineering feat, probably can't compare to whatever was begun at Babel.

"*...nothing will be restrained from them, which they have imagined to do.*"

What could this mean? What were they capable of doing? I don't know. But there is evidence that man after the Flood possessed tremendous knowledge.[10] I suspect that had the people remained united and of one language, with the pre-Flood knowledge that they possessed, they would have reached a level of technological advancement in just a matter of years that is equal to or beyond that which we have reached only in the last 100 or so years. There are evidences that the earliest peoples in this region possessed very advanced technical knowledge, to the puzzlement of modern archaeologists and scholars.

The only thing that prevented a very advanced civilisation from soon erupting was, in my opinion, the lack of personnel and the fact that for many, many years after the Flood, they had to concentrate on breeding the animals and cultivating crops to sustain their lives.

When the time came that these things were established, the people could concentrate on other things. And with every great mind on earth together in accord and of one language, we cannot imagine what they could have done.

We have been "brainwashed" with the idea of early man being primitive and animal-like, but the evidence does NOT show this to be the case.

MISTAKEN POPULAR THEORIES

When we study the archaeological journals and reports, we must be careful to separate the physical evidence from the opinions of the excavators or those writing the reports. They all too often assume that first came the cave-man, then fire, etc. And they assign dates to archaeological sites based on these assumptions.

But think about this! If a rocket scientist suddenly found himself in a world that had just experienced a global disaster, with little but a barren landscape of renewing plant and animal life, would we expect him to find or build launch-pads? If America were covered in dirt and archaeologists one day dug it up, would they date the fancy, modern homes of today as from the same time period as those in Papua New Guinea jungles that have no plumbing or electricity? I suspect they would place thousands of years between them.

The point is, when mankind left their first home near Noah and the Ark, they did have knowledge. What they didn't have were the ready-made resources.

THE TOWER REBELLION

The tower, dedicated "unto heaven" (to the worship of the host of heaven, an astrological system) was the actual headquarters of a rebel movement which aimed to seize control of the world.

Building the tower was a case of clear-cut DEFIANCE of the Creator. In the first place, God had promised never to send another universal Flood; the tower builders said God had lied (and they decided that to protect themselves from another Flood they should build a great tower whose top would reach above the deepest flood waters.) In the second place, the Flood had destroyed only the rebels; The Creator Himself had protected the faithful. The tower builders were saying that they would live exactly as they pleased, and would protect themselves. God was superfluous.

DEITY INTERVENES

Once again, the Creator intervened. It seems to me that He has a timetable for world events, upon which He imposes limits. When mankind had reached the point of almost complete degradation, He sent the global Deluge. When mankind again embarked upon a path SO SOON, which was contrary to His plan, He intervened in a manner that caused them to comply with His command to "replenish the earth".

Nimrod persuaded the people that they could find security without God if they stayed together under his rule. Babel was **a project of clear-cut defiance**.

There was an urgency about being connected. They conceived a plan for a united world government. Oppressive and cruel laws were planned by Nimrod and his henchmen. Had they gone unchecked, they would have demoralised the world in its infancy.

The symbol of their defiance – the tower of Babel – was already reaching high above the plain.

Then it happened. Many factors were involved. But, in brief, there was a catastrophic interruption to their plan.

The population at this time would be anywhere from 4,000 to 25,000.

THE LANGUAGE CONFOUNDED

"Go to, let us go down, and there confound their language, that they may not understand one another's speech. So the Lord scattered them abroad from thence upon the face of all the earth: and they left off to build the city... Therefore is the name of it called Babel; because the Lord did there confound the language of all the earth: and from thence did the Lord scatter them abroad upon the face of all the earth."[11]

The name of the first city that they built was called "Babel", which means, simply, "Confusion" or "Mingled". The people wanted to "make US a name", and they did. Imagine the scene – this city of certainly thousands of people working side by side, building not only their city, but this massive tower, the first ever built after the Flood, whose design was to extend up into the very clouds of "heaven". (The fact that they chose this design may imply that they knew about similar pre-Flood structures.)

Workmen at the top ordered materials from those down below. Then, the materials were despatched to the workmen at the top.

But then, something occurred that no one expected – They no longer could understand each other. There was a sudden multiplication of languages (evidently by miraculous means).

Maybe the ones next to each other could understand one another, but those below them only heard gibberish when the next call came for materials. The scene must have been one of chaos. It is impossible to imagine what it must have been like. All we are told is that at some point after this "confusion" of languages, they ceased work on the city and were scattered "abroad upon the face of all the earth".

Family groups were not able to get on with other family groups. People now wanted to get away from each other. The inevitable result was that those who understood each other moved off together.

So began the DISPERSION from the Mesopotamian plain in all directions across the super-continent.

In a moment, we shall examine more compelling evidence that it was indeed this very area that the different languages originated.

11

From Babel:
The second dispersal (b) -

LANGUAGES AND THE DISPERSION

Imagine a town where SUDDENLY many, many different languages were spoken.

In the confusion, what would you do? Firstly, everyone would find those who speak their own language. Then decisions would be made about what to do next. It would be almost impossible to continue planting, harvesting, building, with those to whom you cannot communicate. Especially back then when there were no translators.

The next step would most likely be to find a separate place to live.

You'd need room to raise your crops; fields for your flocks; and space to build a permanent settlement. Some language groups may set out and settle 25 miles from the original town; others would have to travel 100 miles or even more before they could find a suitable location.

As time passed, the land nearby would already be taken and new groups would have to travel further and further away to find a suitable location. Some might be more ambitious and travel much, much further – perhaps 1,000 miles away.

But, as with all things, there would survive remnants of many, many of the original language groups in the general area.

"LANGUAGES BIRTHPLACE"

And today, nowhere else on earth can you find so many different tongues being spoken in such a small area: "**Many ancient races and tribes still inhabit the Caucasus** [the mountains above Noah's Ark which form the northern barrier of the Araxes plain] **and the Armenian plateau of eastern Anatolia. As many as fifty different** languages and dialects are spoken in this vast and, in parts, inaccessible region."[1] "Strabo informs us (Book XI,5), that **no less than seventy Dialects were spoken in the country, which even then was called the Mountain of Languages**."[2]

The further one travels from this area, the fewer languages we find being spoken in an area (except in cases of immigration, such as in the USA and Australia). This evidence alone is sufficient to show where the languages began.

POST-BABEL WRITING

It would take some time and effort for the various language groups to work out a means of communication with each other.

When true writing systems were organised, many times they contained bi-lingual inscriptions, or the same message written side by side in two or more languages, which indicates the presence of numerous languages in the area.

"In Anatolia, at least, the ethnic and linguistic situation seems to have been exceedingly complex... Although few, if any inscriptions are available for this region before the rise of the Hittite empire, about 1800 (B.C.)... there were certainly a great variety of languages and cultures functioning within a comparatively small area. Tablets from the Hittite archives at Boghaz Keui **are written in at least 17 different languages**, several of which cannot be related to any known linguistic stocks."[3]

Here we have proof that within a few hundred years, there were people capable of translating "at least 17 different languages"!

LANGUAGE GROUPS

The Table of Nations (Genesis 10) gives us a photo-start breakdown of the language groups which were formed into nations at the time of the Babel dispersion.[4]

The figure given in that table of up to 46 basic language groups is not unrealistic in regard to the active language groups in the world today.

From these originals, the languages of the earth have developed.

Of course, there are now thousands of languages, but there is a definite grouping of them (Aboriginal, Sino-Tibetic, Dravidian, etc.,

etc.). Careful study of these basic modern language groups shows that they are not in excess of the number allowed for in Genesis 10.

While the biblical story of the confusion of tongues and the forced worldwide dispersion from Babel is commonly ridiculed by skeptics, there is certainly no better explanation for the origin of the different families of languages. The evolution theory is unable to adequately account for even the origin of human language itself.

NO EVOLUTION OF LANGUAGE

The question is often asked, How did human speech come about? Are there any simple primitive languages that could be a transition from animal speech?

You see, according to evolution theory, human languages are developing from meaningless sounds to ever more perfect languages.

All right, then. If the origin of man, including his ability to speak, occurred by evolution, then may I ask this question: Why are the most HIGHLY STRUCTURED AND COMPLEX languages found among the most primitive tribes?

Why is there no such thing as a primitive language?

The idea of SIMPLE languages among primitive people does not coincide with fact.

Linguists have found the most highly constructed, complex and sophisticated languages among the most backward and culturally "primitive" tribes. Most of them are actually more complicated in grammar than the tongues spoken by civilised people.

In every culture on the planet, the language is complex.

The languages of even the most 'primitive' tribes are extremely complex – and are removed by a great gulf from the chatterings of the most 'advanced' apes, as well as other animals.

All animal sounds are more or less on the same level of complexity. Human speech is absolutely distinct from animal communication. And the ability to articulate and communicate even abstract concepts is the basic aspect of human culture.

Noam Chomsky, a leading linguist of the twentieth century, has indicated that human language and animal vocables are so different, they are not even comparable entities.[5]

No society is known at any point in history which did not have a fully developed language.[6]

We find no support at all for any kind of evolutionary development of language. There is NO EVIDENCE nor any EXPLANATION for such an assumed evolution of language.

Certainly there has been much change, but **not in a simple-to-complex sequence**.

If anything, the evidence clearly shows that languages have become simplified out of a more complex past. We see indications of **deterioration** after a previous higher level which hints at catastrophic events.

In fact, scholars who know **modern** languages (modern Hebrew, Greek, Arabic and neolatinic, etc) **as well as** those same languages' **ancient classical counterparts,** state that the ancient language was the most perfect.

And linguistic authority Suzette H. Elgin assures us:

"The most ancient languages for which we have written texts – Sanskrit, for example – are often far more intricate and complicated in their grammatical forms than many modern languages."[7]

In the light of these findings, may I ask How does language development fit into the "evolutionary model"? How did the diversity and complexity of new languages help humans in their struggle for the "survival of the fittest"?

It doesn't in my opinion. Evolution cannot account for one language, much less hundreds of languages, in any meaningful manner. I mean, who had time to formulate grammar when we were all supposedly running around simply trying to survive the next few minutes of life?

WORLDWIDE TRADITIONS OF THE BABEL TONGUES CONFUSION

The Babel explanation of languages is not just some biblical fairytale. This ancient event has been burnt into the racial memory of mankind as a whole.

The native Mexican chronicler, Ixtilxochitl, in his *Relaciones*, records an ancient Toltec tradition that the descendants of the Flood survivors built a "zacuali" (tower) of great height. After this, their tongues became confused and, not understanding one another, they went to different parts of the world. The 7 families who spoke the Toltec language set out for the New World. They wandered 104 years over large extents of land and water. Finally they arrived at Huehue Tlapallan in the year One Flint, 520 years after the Flood.

Other peoples, such as the Chaldeans, the Hindus and the Chiapa of the Americas, to name a few, were discovered with a tradition which not only agrees with the Scripture account of the manner in which Babel was built, but with the confusion of tongues and the subsequent dispersal.

A clay tablet has been unearthed in Mesopotamia, which reads:

"The erection of this tower highly offended the gods. In a night they [threw down] what man had built, and impeded their progress. They were scattered abroad, and their speech was strange."[8]

From ancient Sumer comes a passage in *Enmerkar and the Lord of Aratta*: "The whole universe, the people in unison, To Enlil **in one tongue** gave praise."[9] While "Enlil" was the "god" to whom "the whole universe" gave praise, another ancient Sumerian text says it was "Enki" (sometimes called "the son of Enlil")[10] who was responsible for the "confounding of the languages": "Enki... **Changed the speech** in their mouths/brought contention into it/Into the speech of man that [until then] had been one."[11]

Berosus, the Babylonian historian of the 3rd century BC, in his history of mankind, noted that the "first inhabitants of the land, glorying in their own strength... undertook to raise a tower whose 'top should reach the sky.' But the tower was overturned by the gods and heavy winds, 'and the gods introduced a diversity of tongues among men, who till that time had all spoken the same language.'"

Even the Fijians recorded a tradition of a building just like the Tower of Babel.

There are also Australian Aboriginal tribal legends which appear to be corrupted memories of those events up to, and including, the time they separated from the other peoples. These legends include the "dispersion of the tongues" which occurred at Babel.

In his writings, the Greek historian Hestaeus speaks of "olden traditions" that the people who escaped the Deluge came to Senaar [compare this with the biblical "Shinar"] but were driven away from there by a diversity of tongues.

Likewise, Alexander Polyhistor (1st century BC historian) writes that all men formerly spoke the same tongue. Some of them undertook to erect a large and lofty tower. But the chief god confounded their plans by sending a whirlwind – and each tribe received a new language.

THE DISPERSION OF THE PEOPLE THROUGHOUT THE WORLD

Geneses 10:10 includes some more information on Nimrod and his kingdom: "**And the beginning** of his kingdom was Babel, and Erech, and Accad, and Calneh, in the land of Shinar."

Where were these cities?

Nimrod was the son of Cush, who was the son of Ham. The Cushites were those who settled in Egypt, Arabia, and Ethiopia.

But Nimrod's cities that were "the beginning of his kingdom" were in "the land of Shinar", which we discussed earlier.

In the next Scripture, we learn that it was FROM this area which contained Nimrod's cities which Asshur, a son of Shem, LEFT to found HIS cities:

"Out of that land went forth Asshur, and builded Nineveh, and the city Rehoboth, and Calah, And Resen between Nineveh and Calah."[12]

The chronology of the Bible indicates that the direction of travel was FIRST from the original home near Noah's Ark to the plain of Shinar; THEN, from this area (where Nimrod's kingdom had its start), Asshur went OUT to found his cities.

This indicates that Nimrod's first cities were between Babel (or in the vicinity) and wherever Asshur's cities were located.

The map shows our location of Babel (marked by the large dot in the map) in the plain on the banks of the Euphrates, within miles of the beginning of the Tigris. Asshur, it appears, simply began to follow the Tigris, leaving the immediate area of Babel in south-central Turkey, and founded his cities to the east.

Our conclusion is that none of Nimrod's cities have been accurately identified.

The peoples who settled the later (well over 1,000 years later) city of Babylon and the region further south were NOT Cushite, as was Nimrod.

And since the Cushites settled in Egypt, Arabia and Ethiopia, it seems most likely that they travelled NOT down along the Euphrates, but instead along the Mediterranean coast through Canaan which is the most direct route to these places.

Also, Canaan was inhabited by the Canaanites, likewise descendants of Ham. So it makes more sense that those of the same family would tend to migrate together, even if they didn't speak the same language.

And, since Nimrod was a "leader", it makes sense that the Cushites would have tended to follow him, at least for a while; then, along the way, finding land they liked in Canaan, they settled while the others kept travelling south.

Since the Cushites ended up in Egypt, Arabia and Ethiopia, it seems likely that he ended up in that region as well. After all, the cities listed as being his are said to be "the BEGINNING of his kingdom" – SO WHERE ARE THE REST?

The ancient civilisation that exhibited the strongest evidences of Nimrod, his wife, and his son Tammuz, is Egypt – where he was worshipped as Osiris (the martyred god) and Horus (the reincarnation of Osiris).

The history of this is covered in my book *The Bizarre Origin of Egypt's ancient Gods*.[13]

But the bottom line is that we have no positive evidence as to the location of his cities – simply because it seems likely there was no writing system of that time left behind to record the facts.

DATE OF THE DISPERSION

Latest research places the date of the Flood at 2345-2344 BC and that of the Babel dispersion at about 2244 BC. And let me assure you, the facts of archaeology do not demand those dates to be earlier. Donovan Courville has shown this clearly.[14]

From her research, Mary Nell Wyatt suggests that the Babel event was around 150 to 175 years after the Flood (say 2195-2170 BC), based on how long it may have taken to have enough people. She considers that the people were at Babel for a number of years before the confusion of languages occurred – and that the "dividing of the earth" occurred a number of years after this.

In two ancient records - the Bible and the *Book of Jasher* - a man named Peleg is linked to this "dividing". And since the chronologies show Peleg as having died about 2004 BC – 340 years after the Great Flood - it had to have occurred by then at the latest. But our timing for the Babel event is only a rough estimate, based upon other figures that are known. The only absolute number of years from the time of the Flood which the Bible gives relating to these events is pegged to the death of Peleg.

Independent calculations by the noted anthropologist linguist, Terrence Kaufmann, support this general period of time in a remarkable manner. A study was undertaken in the language of the Maya of Central America. Norman Hammond reports:

"It is accepted that all Maya languages derive from a single extinct ancestor, known as proto-Mayan, and the antiquity of this ancestor has been estimated by a technique known as glottochronology or lexicostatistics, developed and applied to Mesoamerican languages by the late Morris Swadesh. The basic assumption (not universally accepted by linguists) is that over a given period, say 1,000 years, all languages will change to approximately the same extent, in this case 14%: two languages of common parentage, separated for 1,000 years, will **each** have changed 14% of their vocabulary, and since the same words need not have been changed in each language, they will in fact share 74% of cognate, related words (74% being 86% of the 86% remaining unchanged in each language), according to the calculations of Terrence Kaufmann. Thus the Mayan language family began to break up from the common proto-Mayan before 2000 BC, and retains a common 26% - 35% of cognate words: the linguistic reconstruction suggests that the Maya came into existence as a separate entity more than four thousand years ago, and recent archaeological work not only confirms this, but indicates an even greater antiquity for the Maya as a cultural entity."[15]

The noted archaeologist, Professor W.F. Albright, suggested that the Tower of Babel incident and the dispersion of the races (a story which he took seriously) should be dated to the 22nd century BC.

Interestingly, a surprising number of "new" civilisations that suddenly appear are dated to approximately 2000 BC!

As far as we know, there is no sign that any language spoken today has had a shorter history or a slower development than any other.

LANGUAGE – THE MOST EFFECTIVE WAY TO CAUSE DIVISIONS

Physical distinctives like skin colour are of minor importance compared to language, as the cause of divisions among nations and tribes. If, as the record insists, the Creator decided to enforce a separation and scattering, he did it in the most effective way possible – by confusing their speech.

Then after they were separated into distinct tribal groups, it was possible for distinctive physical traits to develop and become fixed genetically, by interbreeding within each group.

In Chapter 2, we saw that a massive splitting of the continental areas occurred rapidly in historical times, as a result of the violent disruption of the earth's crust in the aftermath of the Great Flood.

This apparently occurred AFTER the confusion of languages, when the people had left Babel and travelled to the various parts of the world.

The continental splitting would result in isolating different groups of people, as well as animals, on continents and islands. And this would account for the survival of some unique species (isolated from predators but wiped out elsewhere) in places like Australia, New Zealand and the Galapagos, that are found nowhere else on earth.

So now we find many races separated and isolated.

According to old records, the Creator's purpose in "dividing the earth" was to ensure that the population continued to spread around the earth instead of migrating back to one central location.

And this continental splitting, it seems, did not take place until sufficient numbers of peoples had spread to the various locations.

* * * * * * *

So far, we have been viewing the events that triggered the second great migration from Asia Minor (Turkey).

And this migration has further surprises for us, as we see next…

12

*From Babel:
The second dispersal (c) -*

THE MIGRATION BEGINS

"This is one of the earliest sites, Frank. And these folk had technology. It just doesn't fit!"

Professor Bruce Doherty shook his head. How would they explain this discovery to their peers?

* * * * * * *

As we have researched and pored over the archaeological journals, there is one concept which we keep coming across in reference to the EARLIEST SITES. It concerns the surprising (to them, not to us!) extent of TECHNICAL KNOWLEDGE possessed by these peoples.

You must remember that today it is taught that man began as an apelike moron who stumbled across fire after a lightning strike. He then progressed to man-like, but was extremely primitive, hunting with crude stone implements, eating the flesh off the bones because he had no pottery or utensils. And then one day he suddenly began to plant crops and raise herds.

I suggest you keep this in mind when you read archaeological reports; and totally disregard the dates they assign to different sites.

We will be wise to concentrate ONLY on the evidence – and what it alone reveals.

NO EVIDENCE THAT CIVILISATION EVOLVED FROM PRIMITIVE STATE

For example, workers have excavated sites in central and eastern Turkey which show absolutely NO evidence of evolving from a primitive civilisation through the various stages to that of a people who possessed advanced technical knowledge.

"In these centres, up to now, no trace of an older civilization has been discovered.... A great problem remains unsolved. How are we to account for the fact that in these regions these [supposed earlier primitive cultures] have left no traces whatsoever?"[1]

DIVERSITY BETWEEN SETTLEMENTS

After Babel, there were groups that obviously left the region entirely, and some that settled in the immediate and nearby regions. Individual abilities within each group would now be limited; some groups would have those experienced in metallurgy, some in pottery, some in art, some in construction, and so on. Thus we must expect to find some diversity in the earliest settlements.

And that is precisely what is found.

However, this has caused puzzlement to the archaeologist who continues to try to date each site based on the premise that man had uniformly evolved through various stages.

We have already noted that at some sites the people built their homes with no doors – they were entered via ladders. Catal Huyuk, about 150 to 200 miles west of the Babel region, is another good example of this. Was this perhaps as protection from the wild animals?

Other sites revealed houses with very thick walls entered through doors. And here we see the diversity that suddenly arose when the people were divided by the language barrier.

Everyone, it seems, has a theory on how something should be done. And each group now had no choice but to do it the only way they knew how – for they no longer had access to that great "pool of knowledge" that man had once possessed when all spoke the same language.

And these homes were **not** primitive. Common building practices included wooden frames with mud-bricks then plastered with lime. Many times they show evidences of having been replastered many, many times, much as we would paint our homes when they begin to flake.

The pottery, which is used as a basis for dating, has also thrown a wrench into the works. It is baffling to the established view, because these early sites display much variation in their styles and decoration.

At one site, when archaeologists reached the earliest level, they found almost no pottery. This led them to believe these people were primitive and used no eating utensils. But then, they discovered carbonised wooden dishes and vessels, along with basketry.

The styles of pottery vary from site to site, considerably. Some are made without straw, while some are made **with** straw. Some are one colour, some are another. Some have beautiful multi-coloured designs while some have none, or simply geometric designs drawn into the clay without any colour at all.

If traditional interpretations were correct, this would mean that each site represented a different time period in the evolution of mankind.

Yet these same sites present some very obvious similarities which show that they existed during the same time period.

For example, **almost all** (except some of the small villages) show evidence of **metallurgy**, which is also quite puzzling to archaeologists. Concerning one site in southern Turkey this statement is made: "The perforation of large objects like maceheads presented no difficulty; but it was another matter with **the drilling** of some of the stone beads, including those of obsidian, which have **perforations too fine for a modern steel needle. It is quite uncertain how this was achieved.:...**"[2]

VERY ADVANCED KNOWLEDGE

The bottom line is this: In the regions extending out from south central Turkey (our site for Babel) the archaeological evidence reveals very early villages and towns whose earliest level (on virgin soil) presents concrete evidences of people who possessed very advanced technical knowledge. "...recent, revolutionary finds have left no doubt that it is in the Southern regions of Central Anatolia that Neolithic civilization achieved its greatest progress."[3]

THE GREAT "POOL" OF KNOWLEDGE
DIVIDED UP AMONG THE PEOPLE

The Establishment has designed its own little system for dating the ages of sites that are excavated. This system is based on the premise of evolution and the idea that man gradually progressed from an ape to a primitive hunter, to a crude agriculturalist, then on to a farmer who domesticated animals, and so on.

But that is **NOT** WHAT THE EVIDENCE SHOWS! In fact, when simple, factual evidence is removed from the theories that are presented with it as fact, a very clear picture emerges.

The evidence shows that when man first appeared in north-eastern Turkey, he appeared with very advanced knowledge. This is evidenced by the sophisticated metallurgy of the region, as well as the completely developed masonry and construction techniques.

But for a moment, we must consider another aspect of the confounding of the languages. While the population as a whole possessed a wide variety of knowledge and abilities, when they suddenly were cut off from one another by the language barrier, they would no longer have access to the great "pool" of pre-Flood knowledge. Members of each language group would have only the knowledge and abilities of those within their own group.

Therefore, we would expect some to excel in metallurgy while others excelled in animal husbandry or crop cultivation. Some groups would have people who were talented artists while others would have those who were knowledgeable in engineering and construction.

From this point on, we would expect more diversity in the early settlements – even in those relatively close to one another.

Traditional archaeologists and paleontologists, not believing the biblical account but instead assuming evolution, classify these various groups of people who may excel in one aspect and display a total absence of another.

Those who mainly hunted (using spearheads and arrowheads of flint, etc) but did little or no farming are classified as "Paleolithic" or stone age. But 20 miles away another settlement that farmed and had domesticated animals are classified as "Neolithic", as though they were thousands of years later than the other group.

One group whose pottery was painted nicer and with more colours than their neighbours whose pottery-maker wasn't an artist and whose designs were crude were dated perhaps 1,000 years after the second group. But, in fact, these folks all lived at the same time.

This situation can be distinctly seen in the region of our suggested Babel site, the area of south-eastern Turkey. Some settlements had round houses, while others were rectangular. Their pottery varied – some displaying great artistic flair, while others were sensible and usable, but not works of art.

ART AND RELIGION

These early settlements demonstrate some very interesting features. For one, there is no evidence of invaders. It appears that they lived here for a while and then simply disappeared, packing up and leaving.

But there are evidences that indicate where at least some of them went. In all of the early sites there have been found strange, grotesque figures of a woman, some standing, some sitting, some with animals, some with children. The indication is that she represents the "mother goddess of fertility".

This concept is represented in the other early religions by the Egyptian Isis, the Assyro-Babylonian Ishtar, the Phoenician Astarte, the Iranian Ashi, the Greek Aphrodite and the Roman Venus, to list a few. But by the time these others appear, they are in an organised system of gods and goddesses. The figure of an early goddess found at Catal Huyuk in Turkey is the original from which the others developed.

It is easy to understand that once Noah's offspring began to slip from the worship of the Creator and fell into paganism, one of their biggest concerns and focal points would be that of fertility.

Remember, they started out on an earth devoid of everything. Their survival depended upon crops and animals, and of course they wanted a large family. The more children, the more to help with the work and the things that had to be done.

And the fact that these figures are found in all of the early settlements indicates that "she" was a common "goddess" among the people prior to Babel. The homes and pottery might differ, but the good old "goddess" is always identifiable.

We know that after the early peoples left Turkey, they eventually scattered all over the world. Since the archaeological evidence shows that these early settlements were not destroyed or conquered by a foreign people, the logical explanation is that at least some of them headed south, north, west and east, taking their "mother goddesses" with them.

MIGRATED WITH MUCH ORIGINAL KNOWLEDGE

Here is something that may be surprise you.

These dispersed groups – ancestors of the Egyptians, Chinese, Indians, Maya and so on - in their traditions, cherished the memory of biblical events. These events included a fall from Paradise, the entrapment by the serpent medium; the expulsion of our first parents from Eden, and the racial memory of a world Flood.

And the many races worldwide remembered the Tower of Babel, the sudden language confusion and the dispersion that resulted. These events are recalled in numerous and widespread traditions.

Biblical events... all of them.

Interestingly, we find among the scattered branches of mankind no knowledge of the POST-dispersion events which are mentioned in the Bible. If this is true history, that's exactly what you would expect - since they were cut off from those later events by the dispersion.

On the religious side, the dispersed groups were familiar with animal sacrifices that foreshadowed a promised divine World Rescuer who was to come... suffer a violent death as a sacrifice for mankind... and ultimately achieve victory over the "serpent". The various races knew these things and taught them to their children.

This explains why most religions, even though they degenerated, practised animal sacrifices and gave special honour (or abhorrence) to snakes.

All of these tend to suggest that the biblical accounts are real history.

I hear someone snigger. The Bible as history? You're kidding!

Yes, it's quite unpalatable to modern taste, I'll grant you that. And a name like Noah is dismissed with an academic smirk.

Evolution theory is the rage. Biblical stories are thumbs down!

Okay, it's time for some news...

Have you heard of the Table of Nations? Essentially, it's a list of primeval nations in the biblical book of Genesis (chapter 10). But did you know that it happens to be by far the most complete and accurate listing of ancient tribes and nations that we possess?

Professor W. F. Albright, one of the leading authorities on archaeology, called it "an astonishingly accurate document."[4]

OLDER THAN CRITICS CLAIM

In fact, this Table of Nations is one of the oldest documents in the world. I said oldest.

Yes, I know. The critics have been saying it was not written until the 6th century BC. That the book of Genesis (of which it is a part) was composed by various scribes from old myths collected in Babylon. And that Babylonian tablets and whatever, are older. That's what modern critics are telling us.

Well, how would you like to do a piece of detective work?

And do you know what we shall find? Simply this: that there is NO WAY this book of Genesis could have been written in the 6th century BC. That's utterly IMPOSSIBLE!

Here's why. Please take this in carefully.

For starters, unique tribal names mentioned in the Genesis Table of Nations. Many of those names of obscure tribes had disappeared from the historical scene many centuries before the 6th century BC. (It is only through modern discoveries that we now know these names once existed – and that they were recorded with such astonishing accuracy in the Table of Nations).

You see, the records of these tribes were written, and then lost as early as 1000 BC. And not re-discovered until modern times. Moreover, even the original tribes that wrote them had vanished altogether from the historical scene, or had been assimilated into other powerful nations and cultures. Yes, they had even lost their names.

By the 6th century BC they were unknown. Forgotten.

The Table of Nations, you understand, was written while these tribes were still known. This document is about as old as you can get.

A 6th century BC forgery? Of course not!

But we won't leave it at that. This Table of Nations makes a sweeping statement...

CRITICS FIND "ERRORS"

The book of Genesis says that from the three sons of Noah "was the whole earth overspread."[5] Then follows the Table of Nations,[6] concluding with this statement: "These are the families of the sons of Noah, after their generations, in their nations: and by these were the nations divided in the earth after the flood."[7]

Did you get that? This tells us very plainly that the nations of earth are all descended from the family of Noah!

Now I'll play devil's advocate and ask this question:

Since the Table of Nations claims to identify all the nations on earth, and their habitats, then why does it OMIT places like the Americas, eastern Asia and Australia? Why does it cover only the area bounded by the Atlantic coast of Europe, Ethiopia and Iran - but no further?

As a critic, I might assert that

(a) THE BIBLE HAD WRITERS HAD A LIMITED, MISTAKEN KNOWLEDGE OF THE EARTH. According to this Table of Nations, Noah's descendants occupied ONLY the Mediterranean/Middle East region. The biblical writer thought (wrongly) that the area from Europe to Ethiopia to Iran was the whole world. So the Bible is mistaken.

(b) OR THE FLOOD WAS NOT WORLD-WIDE, AS THE BIBLE SAYS IT WAS. Since only those inside this region are mentioned as being descendants of the Flood survivors, then all the other nations whose names are omitted must have not been touched by the Flood. So the Flood could not have been NOT worldwide, as claimed by the book of Genesis.

Oh boy! That sounds pretty bad for the Table of Nations and its claims... right?

Okay, so what is the truth?

Just this. The Table of Nations is a snap-shot in time – an instant picture of the nations as they were at the time the Table was written.

It bears within itself the ID of a document written about 2000 BC. It describes those tribes in existence soon after the Babel incident, the regions in which they initially settled, and the nations which had by that time developed from those first tribal settlements.

100% ACCURATE

Now I'll make my own sweeping claim... knowing that it cannot be successfully refuted:

Wherever its statements can be sufficiently tested, Genesis 10 has been found completely accurate (often where, at one time, it seemed most certainly to be in error).

It provides insights into the relationships between peoples that are only now becoming obtainable by other means.

Here are some specific features that testify to its age:

1. The small development of the Japheth races

The Indo-Europeans (descendants of Japheth) were great colonisers and explorers, spreading from north-western Europe to the Indus Valley at quite an early date.

But the Table views them as occupying only Asia Minor (Turkey) and along the immediate Mediterranean coast.

Yet, shift the TIME SETTING to just a few centuries later and such omissions would be inconceivable.

2. Sidon mentioned, but not Tyre

From the 13th century BC onward, Tyre was a major city-state on the eastern Mediterranean coast, which made a considerable noise in the world, whereas nearby Sidon did not.

The omission of Tyre in the Table clearly implies that Tyre had not yet risen to importance – if she existed at all.

Evidently, this Table was written prior to the important Hebrew-Tyre exploits of 1000 BC – and even prior to the 13th century BC..

3. Sodom and Gomorrah said to be still existing

Since these cities around 1897 BC were dramatically destroyed, it is inconceivable that a later writer would mention them and not make some attempt at informing the reader what had happened to them subsequently.

It is more reasonable to accept that he was writing prior to their complete disappearance.

4. The great amount of space given to the Joktanites

If you were to pick up an earlier history book on the settlement of North America by the white man and his inter-action with Indian tribes, you would meet with tribal names like Seneca, Cree, Ojibway, Mohawk, Cherokee and Huron.

But today only a few of these would have any meaning.

Evidently the Joktanites of Arabia were both numerous and important when the Table was written. But within a few centuries they were either insignificant or unknown.

So if a Jewish writer of the 6th century BC had strung off this list of names (even if that were possible), they would mean little to his readers.

When you compare this long list of Arab tribes in the Table with the sparse information concerning the line of Shem to Peleg (the ancestors of the Jews), it is difficult to argue convincingly that the Table was a piece of Jewish propaganda favouring their own ancestry.

It bears the imprint of a document written at a time when these now-forgotten tribes were important to its readers.

5. *The discontinuance of the Hebrew line at Peleg*

Since that character Abraham was so important as the father of all Jewish people, it is unthinkable that a Jewish author who was recording the ancestry of the Jews, would have neglected to indicate where Abraham originated.

The Table lists off the ancestry of the Hebrew race only from Shem to Peleg – just 5 generations. And then stops dead!

Since Sodom and Gomorrah are mentioned in the Table, and since Abraham must have been a figure of some importance before the destruction of Sodom and Gomorrah, we can only conclude that the writer did not know of his existence. And this can mean only one of two things. Either Abraham was not yet alive, or he had not yet achieved prominence.

6. *Jerusalem not mentioned*

This Table concerns itself with the names of people, cities they founded, tribes they gave rise to, and territories they settled in.

Yet, while the Jebusites are mentioned, their capital city (later to be named Jerusalem) is totally omitted.

This is analogous to an early Briton listing the settlements of importance and leaving out London.

The inference is that the writer never knew about Jerusalem. He lived at a time BEFORE it gained relevance to his readers.

FROM AROUND 2000 BC

Well, those are just a few of many evidences that the Table of Nations is much, much older than critics have been willing to admit. At the very latest, the writer of the Table cannot have lived much after the 20th or 19th century BC.

While the Bible is not primarily a history book, modern scholarship has found that when it does touch on history it is remarkably accurate. Increasingly, its stories are seen by leading scholars as solid history, set in backgrounds as real as our own today.

Something else. The detailed Table of Nations could have been composed only if a sustained high degree of communication existed among all these peoples. This implies an early knowledge of geography.

So are we missing something in our school history classes?

13

From Babel:
The second dispersal (d) -

THE MAJOR CIVILISATIONS AFTER BABEL

"These skeletons are radioactive!" The archaeologist almost went into orbit. How did it happen?

Oh, but let me start at the beginning.

After Babel, as we noted, the people began to migrate to the different regions of the world. And closer to Babel, the first major civilisations sprang up.

Discoveries during the past century or so have shown that the EARLIEST and MOST ADVANCED civilisations were along the fertile rivers of THE MIDDLE AND NEAR EAST – areas that were once lush and beautiful, but today are desolate, barren desert regions.

THREE "INSTANT" CIVILISATIONS

Archaeology has revealed three major civilisations that sprang up from "nowhere", so to speak. They were highly civilised, had governments, possessed vast technology and a fully developed writing system.

There can be little room for doubt that these were the three earliest large civilisations formed just after Babel.

What we have discovered in their ancient remains is evidence that these people were highly intelligent and far more advanced than those civilisations that followed them.

THE INDUS VALLEY CIVILISATION

When the numerous groups left Babel, just as when they left their original homes near Noah, they had to follow a river or coastline as much as possible.

Following the Euphrates or the Tigris to the delta region near the Persian Gulf, then following the coastline east through present-day Iran into present-day Pakistan, we find the Indus River.

Along this valley has been found evidence of a very advanced, very unique civilisation that sprang up suddenly and existed at the same time as earliest Sumer – a unique civilisation built by those who left Babel.

Today, this Indus region, north west of modern India, is not a pleasant place. Except for the narrow strip of green along the river where artificial irrigation systems have been built, this is a forbidding, sandy desert, 120 degrees F. in the shade in the summer. It is one of the last places on earth one would expect to find the remains of cities.

Yet, all along this river, a civilisation stretched 1,000 miles in length, covering more than twice as large an area as ancient Egypt or Sumer.

The most famous of its discovered cities, Mohenjo-Daro, was a PRE-PLANNED city.

Some of the houses are so well preserved that they could be occupied today, and use made of the bathroom as well as the irrigation and drainage services.

The city lacked neither grandeur nor comfort. It contained a most ingenious and complete drainage system.

"The brick conduits, arranged under the streets, received the efflux from pipes placed in each house, and were linked to stone sewers. At intervals these sewers were supplied with cesspools which were easy to clean, while it was only necessary to move a few bricks to clean out the small drains in the streets if they became blocked up.... They constructed a whole system of water mains which collected the water from the rain falling outside the city and distributed it via ingenious brick conduits which conducted it to wells in each house.... These water mains fed the bathrooms. Each house possessed its own – and they were much the same as those still in use in India today."[1]

In some houses, a built seat-latrine of Western-type was included on the ground or first floor. And they had a most modern approach to waste disposal.

I suspect that this advanced knowledge of waste-disposal, and so on, came from one who had expert knowledge of the subject, after living with seven other folk over a year in a survival vessel filled with animals of every kind!

Everyday items

These people fashioned elaborate jewellery, augur drills, household utensils, toilet outfits, coins, dice and chessmen.

In one house archaeologists uncovered lipstick. "This stick, one end of which is worn – to whose lips was it last applied five thousand years ago? – lay on a small low table beside vases of kohl (eye make-up), flasks of perfume, hairpins and bronze razors."[2]

They even had cats and dogs in their streets. A brick found in the city of Mohenjo-Daro bears the imprint of a cat's foot slightly overlapped by that of a dog. When the brick was laid out to dry prior to going into the kiln, the cat must have whisked across the bricks at a high rate of speed, followed by the speeding dog, which is evidenced by the deep impress of their footpads.

Only one answer makes sense

Archaeologists and scholars tell the tale themselves, of this civilisation that seemingly "came from nowhere":

"A civilisation as complex as that of the Indus Valley does not spring fullblown out of nowhere. But that is exactly what appears to have happened at Mohenjo-Daro and Harappa. They are cities built from scratch. The archaeologists of the future will have to account for this mysterious improbable breakthrough of civilization in the Indus Valley, circa 2500 BC."[3]

Well, the answer, to this mystery is simple, and, in fact, the ONLY answer. The pieces of the puzzle of mankind will never fit except in the context of the biblical account.

And, as I was about to say, at Mohenjo-Daro, excavations down to the street level revealed 44 scattered skeletons, as if doom had come so suddenly they could not get into their houses. The skeletons, after thousands of years, are still the most radioactive that have ever been found. What we do know is that these cities were destroyed suddenly.

EGYPT

The world has been fascinated with ancient Egypt for the past 200 years, and due to the abundance of artefacts, much is known about this early civilisation.

However, as usual, for the most part the evidences have been "explained" in light of men's theories instead of the eyewitness biblical account. Thus the true picture has been distorted.

For example, when "king lists" have been found, they have been construed to be a continual list – one after another – when, in fact, it is now known that different kings ruled at the same time in different parts of Egypt. Because of this error, scholars proclaim that the Egyptians go back to the time PRIOR TO the Great Flood.

We shall investigate that amazing professional blunder in a later chapter.

Where they came from

It is the earliest period of Egypt that is the least known, but it is from these evidences that we find the information which relates to "where these people came from".

Most of the evidence of this earliest period comes from burials, which have revealed that Egypt's earliest inhabitants were also highly civilised and in possession of technical knowledge. Although their earliest cities have not survived to tell their tales as have those of the

Indus Valley, we have learned from their earliest burials that they had boats, wore elaborate jewellery, make-up and clothes of woven fabric, ate with ivory spoons, and worked in gold, silver and lead, to mention just a few.

The earliest object ever found made of **laminated** wood (plywood) (other than the deck timber from the wreck of the Ark) was in early Egypt – "a coffin whose sides were made of six thin superimposed layers of wood with the grain alternating as in modern plywood".[4]

Their common point of origin is again found. Below is seen some pottery from a pre-dynastic Egyptian burial. Note the ibex (goat with long, curved horns) on the Egyptian vase. Now note the smaller picture of an ibex from the Palanh caves near Adyaman (a little west of Babel).

Pre-dynastic pottery from an Egyptian burial.

Ibex design in Palanh caves at Adyaman, near Babel.

Their common point of origin? The region of Babel.

I could show you other designs that indicate the common point of origin. The **repetition** and usage of animals in designs are SHARED FEATURES that didn't just "evolve" independently among these very separate early civilisations.

These were designs, themes and motifs used when the people were one, united in language and purpose.

After Babel, when they went their separate ways, they carried with them the methods and themes of design used by their families when they lived at their original home in Anatolia.

Another, more impressive, similarity is seen in the knives shown here. The first knife, found in a pre-dynastic Egyptian burial, is made of flint with a gold sheet handle. But of importance is the "snake" design on the handle. Now compare with the second picture of a knife, also from a burial, also made of flint but with a bone handle. And where did this second knife come from? It came from south central Turkey, in a male burial at Catal Huyuk, near Babel.

Pre-dynastic Egyptian flint knife with gold sheet handle. Snake design on handle.

Flint knife with bone handle and similar snake design on handle. From south central Turkey near Babel.

SUMERIA

The appearance around the SAME TIME of Sumerian civilisation was likewise sudden, unexpected and "out of nowhere".

"H. Frankfort (Tell Uqair) called it 'astonishing'. Pierre Amiet (Elam) termed it 'extraordinary'. A. Parrot (Sumer) described it as 'a flame which blazed up so suddenly'. Leo Oppenheim (Ancient Mesopotamia) stressed 'the astonishingly short period' within which the civilisation had arisen. Joseph Campbell describes its appearance as "with stunning abruptness".[5]

LINKS BETWEEN THEM

These civilisations were contemporary with each other. We know this because engraved seals of Indus Valley manufacture have been found in Sumerian cities dating from the time of Sargon (just before 2000 BC). On the island of Bahrain off the east coast of Saudi Arabia are found seals of the Indus Valley designs, along with those of Sumer.

That the three civilisations had a common origin is illustrated by a seal from the Indus Valley with the "lion-slayer" (Nimrod, the great hunter) holding two lions (or perhaps tigers) at bay, one on each side.

The same theme of the "lion-slayer" is seen in the very earliest times of pre-dynastic Egypt. In this drawing from a tomb, we see the typical pose of the hero with the two lions, one on each side or in each hand.

What is so very clear from studying the themes and designs on the earliest objects and artefacts is that certain events took place PRIOR to the dispersion of the people from the Babel area – and these things are found in the artwork of each of the earliest civilisations.

From there, we can see how all the early pagan religions and earliest myths began with the same concepts, such as the "lion killer" and the "earth" or "mother goddess".

After this, however, they begin to develop their own peculiarities and distinctions – the result of being separated by the language barrier.

KNOWLEDGE POSSESSED BY THE EARLIEST PEOPLE

In our book *Dead Men's Secrets* we have catalogued more than a thousand of the incredible exhibits from the lost cities of the dead. Some of these are almost unbelievable, yet they existed or still survive.

TRUE MODEL OF HISTORY

The Bible contains a model of human history. The biblical framework of history is essentially complete – from the time of Creation to the time of Jesus Christ.

It explains where all the time is, in human history. It gives mathematical documentation. If, as now appears from archaeological research, it is a valid historical document, then it is truly the yardstick by which the time framework of all ancient world history can be measured. Including, as well, the history of China, Australia, the United States and EVERY other country.

ENOUGH PEOPLE TO PRODUCE THESE CIVILISATIONS?

Now for a sticky question.

If a total world wipe-out occurred around 2345 BC, which left only eight survivors to start a new world, then how on earth could there have been enough people to build Egypt, Sumeria and the other new civilisations as early as 2000 BC?

Or, as one gentleman wrote in:

"If the eight people on the Ark gave rise to all the races on this earth, work out (using the compound interest formula for geometric progression, with annual rate equal to, say 3%), how long would it take eight people to produce a viable world population of about 500 million people comprising Chinese and all the rest? (I'm fully aware, by the way, that compound interest calculations will easily give the **present** world population, from eight people over a period of 4,300 years. I'm only concerned about the world, as we know it from history, from the supposed time of the Flood to around 2000 BC.)"

You will realise that this problem – of enough people (from only eight survivors) to launch new, high civilisations within just 300 or 400 years – certainly needs to be addressed.

It seems almost impossible, don't you think?

Well, here is the answer. As we noted early in Chapter 7, several factors favoured a rapid population growth in the earliest post-Flood centuries.

There I presented a formula which has been historically validated in modern times (for example, in Canada).

Of course, I cannot claimed these figures are accurate, but they give an idea of how slowly the repopulation of the earth would have begun, and then how suddenly it began to increase.

And something else. The fact of a person dying without having children back in ancient times was so rare that the biblical record specifically makes mention of one in 1 Chronicles 2:10. It appears that the earth, the animals and the people were favoured with a special fertility at that time in order to facilitate the renewing of life on the planet.

In any case, on the basis of this formula in Chapter 7, the world population just 300 years from the Flood (at the beginning of the eleventh generation) could be as much as 300 million people. Certainly large enough to trigger the sudden rise of these civilisations at that time.

Even a population of one tenth that size would have been sufficient.

By the time Abraham went to Canaan, just 427 years after the Flood, we know that quite a number of different nations were already established in their lands.

****

But what about Stone Age people? What about the finds of the first men... not in Turkey, where you are saying, Jonathan... but in Africa!

Good one. Let's see...

14

From Babel:
The second dispersal (e) -

SKYSCRAPER TO "STONE AGE"

"It's way out!" shrieked Mari. "Come, look! This has to be the place."

For as long as the eleven year old could remember, his family had been uprooting and trekking. They were refugees from Babel, you see. No sooner did they find a choice spot to settle, than others would come and edge them out.

This time, it had been a marathon adventure. For weeks they had skirted the coast, travelling east, before coming upon a virgin land of high, awesome peaks.

The setting was terrifyingly wild.

In from the beach, they entered a gorge. It was raging, so much water. Hopefully, they might reach the interior of this passage.

For a full two days, they negotiated it. The beauty of the terrain overwhelmed them. Mid-morning on the third day their passage was blocked by a foaming tributary which exited between cliffs. Finding a ledge, they turned along it.

At times, the ledge widened into sandbanks overhung with trees. Songsters unseen enticed them forward. There was a raucous shriek, as two winged giants swooped down then flew ahead.

Mari and his sister were skipping ahead of their elders. At each new marvel they would turn and call back. The tiny group had been pushing up this tributary for most of the day now.

Suddenly Mari stopped dead... and gasped. Before him opened a basin, walled in by an immaculate snowy range. And into it a waterfall of awesome beauty plunged down among palms and kapok trees.

Imagine it! They must be the first people to see this place! No wonder Mari shouted excitedly! Here they just had to remain.

* * * * * * *

OFFSHOOTS OF MAINSTREAM CULTURE
In the ongoing migration from the Babel region, some family groups were pushed out further by those following.

There were bands of scattering families who lost touch with civilised communities. The further they wandered, the more barbaric and debased they became.

And that brings us to an important question we should ask before going further.

WHAT ABOUT THE "MISSING LINKS" THEORY?
What about the claims that ancient "primitive" men are missing links in the evolutionary ladder?

Fascinating, isn't it? Sometimes when ancient remains are discovered, they are loudly hailed as "missing links" between man and his imagined ape-like ancestors. Unfortunately, such "missing links" have a habit of being discredited.

For example:
- Java man: proved to be the skullcap of a giant gibbon.
- Cro-magnon man: human 100 per cent.
- Piltdown man: After 41 years as "proof" of evolution, it was exposed as a fraud.
- Nebraska man: The discovery consisted of no more than a single tooth – later proven to be that of a pig!

When will we learn? Evolution? The fossils say NO![1]

Well, before we leave that topic, we'd better squarely face this one:

DID MAN BEGIN IN DIFFERENT PARTS OF THE WORLD?
A fascinating report appeared some years ago in *Time* magazine. (I think the article was called "Adam's Genes".) Anyway, it reported that scientists had dealt a blow to the idea that modern humans simultaneously arose in different parts of the world.

Analysing a gene on the Y chromosome of 38 men from all over the globe, they found no variation – and thus concluded that humanity's ancestors formed one small, concentrated population.

Earlier studies had reached the same conclusion by looking at a different sort of genetic material in women.

No, mankind did NOT evolve in different parts of the world.

DID MAN BEGIN IN AFRICA?

Also, you've probably heard the theory... "Man began in Africa. That's where the oldest remains of man emerging from his ape-like ancestors have been found."

It's all cut and dried, we're told. Africa...

Not quite, I'm afraid. For long years, other evolutionists have been just as strongly disputing that idea. And with good reason.

CRADLE OF MANKIND NOT IN AFRICA, THE AMERICAS, EUROPE or EAST ASIA

As far back as 1932, Henry Field wrote:

"It does not seem probable to me that any of these localities could have been the original point from which the earliest men migrated. The distances, combined with many geographical barriers, would tend to make a theory of this nature untenable. I suggest that an area more or less equidistant from the outer edges of Europe, Asia and Africa, may indeed be the centre in which development took place."[2]

It is true that Field's assessment was written before the bone finds of Leakey and others in Africa. But fossil discoveries in Africa over recent years have not changed this.

FROM THE MIDDLE EAST

So here is the position. Human beings must have migrated from one common point.

And it is hopeless to assume that this point of origin was at the extremities of man's geographical range. It is much more likely that man came from some point midway... which is Asia.

We have already seen some compelling evidence of our origins in the Middle East, and in particular, Turkey.

But now we see the same story from global migration patterns!

All lines of migration that are in any way still traceable are found to radiate from the Middle East.

Along each migratory route, settlements have been found, each slightly different from the one that preceded it or followed it.

Generally, the direction of movement tends to be shown by a gradual loss of cultural artefacts.

As several lines radiate from a single centre, there can be traced more or less a series of ever increasing circles of settlement, each sharing fewer and fewer of the original cultural artefacts which are seen at the centre.

MORE PRIMITIVE ON THE FRINGES

As we have seen, the cradle of mankind was in Asia Minor (modern Turkey).

Any evidence of primitive types elsewhere in the world, whether living or fossil, is evidence, not that man began there, but that man became degraded as he departed from the centre.

In marginal areas where individuals or families were pushed by those who followed them, circumstances often combined to degrade them physically and culturally.

A series of zones is found globally, in which the most primitive are found furthest from Asia, and most advanced nearest to Asia.

Professor Griffith Taylor of the University of Toronto, put it this way:

"A series of zones is shown to exist in the East Indies and in Australasia which is so arranged that the most primitive are found farthest from Asia, and the most advanced nearest to Asia. This distribution about Asia is shown to be true in the other 'peninsulas' (i.e. Africa and Europe, ACC)....

"Which ever region we consider, Africa, Europe, Australia, or America, we find that the major migrations have always been from Asia."[3]

He says further:

"The first point of interest in studying the distribution of the African peoples is that the same rule holds good which we have observed in the Australasian peoples. The most primitive groups are found in the regions most distant from Asia, or what comes to the same thing, in the most inaccessible regions....

"Given these conditions, it seems logical to assume that the racial zones can only have resulted from similar peoples spreading out like waves from a common origin. This cradleland should be approximately between the two 'peninsulas,' and all indications (including the racial distribution of India) point to a region of maximum evolution not far from Turkestan. It is not unlikely that the time factor was similar in the spread of all these peoples."[4]

So how can one most logically explain the geographical distribution of "primitive" human fossil remains?

These were the marginal representatives of a widespread dispersion of people from a single population established at a point central to them all.

As the central population multiplied, it sent forth successive waves of migrants. Each wave drove the previous one further toward the outer edge.

Those who were driven into the least hospitable areas, suffered physical degeneration under the conditions they were forced to live.

We find these today as the most degraded fossil specimens, or as the most primitive societies still alive today.

And there are extraordinary physical differences among them. Doubtless because they were members of small, isolated, strongly inbred bands.

Yet the cultural similarities which link together even the most widely dispersed of them indicate a common origin for them all.

Throughout the great migrations, "prehistoric" or historic, there never were any human beings who did not belong within the family of Noah and his descendants.

TIME TAKEN TO MIGRATE

So how long did it take for these ex-Babel folk to disperse to the ends of the earth?

From the Middle East "Cradle of Man", the most distant settlement by land is the very southern tip of South America, 15,000 miles approximately.

How long would such a journey take? It has been estimated that men might have covered the 4,000 miles from Harbin, Manchuria, to Vancouver Island, Canada, in as little as 20 years.[5]

And the rest of the journey southward? Says Alfred Kidder:

"A hunting pattern based primarily on big game could have carried man to southern South America without the necessity at that time of great localized adaptation. It could have been effected with relative rapidity, so long as camel, horse, sloth, and elephant were available. All the indications point to the fact that they were."[6]

So, as with everything else, migrations did not require vast aeons of time.

SOME SOCIETIES BECAME PRIMITIVE, OTHERS RETAINED CIVILISATION

Among the family groups which dispersed over the earth, some developed into nations.

In a remarkably short time the Hamitic branch of mankind (the coloured races) had established beachheads of settlement in every part of the world.

Some who penetrated wilderness areas did not maintain their civilisation in the new isolated environment, but over generations became more and more savage and depraved.

Many of the dispersing groups were plunged into an "instant stone age" through loss of metal technology (or loss of its easy availability).

With little or no technology when they arrived (but with knowledge they had brought), they used stone or whatever was handy. Top priority was survival.

But as time passed and survival was secured, and they had time to sit down and work again with metals, they did so.

To a modern archaeologist this might appear as development of culture, whereas it was really just an expression of culture, now that the question of survival had been settled.

So, on the evidence, it is **not** necessary to assume that men developed over long periods of time. Around the world, men could be at different levels of technology at the same time – just as they are today. AND THE EVIDENCE FOR THAT IS OVERWHELMING

It is almost amusing to watch how industriously and seriously evolutionists try to discover ape-like features in the remains of such people.

I tell you, there are men alive TODAY whose skulls would qualify as "connecting links between man and his alleged ape-like ancestors".

A theory can certainly have a strong influence upon a man's judgment.

CIVILISATIONS BECOME ISOLATED BY DISASTER

It appears that even after many migrating tribes became trapped in their new surroundings, knowledge of world geography was never completely lost.

The great maritime powers around 2000 BC were the Minoans (Cretans), Mycenaeans (Greeks) and Egyptians. There is evidence also of possible cross-world travel by the Indus Valley civilisation and the Mesopotamians (from the Babel region).

Oh, yes. And something else. People all over the world have retained separate memories of a period when aviation was a well-known concept, and flight was a frequent occurrence.[7]

At first a number of highly civilised nations flourished. But their descendants became embroiled in destructive wars. Large cities were reduced to ruins. Commerce on the air and sea lanes fell into disuse.

Although a great part of the evidence is unsatisfactory and mixed with vague tradition, yet for some of it there seems to be substantial and independent proof - even to solid artifacts.[8]

THE LANES REOPENED

Many centuries would elapse before Phoenicia, the new great naval power, would reopen the long ocean lanes.

While a few nations retained some memory of their past heritage, it was the Phoenicians who most aggressively used it to their advantage.

In the time of Solomon of Israel (10th century BC), the Phoenicians reopened the lines of commerce that had existed a thousand years before.

TESTIMONY OF THE MAYA

Votan, the first historian of the Maya civilisation, wrote a book on the origin of the race. This ancient volume, written in the Quiche Language, was found by the Spaniards after their conquest of Mexico.

Votan founded a settlement at Palenque about 1000 BC. Later he made four or more visits to his former home of Chivim (Tripoli of Syria, a town in the kingdom of Tyre, in the eastern Mediterranean). During these trips he visited a great city wherein a magnificent temple was in course of erection. He next visited an edifice which had been originally intended to reach heaven, an object defeated, says Votan, when "to every people a different language was given." Upon returning to Palenque, he found that several more of his nation had arrived. Legend and pictorial evidence suggests that they were akin to Carthaginians.[9]

From this time onward, spreading at a more leisurely rate, the Indo-European races (descendants of Noah's son **Japheth**) and the Semites (Hebrews and Arabs mainly, descended from Noah's son **Shem**), settled slowly into the areas already opened up by the **Hamites** (the coloured races). We shall consider this in the next chapter.

NORTH AMERICAN INDIANS

Concerning the New World, there is good evidence that the colossal buildings now found there were constructed no later than about 1200 BC.[10]

Little is known of the ancestors of the Red Indians who spread over North America. They dwelt in enormous cities, with temples and fortresses. They were expert agriculturalists, they domesticated animals and worked mines.

Western experts are very ignorant on American pre-Columbian history. Red Indian history is only explained to white men whom the Indians grow to trust. To others, they will deny all knowledge of their history, including that of the Mounds.

THE POLYNESIANS

Mistaken concepts also prevail among "experts" concerning Pacific history. Scholars say that the long-ago voyages from Hawaii to French Polynesia, from Samoa to Raratonga, and from the historical but unauthenticated Hawaiki to Raratonga and then on to New Zealand, were either legend or haphazard voyaging. The Polynesian people do not agree and claim they were deliberate and skilful.

We should not place too much reliance on academic historical theory. Native genealogy and history, backed with archaeology, work much better.

* * * * * * *

Now here is a prophecy given by Noah himself, that reaches right down to us today. History foretold before it happened.

Would you like to know what that wise old man foresaw?

15

Racial history foretold -

AN ASTONISHING PROPHECY COMES TRUE

After the Flood, when Noah drank from the vines he had grown, it may have come as a surprise to him that under the new atmospheric conditions fresh juice fermented more readily.

Soon he was drunk. His son Ham, seeing the father's nakedness, neglected to cover him, but instead went and told his brothers. Respectfully backing toward their father, they covered his nakedness.

"When Noah woke from his wine, knowing how his youngest son had treated him, he exclaimed, 'Cursed be Canaan [**Ham's** family]! May he be a servant of servants to his brothers.' He then added, 'Blessed be the Lord, the God of **Shem** and may Canaan be his servant. May God make **Japheth** so great that he shall dwell in Shem's tents; and may Canaan be their servant.'"[1]

This prophecy and its fulfilment will give you a better understanding of human history.

The initial family pattern set from three sons and their wives, gave rise in the course of time to three distinct racial stocks.

SHEM is represented by the Semitic people (Hebrews, Arabs, and ancient nations such as Babylonians, Assyrians, etc.). HAM is the progenitor of the Mongoloid and Negroid groups. JAPHETH is represented by the Caucasoids (Indo-Europeans).

In Noah's prophecy we do seem to have a summary of history right down to our day, as it has since turned out.

THE DESTINY OF HAM

The prophecy: "*A servant of servants shall he be unto his brethren.*" Being a servant may be considered less honourable than to be a master, yet the opposite may often be the case. In which case, the curse may be not as severe as it seems. Ham's progeny was given responsibility for man's physical well-being. His race was to render outstanding service to the races descended from his brothers Japheth and Shem, but were to profit so little by it themselves.

The races descended from Ham were given the pioneering task of opening up the world, subduing it and rendering it habitable.

History: Hamitic pioneers (Mongoloid and Negroid) blazed trails and opened up territories in every habitable part of the earth. At a basic level they made maximum use of the raw materials and resources of that locality.

This seems to have been done under pressure, since in a remarkably short time the descendants of Ham had established beachheads of settlement in every part of the world.

Ham's contribution is essentially practical – technological. Wherever they went, they seem to have had a remarkable skill in adapting local raw materials for survival.

They invented most of the world's basic technology, that the Indo-Europeans subsequently adopted and refined. In fact, generally speaking, and with few exceptions, the inventions developed in the Western world owe their original inspiration to the prior, basic technology of the Negroid or Mongoloid cultures.

Centuries later, spreading at a more leisurely rate, Japheth's descendants settled slowly into the areas opened up by Ham's descendants.

In every part of the world where Japheth has subsequently migrated, he has always been preceded by Ham. He has adopted Ham's local survival techniques and modified them. In a few cases, Japheth almost obliterated the high civilisation which Ham had established.

Japheth is indebted to Ham for his pioneering contribution in mastering the environment.

THE DESTINY OF JAPHETH

The prophecy: "God **shall enlarge Japheth**, and he shall dwell in the tents of Shem; and Canaan [Ham] shall be his servant." So Japheth will be enlarged. And something else: he will occupy a position originally possessed by Shem.

Japheth was destined to contribute to mankind's mental, or intellectual enrichment.

History: Japheth's spread over the earth was more leisurely.

In the course of time, they peopled the northern shore of the Mediterranean, the whole of Europe, the British Isles and Scandinavia, as well as the larger part of Russia. They even settled in India, displacing a prior settlement of Hamites in the Indus Valley. Isolated groups of Japhethites (Caucasians) wandered further eastward, settling in small pockets which were mostly, if not all, later swallowed up by Hamites.

Very possibly they contributed characteristics found in people of Polynesia. The Miautso of China represent remnants of these Japhethites, as may the Ainu of northern Japan.

Following the Hamites to the ends of the earth, they built upon the Hamite foundation. They took advantage of the basic technology they found in use, in order to raise, in time, a higher civilisation. Sometimes they displaced the Hamites entirely. Sometimes they educated the Hamitic races' teachers to new ways, and then retired. Sometimes they absorbed them so that the two racial stocks were fused into one.

The contribution of Japheth has been in the realm of the intellect. From the family of Japheth have arisen the great philosophical systems.

As they followed the Hamites, they took with them cultural refinements.

Japheth's enlargement has been accelerated geographically in recent centuries, often at the expense of the Hamites. This power of expansion at the expense of others has resulted from a far superior technology – gained by building upon the basic foundation provided by Ham. It is certainly not from any superior genius on Japheth's part.

This "enlargement" has also brought its own undesirable consequences. Perhaps this is because the spiritual responsibility and leadership of the nations taken over from Shem, has never been completely undertaken, but rather abused.

THE DESTINY OF SHEM

The prophecy: A covenant relationship with the Creator. Shem was appointed with responsibility for man's religious and spiritual well-being.

The contribution of Shem was essentially in the realm of the spirit.

But this would be interrupted, so that Japheth would one day assume the responsibility that had been appointed for Shem.

History: A branch of the Semitic family, Israel, was given the responsibility to prepare the world for the promised Deliverer (who was expected by all nations). For this reason, they were allotted an area in the Middle East, at the crossroads of the early world – where Europe, Africa and Asia met, to accomplish this task of blessing the nations.

But when they failed to recognise the Deliverer (Messiah), their covenant responsibility was taken away and given to Japheth.

LANGUAGE LINK TO THE "FIRST TONGUE"

In Chapter 8 we found how researchers on six continents have been discovering script in the "First Tongue".

This would be the language of the Flood survivors and their early descendants BEFORE the Tower of Babel fiasco.

May I now ask a pertinent question: Why did all attempts to translate the "First Tongue" fail – until the key was found in an old Hebrew dialect?

Simply this: that the "First Tongue" and that old Hebrew tongue shared the same roots.

To put it another way, the language that everyone spoke BEFORE the Babel rebellion was something akin to old Hebrew.

And this old Hebrew was, I suggest, the only link to the mother tongue that survived, unaffected by Babel.

And when you think about it, isn't this precisely what one should expect?

After all, the Hebrews were Semites, descended from Shem, a man who professed loyalty to the Creator. So Shem's line, not so involved in the Babel rebellion, would have generally escaped the language decimation.

It makes sense, then, that the Hebrews would have inherited the largely original, uncorrupted language of Shem – unlike most others, who had their language shattered at Babel.

I hope you can see the significance of this discovery. It is further evidence that the events we are discussing are solid, historical truth!

BALANCE NEEDED

We have noticed three dimensions to history, seen in the character of the three main branches of the human race. Even for each of us as individuals, life at its fullest comprises three dimensions – physical, mental and spiritual. Whenever these three personal needs are equally cultivated, a full personality develops. To neglect any one of them brings an imbalance.

History shows that nations, as well as individuals, have personalities.

Whenever the contribution of Ham, Shem and Japheth has been blended into a single, organised way of life, a high civilisation has resulted. But whenever a culture over-emphasises one aspect of life, to the detriment of the other two, that civilisation has for a brief period appeared to burst ahead, only to collapse.

Neither the spiritual contribution of Shem, nor the intellectual contribution of Japheth, nor the technological contribution of Ham, really benefit man as they should, without the balancing constraint of the other two.

The issue is not one of inferiority or superiority, but of uniqueness of contribution. Each race was commissioned to make a contribution of immeasurable benefit to itself and to mankind as a whole. In isolation, none of the three races produces what they CAN produce when they cooperate.

* * * * * * *

Of course, we've only touched on this subject. It deserves better. If only we had more time and space!

But we must move on.

What if I were to show you that far from Noah being a hazy legend from the past, there are several carefully preserved national genealogies which trace back – unbroken – to Noah's son Japheth?

We are still on the second migration wave from Turkey. Where does it take us now?

16

Scattered races remember their origins -

ROYAL FAMILIES TRACE BACK TO NOAH'S SON

Ararat was, according to the ancient book of Genesis, the springboard of the post-Flood culture.

From the generation list of Noah's descendants, it appears that the new population multiplied fast and spread rapidly across the globe. Within just two centuries after the Deluge, they had resettled in lands from northern Europe and Spain to Ethiopia and Iran.

A MYTHICAL HISTORY TOOK OVER

Of course, some tribes retained their national or tribal identities – but, even then, they soon lost all trace and memory of their own beginnings – and went on to invent fantastic accounts of how they came to be. It's amazing, but true. This mythological invention emerged early and grew rapidly in many cultures.

Perhaps you weren't aware of this. Their true histories were obscured beyond all recognition.

Thus we find Josephus complaining that this had happened to the Greeks of his day. And he lamented that by obscuring their own history, they had obscured the histories of other nations also.[1]

REAL HISTORY

But some of the early nations DID NOT LOSE their records. And they provide independent confirmation of the early history I am revealing to you.

It is fashionable to deny that Noah, and his three sons who survived the World Flood, ever existed. And, if they are proved to have lived, certain people will still say you could never know their real names.

Really? Let's see...

OTHER INDEPENDENT RECORDS TRACE THE SAME ORIGINS

INDIA: There is an Indian account of the Great Flood. It says Noah (known as *Satyaurata)* had three sons – **Iyapeti** (**Japheth**?), **Sharma** (**Shem**?) and **C'harma** (**Ham**?). To Iyapeti he allotted the regions north of the Himalayas and to Sharma the country of the south. The father cursed C'harma, who had laughed at him when he was accidentally inebriated with strong liquor made from fermented rice.[2]

How strikingly close to the biblical account of the cursing of Ham!

GREECE: Homer, in his *Iliad*, shows us that the Greeks likewise recollected three brothers. To each was given a domain when the world was divided. The Greeks trace themselves back to **Japetos**.[3]

The Hindu **Iyapeti** and the Greek **Japetos** are recognisable as the biblical **Japheth**, son of Noah.

CHINA: The Miautso people of China (who first settled in what is now Kiangsi province, until driven out by the Chinese) are another early people who regard themselves as being descended from Japheth. They also remember some of the other early patriarchs whose names appear in the biblical record.

When first contacted by the outside world, they were in possession of surprisingly accurate recollections of the Creation and the Great Flood. And some of the close detail of their world history coincides almost identically with the Genesis record.

The accuracy of their oral history owes its purity to the fact that it has been recited in full at weddings, funerals and other public occasions, since the earliest times.

Their names for **Shem, Ham** and **Japheth**, Noah's three sons, are **Lo Shen, Lo Han** and **Jah-phu**.[4]

Thus, in regions as far distant from each other as Greece, India and China, the names of the three sons of Noah have been preserved, in agreement with the Hebrew book of Genesis. This points to an historical common point of origin after the Great Flood.

EUROPE: Also, certain European peoples kept an accurate record of their beginnings. They wrote down the names of their founding fathers and continually brought their genealogies up to date with each new generation. And these preserved lists, annals and chronicles give us a surprising link between the early post-Flood era and more modern times.

During more than 25 years, British researcher Bill Cooper amassed astonishing evidence showing how the earliest Europeans recorded their descent from Noah through his son Japheth in meticulously kept records. He investigated in detail these various records and was able to establish good evidence for their antiquity and authenticity.[5]

Of course, the Table of Nations in the book of Genesis originated in the Middle East. But these independent records originated in Europe – and pre-date the arrival of Christianity in Europe, which nullifies the argument that they may have been medieval forgeries.

These records contain the early post-Flood history of Europe. They bear unsuspected and striking marks of authenticity – and contain certain material that can be dated at least to the 12th century BC – with important details that no later forger would have been aware of.

The Britons left to posterity a list of the ancestors of the early British kings as they were counted generation by generation, prior to their migration to Britain, and back all the way to Japheth, the son of Noah. These pre-migration records are in the form of genealogies and king-lists.

Cooper researched the lists of six separate Anglo-Saxon royal families whose kingdoms were hundreds of miles apart, who spoke different dialects and whose people rarely wandered beyond their own borders unless it was to fight. Each had a list of ancestral names that just happens to coincide in its earlier portions with that of every other.

And each goes back to Japheth, the ancestor of the Indo European races. For example, "This **Sceaf [Japheth]** was Noah's son, and he was born in the Ark."[6]

These pre-migration ancestral lists of the Anglo-Saxon kings would be astonishing records even if they existed on their own. But, in addition, there are the separate genealogies of the pre-Christian Norwegians, Danes and Icelanders. And the genealogies of these diverse nations, in their earlier portions, though strictly individual, are practically identical.

THE DISPERSAL: AFTER 5 GENERATIONS
And please note this. When we compare the genealogies of the early Irish with those of the continental Europeans, we see the same ancestral names for the first FIVE generations. The genealogies show a mixing between the various children of Japheth – a uniting into a single people – just as the Bible their intention was, before Babel. But after generation FIVE the pedigrees diverge. And this is remarkable!

You see, it was only after Babel that the nations were separated. From this moment in time, the pedigrees branched away from each other in an emphatic way. And in the book of Genesis, the dispersal is likewise depicted as having occurred in the FIFTH generation after the Flood.

To repeat, after the FIFTH generation, the lines of the Irish and the other Celts diversify, exactly in accordance with the historical movement of nations as depicted in Genesis.

TWO DIFFERENT BRANCHES
OF JAPHETH RECORDED

Something else of interest. The biblical Table of Nations begins:

"Now these are the generations of the sons of Noah, Shem, Ham, and Japheth: and unto them were sons born after the flood. The sons of Japheth; Gomer, and **MAGOG**, and Madai, and **JAVAN**, and Tubal, and Meshech, and Tiras."[7]

Quite independently, in their records, the Irish Celtic kings – decidedly pagan – traced their origins back through MAGOG, the son of Japheth.

This descent through MAGOG in the early Irish chronicles is in direct contrast to the claims of the Saxons and other European nations, whose genealogies were traced back to JAVAN, another son of Japheth.

Modern archaeology (not genealogy) has confirmed that the early Irish, the early British and some other Europeans were Celts.

But the Saxons were not Celts.

These two groups were each from a different line – confirming what their genealogies show.

Celts and Saxons. Both these pagan sources independently confirm the biblical record of history.

ACCURATE RECORDS KEPT

Were these ancient Celts serious enough to take the trouble to keep records over long periods of time, that were accurate? Let the scholar Cusack answer:

"The Books of Genealogies and Pedigrees form a most important element in Irish pagan history. For social and political reasons, the Irish Celt preserved his genealogical tree with scrupulous precision. The rights of property and the governing power were transmitted with patriarchal exactitude on strict claims of primogeniture, which claims could only be refused under certain conditions defined by law… and in obedience to an ancient law, established long before the introduction of Christianity, all the provincial records, as well as those of the various chieftains, were required to be furnished every third year to the convocation at Tara, where they were compared and corrected."[8]

It is impossible to see how anyone could have contrived even a minor alteration to their pedigree without every one else becoming immediately aware of the fact.

These records may be relied upon, therefore, to be as accurate as any record can be.

WORLDWIDE AGREEMENT
WITH THE GENESIS ACCOUNT

So we are faced with this fact: That so many peoples from diverse cultures actually recorded their descent from the patriarchs of the biblical book of Genesis long before they could have heard of the Bible or have been taught its contents!

I have a question for the skeptic who asserts that the biblical characters are fictitious. What knowledge could pagan Saxons (and all the other races) have had of supposedly non-existent biblical characters?

Thus, in regions as far distant from each other as Greece, India, China, Britain, Ireland, Denmark, Norway and Iceland, the name of Japheth the son of Noah has been preserved, in agreement with the Hebrew book of Genesis. This points to an historical common point of origin after the Great Flood.

All of these sources differ from one another in many and various points – which rules out inter-dependency or copying. But they also agree on many independent points – which demonstrates the historicity of the patriarchs who are listed.

How come that the biblical patriarchs are listed amongst such diverse and independent sources?

Think about this. The historicity of many other characters from the ancient world is accepted on much less evidence than this – often merely upon the single appearance of a name.

What precious insights into our origins this information gives us!

ALL RACES DEVELOPED SINCE NOAH?

This brings us to a fascinating question:

IF THE WORLD WAS WIPED OUT, EXCEPT FOR A SINGLE GROUP OF SURVIVORS, THEN HOWEVER COULD ALL TODAY'S VARIATIONS IN THE HUMAN RACE HAVE OCCURRED IN JUST A FEW THOUSAND YEARS SINCE THAT TIME?

Now, this question was covered in Book 1 of this series. But it so frequently asked, that I shall repeat it here.

To put it another way, IF THERE WERE ONLY EIGHT PEOPLE AT THE START, WHERE DO ALL THE COLOURS COME FROM AND WHY ARE THE RACES SO DIFFERENT?

What about the Australian Aborigines, for example, and the Chinese, and so on?

Frankly, I must confess that for ages I found this to be a tremendous problem for scientific acceptance of a Great Flood total wipe-out. That's because I did not know enough about genetics.

Take *skin colour*, for example. Actually, if you didn't know, mankind has only one skin colour. That colour shows up as different shades in proportion to the *amount of melanin* in the skin. (Melanin is a colouring compound.)

Melanin protects our bodies by absorbing ultra-violet (UV) radiation from sunlight which falls on the skin.

Darker-skinned people have more melanin, which renders their skin more sunlight resistant. Thus they are better suited to hotter climates. Lighter-skinned people are better suited to a cooler environment.

Governed by two pairs of genes

John Mackay B.Sc. writes that "if a person from a pure white European background marries a person from a pure black Negro background, their children will be an intermediate brown colour. This brownish colour is called 'mulatto'. If two MULATTOS marry, unlike their parents they DO NOT produce children which have the same colour. The offspring can be ANY OF NINE COLOURS, from pure white through to pure black." (That is, there are 19 alleles for skin color.)

Thus "if we started today with one pair of middle-brown coloured people (similar to the mulattos), we could produce all the racial colours in the world, NOT IN MILLIONS OF YEARS, NOR IN THOUSANDS OF YEARS, BUT *IN ONLY ONE GENERATION*."[9] Did you get that? In just one generation!

How it works

A child receives half its genes from each parent. Let's call these genes A and B. The genes have partners, a and b.

Genes A and B are good at producing melanin (which darkens the skin). Result: A person with two pairs of genes *AA and BB* will have *darker* skin.

Genes *a and b* both produce less melanin. Result: A person with two pairs of genes *aa and bb* will have *very light* skin.

A person with gene pairs *Aa and Bb* (let's write it as *AaBb*) will have *medium-coloured* skin.

And so on.

Now, *suppose both parents are AaBb* (medium-brown).

The mother gives the child two genes for skin colour – one from type A or a, the other from B or b. The father likewise gives two genes for skin colour – one from type A or a, the other from B or b.

So each of these middle-brown parents with *AaBb* can give his/her children any one of the following pairs of gene combinations: AB, Ab, aB or ab.

For example, suppose each parent passes on the AB combination to the new child. The mother gives the child *AB*. The father gives the child *AB*. Result: The child will be born with *AABB* – and thus will be *PURE BLACK*.

But if both parents pass on the ab combination (the mother giving the child *ab*; the father giving the child *ab*), then what? Result: The child will be born with *aabb* – and will be *PURE WHITE*.

... EVEN THOUGH BOTH PARENTS WERE MEDIUM-BROWN SKINNED!

How colour becomes permanent

Notice that the PURE BLACK child is born *AABB* – that is, he has *no genes for lightness*. If a group of pure black persons is isolated, their offspring will be only black. These children will have *lost* the ability to be "white".

Likewise, when *aabb* children marry their own type (pure white) and move away to interbreed only among themselves, they will produce from now on only white offspring. They have lost their ability to be black. They no longer have genes to produce a great deal of melanin.

If we started today with just two MIDDLE-BROWN parents, they could produce extreme racial colours (BLACK and WHITE), in a way that races would have PERMANENTLY DIFFERENT colours.

A fixed middle-brown colour could also be produced. If the original middle-brown parents produce children of either *AAbb* or *aaBB* and these offspring move away and interact only with their kind, their descendants will be a fixed middle-brown colour.

Reversing the process

Despite marked differences, the races would disappear if total inter-marriage were practised today. There would reappear a brown coloured majority, with a sprinkling of every other shade permitted within the genetic pool.

The genes for Chinese almond eyes, black skin or white, etcetra, would still exist, but the combinations would be different.

Interestingly, you can find the characteristics of ANY race in EVERY race. For example, some Europeans have broad, flat noses, and others have short, frizzy hair, but on average Europeans do not have these features. The same sort of genetic recombinations that have produced skin colour variations have produced other body variations – straight hair, wavy hair, eye shape, eye colour, body height, and so on.

It may be of interest to note a comment by Professor William C. Boyd, Professor of Immunochemistry at the Boston University School of Medicine:

"We should not be surprised if identical genes crop up in all corners of the earth, or if the over-all racial differences we detect prove to be small. We do not know the total number of gene differences which mark off a Negro of the Alur tribe in the Belgian Congo from a white native of Haderslev, Denmark. Glass has suggested that the number of gene differences even in such a case is probably small. Besides a few genes for skin colour, he thinks that there may be a dominant gene for kinky hair and a pair or two of genes for facial features. He considers it unlikely that there are *more than six pairs of genes* in which the white race differs *characteristically* from the black. This estimate errs somewhat on the small side, in the opinion of the present writer. Probably, however, it is of the right order of magnitude, and any outraged conviction that the difference between the two races must be much greater than this, which some persons might feel, is likely to be based on emotional, rather than rational, factors."[10]

Genes for all races existed at the start

The first man was designed with the best possible combination of skin-colour genes for his perfect created environment.

The Great Flood radically altered that environment.

Evidently, Noah's family possessed genes for both light and dark skin, dark enough to protect them, yet light enough to ensure sufficient Vitamin D.

All racial varieties could appear in just one generation

From the above data it can be seen that all the known varieties of skin colour could come from one pair of mid-brown parents IN ONE GENERATION.

In general, racial characteristics are recombinations of pre-existing, created hereditary (genetic) information. They have not evolved and they do not require a long time to become apparent.

You can be clear on this. There has been *no evolution of genes that did not previously exist*. All that has occurred is the *recombination* and degeneration of created genetic information.

And the differences did *not* take countless ages to produce.

AFTER BABEL

It is now known from observation that
(a) a small population tend rapidly to vary to the utmost extent of their possible limits and then to remain stationary for an indefinite time.
(b) When a few members of it shift to a new environment, wide varieties again appear, which become stable only with time.

The splitting up of a large group into many smaller groups who became isolated from each other would provide the ideal condition for the RAPID APPEARANCE of many different racial groups with distinct characteristics.

This is doubtless what occurred. There is overwhelming archaeological evidence for a common origin for *all* races on this planet.[11]

The scattering of mankind shortly after the Great Flood, when their language was suddenly confused, was the catalyst that produced the variations now seen.

Each of these groups migrated into areas which offered them new and different climates, as well as different diets from those they had been used to. As we noted, the global environment had drastically changed. From now on, it was unlikely that any two groups would find identical areas to move into.

So would such a change in climate, environment and diet have any effect on skin colours? Very little, actually. But there would be some effect.

Studies have been made on the relationship between skin colour and health or diet in a given environment. So we can postulate the following influences.

Those who, after Babel, moved to colder regions but had darker skin, could suffer from vitamin D deficiency, such as rickets. The Neanderthals are a classic example of this.

By the way, Neanderthals were not emerging primitives. That's fiction. They had a skull capacity (with its inferred brain size) larger than that of modern man. Classic descriptions of so-called Neanderthal man were based in large part on the skeletal remains of a man suffering from severe osteoarthritis. He had degenerated. In fact, there are folk who would pass for Neanderthals, alive today. It has nothing to do with history or intelligence, but rather, health!

But back to our subject.

The skin, as you know, produces vitamin D from sunlight. So any person with a darker skin is worse off in a cold region, because there is less sunlight. Because a dark skin is more sunlight resistant, it can produce less vitamin D.

So a colder environment, with less available sunlight (and not forgetting the available diet), would tend to favour those who inherited fairer skins.

Dark-skinned people in such an area would therefore tend to be less healthy and would have fewer children. This means that gradually the number of black people in any group going to a cold region would be outnumbered by the white.

Similarly, people with darker skins who went to sunnier or hotter regions would survive better – for one thing, getting less skin cancer. Gradually, the fairer persons would dwindle from the population and a black race would result.

But the bottom line is, such differences did *not* take countless ages to produce.

* * * * * * *

Speaking of cold regions, how long ago was the Ice Age... really? How long did it last? Have there been many Ice ages... or just one? Why can't you have an Ice Age without HEAT?

Rug up warm... here we go!

17

The Ice Age -

SHIVER ALL SUMMER

No bikini-clad beauties soaked up the sun on Tiahuanaco's beaches. This Pacific seaport was as dreary as every other city on earth... at that time.

Don't get me wrong. This was a city of startling dimensions. Giant buildings, imposing colonnades and lifelike statues of men and women in a thousand poses. There was partying, action and excitement.

But just go outside... How tiresome it must have been, seeing in the sky nothing but clouds - night and day! Generations of children grew up to endless heavy clouds, hanging low overhead. Dark nights. Dismal summers. And very stormy - all through the year.

The racial memory of the Cashinaua Indians of Brazil recalls the deafening thunder, the lightning and a "collapsed sky".[1]

And the African Ovaherero tribe says the sky "fell down". In fact, myths of this falling sky are found amongst the Celts, the Eskimos of Greenland, the Lapps of Finland, ancient peoples of Tibet, China and Mexico, as well as tribes of Samoa and western and eastern Africa.

In the aftermath of the Deluge, large areas of the oceans and seas would have boiled and steamed.

Massive evaporation of the waters inevitably resulted in the formation of thickening cloud cover.

The general release of heat, smoke and dust initiated atmospheric pollution that would last for decades.

And the sheer weight of this polluted atmosphere would have forced the cloud base down to unprecedently low levels.

Much of the high latitudes of Earth were enveloped in a gloomy shroud.

An Australian Aboriginal legend tells how "in those days the sky was close to the ground and everything, both man and beast, crept and crawled on the earth; and only stunted shrubs covered the land" - until Yondi the warrior "raised the sky"[2]

The clouds were so thick that when they were dispersed one day, men discovered the stars - the stars that they had never seen before.

A South American tradition recalls that Tiahuanaco existed **before** the stars. Before the stars? Absurd, of course. That is, if we take it literally. But not so absurd if we imagine that in the not too distant past men had seen the cloud cover dissolve and a star-strewn sky sparkling above them for the first time.

And so the stars became visible again!

According to the Aztecs, "'There had been no sun in existence for many years... [The Chiefs] began to peer through the gloom in all directions for the expected sight, and to make bets as to what part of heaven [the sun] should first appear... but when the sun rose, they were all proved wrong, for not one of them had fixed upon the east.'"[3]

Why no sun and no stars? Actually, it was the same thing that caused the Ice Age... and why did the sun rise in a new direction? That will follow.

ICE AGE

A glacial period came on suddenly.

The origin of glaciation (contributing to an ice age or ages) has been explained by changes in temperature in the past.

But what on earth caused it? There is plenty of speculation. Sixty different theories, in fact. But to the uniformitarian (evolutionist) the cause of the Ice Age remains a "mystery". As Reginald Daly puts it:

"At present the cause of excessive ice making on the lands remains a baffling mystery, a major question for the future reader of earth's riddles."[4]

Charles H. Hapgood admits:

"We do not have an integrated, effective theory of the earth we live on... [in the last 100 years] at least fifty theories have been produced to explain the 'ice ages' but none of them has been satisfactory."[5]

No theory has been able to explain why an Ice Age failed to occur in the coldest place on earth (northeastern Siberia), yet laid areas of ice over parts of warmer latitudes.

No sufficient cause, except...

The truth is, there is no cause that could sufficiently lower the temperature to produce an Ice Age - apart from thick clouds of dust enveloping the earth to keep out the sun's rays. And that calls for global catastrophe (which is against uniformism, the basis of evolution).

To complicate the problem, adherents of the Ice Age theory have been forced to suggest **several** Ice Ages, in an effort to account for various "mystery" phenomena.

However, such mysteries vanish when we realize this: Marks which are supposed to be evidence of ice are explained more easily as evidence of flood water.

If we consider all the evidence, the most reasonable view is that there was one Ice Age, which followed the Great Flood.

But unfortunately, evolutionary geologists resist the Great Flood concept. You ask, why? Because a Flood-based geology destroys the essential uniformitarianism basis of the theory of evolution. One cannot logically believe in the global Flood and also believe in evolution.

HEAT NECESSARY

One vital ingredient needed for an Ice Age would be heat. John Tyndall, a nineteenth century British physicist, understood this:

> "The enormous extension of glaciers in bygone ages demonstrates, just as rigidly, the operation of heat as well as the action of cold. Cold [alone] will not produce glaciers."[6]

The thickness of ice which formed on the land is estimated at 6,000 to 12,000 feet! The amount of water contained in so much ice is enough to have required the ocean level to be 300 feet lower than now.

To originally evaporate so much water (which was redeposited as ice) an enormous amount of HEAT was necessary.

Tyndall demonstrated that the same amount of heat necessary to melt 5 pounds of cast iron is required to produce one pound of vapour. Thus to evaporate water into clouds that would fall as snow and ice, there was needed a quantity of heat sufficient to melt a mass of iron 5 times greater than the mass of ice.

Without such enormous heat, said Tyndall, there could have been no Ice Age. Even if the sun disappeared and the earth lost its heat to outer space, the oceans and water bodies would freeze, but there could have been **no ice formation on LAND**.

Astronomer D. Manzel of the Harvard Observatory, referring to the so-called "ice ages", preferred to think that "increased warmth brought them on, whereas a diminution caused them to stop."[7]

Ice from heat!

The bottom line is this: Large stretches of the earth and its oceans must have been heated as a furnace; vast "areas" of ocean bottom must have bubbled with lava - both during the Flood and for some time later.

It was these post-Flood warm oceans that initiated the Ice Age.

COLD ALSO NECESSARY

But heat evaporation was not enough. Copious and rapid condensation of the vapours had to follow.-

Tyndall explains:

"We need a condenser so powerful that this vapour, instead of falling in liquid showers to the earth, shall be so far reduced in temperature as to descend as snow."[8]

Immanuel Velikovsky pinpoints the only conditions under which an Ice Age could have taken place:

"An unusual sequence of events was necessary; the oceans must have steamed and the vaporised water must have fallen as snow in latitudes of temperate climates, This sequence of heat and cold must have taken place in quick succession."[9]

CAUSE OF ICE = VOLCANOES

Let us, then, observe what occurred as the Great Flood was subsiding.

We saw in Book 2 of this series, *Surprise Witness*, that the Great Flood was a cosmic catastrophe, involving an estimated 30,000 volcanoes, which shook and tore at the foundation of the earth, roaring with incessant thunder, belching forth dust, steam, boulders and lava - and lighting up the darkened sky with their terrifying and lurid flames.

This is not imagination. The rocks of our earth show that it happened.

And even after the Flood, volcanic activity persisted. This intense volcanism produced dust, which effectively reduced the sun's radiation.

Day and night, the whole planet was enveloped *in a cloud covering* as thick as that of Venus. The dense cloud of steam and dust deflected the sun's heat away from the earth. Atmospheric temperature dropped.

Interestingly, volcanic dust is said to be 30 times more effective in shutting out solar radiation than in keeping terrestrial heat in.

A mean temperature drop today of 5 degrees Fahrenheit (if moisture conditions were favourable) would cause great areas of ice to form on mountains and tablelands of the earth's temperate zones.

Modern examples

After studying the records of three centuries, Dr. W.J. Humphrey of the U.S. Weather Bureau compiled a report showing that, virtually without exception, periods of volcanic activity were followed by cool and rainy summers .
- Volcanic activity from 1500 to 1912 is believed to have lowered the earth's temperature 2 or 3 degrees. Polar Sea ice grew sufficiently to block off Greenland; European glaciers overran small villages. Since then, with fewer major eruptions, the climate has warmed up.
- In April, 1815, Tambora Volcano in Indonesia exploded, in one of history's most violent eruptions.

A year later (the usual time lag) record low temperatures were felt in various places. That was a year without summer.
- After the 1883 Krakatoa eruption, dust particles suspended in the

atmosphere almost worldwide reduced the normal amount of solar radiation for THREE YEARS or more, by 15 percent.
- When Mount Katmai in Alaska erupted on June 8, 1912, the thermometer fell 10-12 degrees Celcius as far away as Algeria. According to meteorologist W. Humphrey, the effect was to diminish by 20 percent the amount of heat received by the earth from the sun. In some parts of America, they did not see the sun for 40 days. L. Don Leet, in *Encyclopedia Americana*, referring to this event, says: "If it were effective for a long enough period of time such a fall (of temperature) would bring a large section of the present temperate zones within a region of year-round ice."[10]

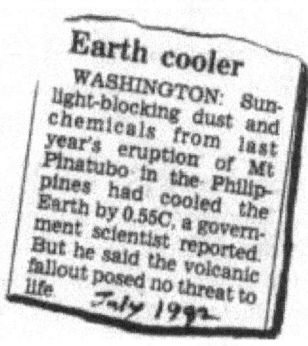

A more recent news report

The combination of causes

At the close of the Deluge:
1. Large quantities of stranded water filled all low continental areas.
2. Volcanic activity evaporated enormous quantities of water into steam clouds.
3. It also produced dust, which reduced solar-radiation and lowered temperatures.
4. The cold air and warm oceans caused heavy precipitation of snow and ice.

Volcanic winter

Falling again and again in a sunless world, the snow finally cooled the ground to the point where it could turn to ice.

As a result, snow rapidly piled up in the mountains and formed glaciers. And millions of square miles of ice formed over areas of land. Earth experienced a "volcanic winter".

It was freezing and wet. Snowfall continued through winter and summer alike, uninterrupted for years.

Glaciers pushed down into the valleys and scoured the landscape. Glaciers ground rocks into powder which was spread over the landscape by melt water.

When it dried, winds lifted the powder and dropped it to form loess deposits, such as are found, for example, in Mississippi.

This Ice Age, as it is called, set in **before** the break-up into continents.

RAIN TOO

In the counter-action between heat and cold, snow would fall in some areas of the earth and torrential rain elsewhere. And this is just what scientists have found from their field studies.

This Ice Age, as we term it, set in **before** the break-up of the super-continent, and spread into Antarctica **after** that region was wrenched southward.

Historical and archaeological evidence shows that Antarctica escaped a continental freeze-over for some centuries, during which period human colonies, apparently, were established.[11]

The peopling of the Americas as well as Antarctica took place amazingly soon after the Flood.

According to Polynesian traditions, there was a time when Antarctica was not covered with ice, and several nations inhabited it.[12]

Antarctica was settled before the continents became separated.

But with the wrenching apart of the continental mass, the upthrusting of mountain ranges and the rifting, severe climatic changes came to Antarctica. The location of the poles had altered. And both Arctic and Antarctic regions, cut off from the heat of the sun, were plunged into a prolonged night of devastating cold.

Although it took some time for ice cover to advance, the Antarctica civilisation was destroyed by the expanding walls of ice.

SEVERAL ICE AGES OR JUST ONE?

Here's another puzzle that has uniformitarian geologists scratching their heads:

A worldwide warm climate seems to be indicated in practically every **so-called "age"** in the geological fossil column. Yet there is the *"Ice Age" in the most RECENT portion* of that column, the Pleistocene epoch.

"Jonathan!" I hear someone say. "There's evidence of earlier ice ages - the Permian ice age and the ones in the pre-Cambrian."

Well, that statement deserves our attention. So let's see.

Okay, first of all, we should note that striated bedrock and conglomerates are often quoted as being indicators of glaciation. But these may be produced by causes other than glaciers - for example, FLOODS. For instance, 55 thousand million cubic metres of coarse sedimentary rock in Australia was formerly interpreted as a 'tillite' originally deposited in an ancient glacial period. However, these have now been shown to have been formed by underwater mud flows.[13]

But, despite this, some academics will dig in their heels and insist on several Ice Ages. Why? Because they don't want to face the implications of a global Flood. Honestly, you have only that choice - several Ice Ages, or a worldwide Flood. (The Global Flood, you see, pulls away the mat from under the evolution theory. We explained how in *Surprise Witness*.)

When you consider the requirements we have just discovered which are necessary to produce just one Ice Age, it becomes obvious: Surely, several periods of worldwide glaciation would require a miracle (or series of miracles) greater than that needed to bring on the global Flood.

To accomplish some of the feats demanded of ice by those who insist on these Ice Ages, ice would not only have had to climb high mountains 3,000 to 4,000 feet higher than itself *against gravity*, but it would need to act contrary to all laws of nature seen in action today.

Be sure of this. Uniformitarian causes are totally inadequate. The result is an almost INSOLUBLE problem.

On the other hand, there is good scientific basis for suggesting that the supposed evidence for these presumed "Ice Ages" (especially the "earlier" ones) could be **better explained by water action**.[14]

However, I shall grant this: the glacial till from the ***"last"*** ice sheet is of a different type from the others. This one probably does indicate true ice conditions.

During this ***one Ice Age***, volcanic dust was also blowing in from time to time to ***interbed*** with the ice. From one direction a shower of snow might blow in, followed by a layer of volcanic ash from another direction. One might also expect oxygen levels, like other factors during those centuries, to be unstable and variable.

Short-lived Ice Age

But evidence strongly suggests that this one and only Ice Age was short-lived. Assumptions of long periods of glaciation are not provable by dating methods, states Frederick Johnson, writing with Willard Libby, the most recognised authority on carbon dating.[15]

Evidence from a number of authorities suggests that the glacial period ended "abruptly". Wallace S. Broeker, Maurice Ewing and Bruce C. Heezen speak of the "rapid ice retreat" and "the warming which occurred at the close of Wisconsin glacial times" as "extremely abrupt".[16]

HOW LONG AGO WAS THE ICE AGE?

The French scholar Francois Forel thought that the ice sheet of the last glacial period began to melt 12,000 years ago. This was estimated from the deposits of detritus carried by glacial rivers and deposits in lakes.

But Velikovsky notes that "the mud must have assembled on the bottom of a lake at a faster rate in the beginning when the glaciers were larger, and if the Ice Age terminated suddenly, the deposition of detritus would have been much heavier at first, and there would be little analogy to the accumulation of detritus from the seasonal melting of snow in the Alps. **Therefore the time that has elapsed since the end of the last glacial period must have been even shorter than reckoned.**"[17]

Let's digress for a moment concerning Antarctica. I saw in an encyclopaedia published in 1976, the confident and absolute claim that ANTARCTICA had been under ice for 50 to 60 million years!

But in 1990 two geologists made a discovery that completely reopened the question of the age of the ice-sheet. Working just 250 miles from the South Pole, the geologists discovered the frozen remains of forest that was later dated to be between 2 and 3 million years old.

That encyclopaedia was wrong by as much as 58 million years! The absolute, ancient age of the Antarctic ice-cap wasn't so absolute after all.

In fact, C.H. Hopgood had already announced that Iconium dating of cores taken from the bottom of the Ross Sea showed that the "most recent" Ice Age in Antarctica **began** no more than 6,000 years ago.[18]

It doesn't take long for ice to build up.

A pole erected early last century in the Australian Antarctic Territory is reported to be now covered in ice over 100 feet deep.

Similarly, not much time would be required for an Ice Age to end.

Witnesses recorded it

In this connection, I shall mention again some very ancient maps. In *Dead Men's Secrets*, we noted that these maps were drawn by surveying parties who used longitude, latitude and a spherical earth map projection system. The maps indicate that those early explorers possessed a knowledge of cartography comparable to our own; they knew the correct shape and size of the earth; and they must have had at their disposal advanced geodetic instruments. In short, they were sophisticated.

According to the maps, survey expeditions that roamed the planet began to record ominous changes in both of the polar regions.

These maps, the origins of which are thousands of years old, show Antarctica firstly free of ice, secondly, the centre of Antarctica beginning to fill with ice (rivers and fjords being shown where today mile-thick glaciers flow) and thirdly, Antarctica after it had become mostly covered in ice. The U.S. Hydrographic Office declared one of these maps to be over 5,000 years old.[19]

Similar ancient maps show Greenland before it was covered in ice; glacial actions in the Baltic countries; and northern Europe being covered by the Ice Age glaciation's furthest advance. They were recording it as it occurred! Undoubtedly with sophisticated mapping instruments!

Physical evidence documented by Velikovsky suggests the Ice Age occurred only 4- to 5,000 years ago.[20] This overlaps the date of the Great Flood (4,350 years ago), which was the catalyst for the Ice Age.

Our map on page 24 reveals this interesting fact: **Before** the *final* tearing apart of the continents, the Ice Age had begun.

Temperatures were dropping.

The book of Job, so far as we can ascertain, is the oldest surviving book in the world. From the various astronomical references in the book, different astronomers claim to be able to calculate the time in which Job lived, which they give as from 2200-2100 BC.[21]

In his Ice Age book, Job recorded that "the waters [of the sea] harden like stone, and the surface of the deep [ocean] is frozen."[22]

As immense ice sheets came to cover Europe, at the same time in the Middle East, hail, snow and storms would be frequent. And the sea froze over in winter.

The later receding of the ice sheets over northern Europe seems to have been witnessed by some of its earliest colonists, who have left intriguing records for us to discover.

One example that can be dated with fair precision relates to Partholan's coming to Ireland (15th century BC). He counted "but three laughs [lochs, or lakes] and nyne Rivers in the Kingdom." But then, during the later second colonisation of Ireland, we are told that "Many Laughs and Rivers broke out in their time."[23]

Let's face it. Lakes and rivers don't just suddenly 'break out' in a short period of time without a source of water that is truly vast. So it would seem, therefore, that we are given in the **early Irish records an intriguing glimpse into the melting of the north European ice-sheets** which occurred some short time after the 15th century BC.

The Britons did not settle under Brutus in those islands until some three hundred years later (c.1104 BC), which is doubtless why their records contain no allusions to **ice or a sudden burgeoning of rivers and lakes** as do the earlier **Irish accounts**.

****

Ice all through summer is one thing. But when your life expectancy starts plummeting, that's a scary story. As we shall now discover...

18

After-shocks continue (a) -

HUMAN LIFE-SPAN SLASHED

Many hundreds of years would be required for our planet to settle down to relatively stable conditions following the Flood.

The new layers of rock and mountain, as well as rearranged land and sea, produced tensions. These needed to find release and adjustment.

The result was continuing earthquakes and volcanic lava flows - concentrated mainly at the polygon boundaries.

This stress relief was on an enormous scale. There were some massive local catastrophes. On practically every island, continent and seabed, the scars of this period remain.

As you can see, the Deluge was more than a single event. Rather, it involved a series of inter-related activities that still play their dying notes today.

CONTINENTAL BREAK-UP

In Chapter 2, I suggested what might seem at first outrageous. It was this: the Flood catastrophe probably triggered the beginning of the break-up of the original continental land mass.

There is evidence that a short, violent burst of tectonic activity occurred soon after the Babel dispersion had begun.

It was this violent upheaval that tore the earth apart.

In the genealogy of Genesis 10, there's an intriguing notation tucked away, so casually, as though it was then well known. In the fifth generation after Noah, a man was given the name Peleg (meaning "division"). It is stated bluntly that he was thus named because "in his days was the earth divided."[1]

It does appear that around the time of Peleg's birth the people of the earth were "scattered" from Babel.

But "the **EARTH** DIVIDED" - that has the hint of something else.

We have already discovered that there was undertaken in the early post-Flood centuries, a geographical survey, in the process of which the globe was divided into longitude and latitude. In *Dead Men's Secrets* a hint was made of a possible connection with the name "Peleg" ("division"). Certainly two other characters, Mizraim and Almodad can be linked to that event.

I am indebted to Scriptural linguist Dr. Bernard Northrup for pointing out that the root "PLG" means "to cleave, divide or separate", in connection with water. The root "PALA" means "to tear, or cut in two, to tear asunder". (We find a similar meaning in the word "pelican" - a bird that splits the sea when diving for fish.)

The name "PELEG" means "earthquake", "division", or "channel of water". It is the root word for Pelagos, which was the ancient Grecian term for the Mediterranean Sea.

In harmony with this understanding of the name "Peleg" is a statement in the ancient *Book of Jasher*. This document, which is referred to in the Bible[2] is, from internal indications, some 3,400 years old.

Within human memory

The *Book of Jasher* 'remembers' the events of Peleg's life as fairly recent. It records that "in his days the sons of men were divided, **AND in the latter days**, the earth was divided."[3]

You will observe that two events are stated.

According to the biblical chronology, Peleg was born in the 101st year after the Flood, that is, 2244 B.C. It would be fair to conclude that the human dispersion from Babel occurred at this time. He died in 2005 BC, some time after the continental land mass was finally wrenched apart.

The Egyptians also hint at this second event, calling it the work of their god Thoth Tehuti, "cleaver of the earth"! In times more stable, he was referred to as Thoth-Hapi-Tem neb Yut, "lord of the horizon".

Racial memories of this event are preserved in ancient cultures such as the American Indians and in the Dreamtime accounts of Australian Aborigines.[4] An American Indian account describes their survival on a drifting island under traumatic conditions. They finally escaped when their land-mass collided with a much larger one, namely the continent of North America, where they now live.[5]

There are numerous legends worldwide concerning the sun and stars shifting their position in the heavens.

Caius Julius Solinus, a Latin author, writing in the 3rd century, spoke of the people living on the southern borders of Egypt: "The inhabitants of this country say that they have it from their ancestors that the sun now sets where it formerly rose."

Between 939 and 1038 the rabbinical authority Hai Gaon referred in his *Responses* to cosmic changes in which the sun rose in the west and set in the east.

And Plato wrote in his dialogue, *The Statesman (Politicus)*: "I mean the change in the rising and the setting of the sun and the other heavenly bodies, how in those times they used to set in the quarter where they now rise, and they used to rise where they now set."

These could well be a reflection of the sudden moving of land masses to the new location, in which the land faced a completely new direction.

There is evidence that some post-Flood catastrophes devastated wide areas.

Ancient Scriptures vindicated

According to both ancient documents (the biblical Genesis and the *Book of Jasher*), the continental break-up occurred in one man's lifetime.

In Chapter 2 of this present work I touched on some scientific indications that continental separation occurred in "recent" times.

And now we discover that this event has already been recorded in the books of Genesis and Jasher for thousands of years!

Only since the 1960s, have evolutionist writers also seized upon this concept of splitting apart of the land mass and called it Continental Drift.

How interesting that ancient Scripture once more sounds remarkably vindicated - even by its antagonists!

The order of events

We noted in Chapter 2 that a rapid earth expansion was probably the agency which started the rifting of the continental platform and enlarged the sea bed. This caused the Flood waters over the mountains to recede. As water rushed off into these expanded lower basins, areas of the continental mass were exposed as dry land.

However, large volumes of water remained trapped on the continental land mass. Consequently, the higher margins of the new ocean basins remained free of water cover for some time. (Evidence: dry land relics thousands of feet below present sea level.) Later, the run-off from the continental lands caused the ocean level to rise and cover these higher margins.

Eventually, the ocean level stabilised to form a shoreline around the world a little higher than now. (Evidence: global shoreline 20 feet above present sea level) This probably functioned until the "latter days" of. Peleg.

Then followed another burst of tectonic activity, triggered probably by continuing inner earth expansion.

More rifting follows

There was more tensional rifting. This can be seen on a massive scale on the continents; for example, the East African Rift Valley. In this rifting, there was a final wrenching apart of the land areas.

Did you ever see that T.V. series, *The Incredible Hulk*? As the hero's muscles expanded, his shirt was ripped apart, exposing more of his body between. Simple physics. In global expansion, more ocean basin area would be exposed. And that would wrench the continental masses further apart.

Sea level again drops

The existing water in the oceans now had an enlarged lateral space to fill. As water spread through the widened sea basins, the total depth of water would be reduced. The lowering is estimated at around 500 to 600 feet.

Rifting separating Australia from Indonesia is one of the probable events which occurred during the lifetime of Peleg. Such post-Flood geological activity would have divided geographical regions and isolated human and animal populations. This would explain many biogeographical enigmas which concern biologists today.

LOSS OF LIFE SPAN

The Flood and its traumatic aftermath was taking its toll. Man rapidly, from generation to generation, began to decrease in size. His lifespan was also shortened. The first three generations after Shem showed an approximate 25 percent decrease. There was another sharp drop in longevity in the time of Peleg.

Before the Flood, each new generation began and ended progressively later than the one before it, just as occurs in our day.

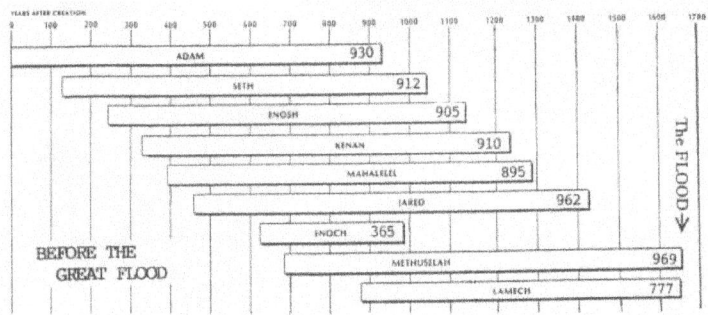

It appears that the Creator had endowed man with so great a life force that, even after the entrance of rebellion (with its physical and spiritual poison effect), people lived for nearly one thousand years.

But now something unprecedented was being experienced. The older patriarchs were living to see their grandchildren and great-great-great-grandchildren (those born in the new, impoverished world) dying before them. And this trend was worst of all in the very latest, youngest generations.

Such a rapidly deteriorating life span must have been viewed with some alarm.

The fact that we have the names of men, together with their ages at the birth of their first sons and their total life spans indicates that a geneological record was kept throughout this period.

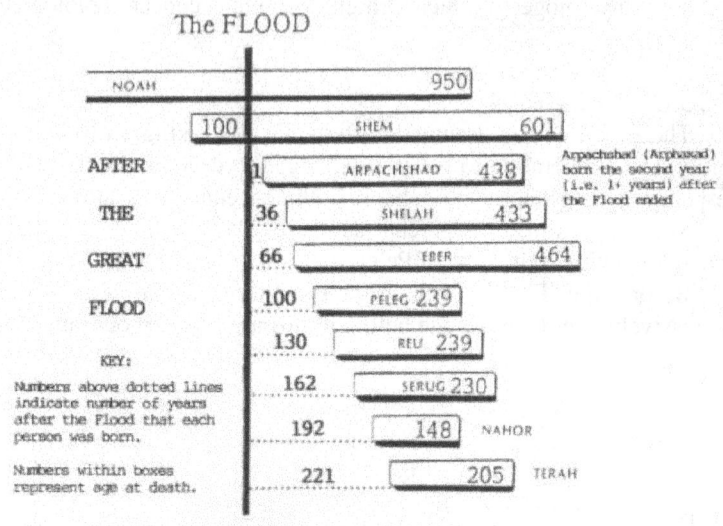

Genealogical records of this frightening trend (as it then must have been) come to us from the Hebrews, but other nations recorded it as well.

An official enquiry proposed

In China, the abrupt change in longevity was also a source of concern. The oldest account of this phenomenon is recorded by Emperor Ho-ang-ti who, according to the chronology of China, was a contemporary of Reu, Peleg's son. In his medical book he proposed an enquiry "whence it happened that the lives of our forefathers were so long compared with the lives of the present generation."[6]

The water-vapour canopy was no longer there to absorb dangerous cosmic radiation and man had begun to suffer an increased rate of mutation of the genetic material in the cells of his body.

This effect accumulated over succeeding generations, and, together with the generally harder way of life, ensured a steady decline in man's life span.

Over a number of generations this decline continued until a new life span was reached, now a mere one tenth of its span before the Deluge.

Residual gigantism

Gigantism or massiveness as a general or at least a widespread character of mankind probably continued for the first century or two after the Flood.

A remnant of giants remained in the time of Joshua, about 1400 BC. The houses of the legendary giants of Bashan still stand, intact, in southern Syria. Remains of ancient giants are excavated from time to time on all continents. This intriguing topic is covered in my book *The Lost World of Giants*.[7]

EARTHQUAKES

It was a traumatic period. After the Deluge, earthquakes took place continuously. Wonderful cities perished in their heyday and were erased from the memory of mankind.

Eduard Suess, the noted Austrian geologist, recognises the unparalleled violence of these earthquakes. He writes:

"Numerous examples of great mountain chains suggest by their structure... episodal disturbances of such indescribable and overpowering violence, that the imagination refuses to follow the understanding...."[8]

Early human records such as Babylonian writings from the library of Nineveh testify to this high earthquake incidence in remote times.

From comparison of ruins, it appears that on several occasions the entire region of the ancient East was shaken by titanic earthquakes. Cities such as Ugarit in Syria and Troy near the Dardanelles, 600 miles away, came crashing down at the same time.

Compared with the largest areas affected by modern earthquakes, these ancient quakes covered an area unusually large.

On Crete, earthquakes laid low whole cities several times in succession. Knossos and Phaestos come to mind. More than once was Troy destroyed by earthquakes.

From excavations in scores, if not hundreds, of sites all over the ancient East, Claude Schaeffer has identified six separate upheavals since shortly before 2000 BC, each of which encompassed the entire region of Asia Minor, the Caucasus, across to Iran, through Mesopotamia, down to Egypt and out into the Mediterranean. Some of them were so violent as to terminate great centres of trade and to lay civilisations prostrate. Loss of human life must have been enormous.

Truly, an earthquake of such magnitude has no modern parallel.

To recover equilibrium

Schaeffer, wondering at the enormous extent of the earthquakes, asked:

"Could it be that in earlier times earthquakes were of very much greater force and wider spread than they are now because geological strata, originally out of equilibrium, were settling with the passing of time?"[9]

Did you get that? Quite independently, Schaeffer has struck the same truth. **Yes, the earth was thrown out of equilibrium just a few thousand years ago, and relief of stress had to follow**.

Two particularly intense periods of seismic and climatic disruption have been identified by Gams and Nordhagen, Sernander, Paret, Velikovsky and others. These occurred around 1500 BC and between 800 and 700 BC.

H. Gams and R. Nordhagen have documented very thoroughly that about 1500 BC and again about 800 BC, the lakes of Europe were tilted. Many of them were emptied of all their water. Many changes of river beds "are indicative of ground movements on a grand scale."[10]

Undoubtedly minor segments of the fossil record can be attributed to regional disturbances stemming from such after-effects of the Deluge.

The plain fact is that earthquakes are readjustments of the earth's crust, a response to stress. And this stress had its origin not more than a few thousand years ago.

The adjustment went on. Considerably later, it was recorded that in a single year (217 BC) 57 earthquakes occurred in Rome.

Subsequently, earthquake activity diminished very quickly in intensity as well as in the number of occurrences. Both earthquakes and eruptions have since taken place periodically, but with subsiding activity. *Historically speaking, both have been on the wane.*

As says Eduard Suess:

"The earthquakes of today are certainly but a faint reminiscence. . ."[11]

VOLCANISM

Likewise with volcanism. The activity curve points to volcanism on a cataclysmic scale just a few thousand years ago. Then an exponential decline.

The destruction of Thera in the eastern Mediterranean between 1800 and 1500 BC was one such cataclysmic disaster. Thera (Santorini) was a circular island surrounding a 5,000 foot mountain. On the slopes were houses of the wealthy, with gardens of figs, olives and grapes, as well as therapeutic hot springs. Below, on the coast, was a highly sophisticated urban community.

When the mountain blew apart, it opened a pit 47 miles across, which sucked in the sea. Some of the island sank into the newly opened undersea crater, and some was buried under a mass of volcanic ash ten stories deep.

Compared to our celebrated Krakatoa, Thera's explosion was a GIANT. Krakatoa lost eight square miles; but thirty-two square miles of Thera fell into the sea. Thera's crater was five times as big as Krakatoa's. The tidal wave from it must have been stupendous. For centuries afterward, Thera was a dead island.

Today, most of the mountain is gone. A broken, steeply plunging crescent encloses the sea. The bottom is 1,300 feet down.

Our world is splattered with volcanoes, untold thousands in number, most of them extinct. You'll notice that they're along the boundaries of the primary polygon features and along some 'swell' features of the secondary polygons. Tiny Iceland had 107 volcanoes. Auckland, New Zealand, is pockmarked with 60 dead volcanoes just within the built-up suburban area!

Later decline

The earth went on shuddering for centuries, slowly quieting down. As time passed, one volcano after another burnt itself out.

Even just a few centuries ago, a considerable number of today's dead volcanoes were still spouting strongly.

Today 400 to 500 are considered active or dormant. Many of these will not endure another hundred years.

****

Even then, some astonishing things still happen. As we shall soon discover...

19

After-shocks continue (b) -

THE MUMMY ROSE FROM THE SEA

We're going to CRASH!" she screamed.

"Hope not," he replied. "My souvenirs are in the cargo hold."

I looked out. On both sides of the plane pressed steep Andean mountains, ominously close. It seemed that any second the wingtips of our DC3 would scrape them.

Next to me a Peruvian man looked about to faint. My stomach was in the back of my throat.

It was a great comfort to know that (a) this aircraft was a second-hand "cast-off" from some North American airline and (b) crashes were not uncommon in these parts.

I was now gasping for breath. The Peruvian lay back with his eyes shut tight. His knuckles were white as he gripped the seat rest.

A rocky spur raced toward us. The plane dipped its wing. The oxygen masks popped down. I ravenously grabbed mine and sucked in deeply.

Above us, two miles high in the clouds, stretched Lake Titicaca…

* * * * * * *

Titicaca. At 12,000 feet altitude, it is the highest navigable lake in the world.

But did you know that 4,000 years ago Titicaca was on sea level? We'll discover, in this chapter, what happened.

MOUNTAINS RAISED "RECENTLY"

The evolution theory speculates that mountain uplifts occurred over millions of years, until about a million years ago.

But listen to the eminent geologist Bailey Willis, regarding the Asian mountains:

"The great mountain chains challenge credulity by their extreme youth."[1]

We need to be clear on this. All our present mountains appear to have been thrust up AFTER all the fossils were buried. They are made up of massive Flood-laid layers. Many are loaded with evidence of volcanism under water.

Though serene looking today, all mountains are the result of **violent** crustal upheavals. The Andes, for example, most probably rose when magma (molten rock) invaded the strata and lifted them. The Andes abound in exceeding high and enormous volcanoes.

On the former surf line of the raised beaches at Valparaiso, Chile, now at 1,300 feet, the seashells are not even decayed - a clear indication of a "recent" up thrust.

Geologist J.S. Lee reports convincing evidence that "the mountain ranges in western China have been elevated **since the Glacial Age.**"[2]

In Kashmir, Helmut de Terra found deposits of a sea bottom at an elevation of 5,000 feet or more and tilted, at an angle of 40 degrees. And the shock is that:

"These deposits contain paleolithic ['Old Stone Age'] fossils."[3]

Thus, the change occurred in human times, "however fantastic changes so extensive may seem to a modern geologist."

Citing extensive evidence, Immanuel Velikovsky concludes that "the great massif of the Himalayas rose to its present height **in the age of modern, actually historical man**. . . With their topmost peaks the mountains have shattered the entire scheme of the geology of the 'long, long ago'."[4]

A shock indeed! It can be demonstrated that the mountain chains of the Caucasus, China, Tibet, the Rockies, the Alps and the Andes all rose to their present heights in historical times. We have the same "late" dating from all parts of the earth.

The Andes range

Certainly the Andes must have risen abruptly in comparatively "recent" times.

At 11,500 feet, a curious whitish streak runs along the side of the mountain range for over 300 miles. It is composed of the calcified remains of marine plants. This shows that these slopes were once part of the seashore.

In fact, many lakes up in the Andes region are completely salt.

One such lake is Titicaca. It stretches 138 miles in length and is in places 70 miles wide. At 12,500 feet altitude, Titicaca is the highest navigable lake on earth.

A watermark of salt along the lake shore now runs at an angle to the water level. Originally it must have been horizontal. Clearly the land was not only thrust up to its present altitude, but was tilted in the process.

Not only is the water saline. On the beach of this lake high in the mountains, there are seashells as well as traces of seaweed. The lake must have been a bay or inlet of the sea.

Even today, various sea creatures (including sea horses) survive in the lake.

Today this lofty, almost sterile region is capable of sustaining only a scant population.

Yet here we are confronted with a colossal mystery. Traces of a huge city lie at the southern side of the lake.

In the fifteenth century, Spanish conquistador Cieca de Leon reported his astonishment at seeing ancient gateways hewn from solid stone 30 feet long and 15 feet high and pivoting.

These ruins of Tiahuanaco, in Bolivia, are extensive. It is obvious that a great city once existed here. But here is the mystery. At an altitude of 13,000 feet, maize will not bear fruit. Yet endless agricultural terraces, now abandoned, rise as high as 18,400 feet above sea level, and continue up under the snow to some unidentified altitude.

Such an abundance of cornfields must have supported a huge population. The region is too high and too barren to do this now. Could the site once have been lower? You see, if the Andes were 2- to 3,000 feet lower than now, maize would ripen around Lake Titicaca and the city of Tiahuanaco could support the large population for which it was evidently built.

Once a seaport

But how about this? Here is an even greater surprise... the remains of an ocean quay. That's right, an ocean quay. It suggests that the city, when built, was at sea level - 12,500 feet lower!

The remains near the stadium of Tiahuanacu show five distinct landing places, harbours with moles and a canal which heads inland. The docks are vast - and one wharf is big enough to take hundreds of ships.

So we're faced now with a sea harbour at 12,500 feet altitude and 200 miles inland! Staggering, isn't it?

Well, someone says, perhaps these gigantic docks were intended for ships on Lake Titicaca. Good try. But I'll tell you why not. You see, they face in the opposite direction from the lake. Not only that, the mooring rings on the stone piers were so large that they could only have been used by ocean-liner sized vessels.

This place - I tell you - was a seaport on the Pacific coast. AND IT WAS THRUST, SO TO SPEAK, TWO MILES INTO THE SKY! Now, how about that?

You've probably heard it said that mountain making took "long ages". That in the case of the Andes (the second highest mountain range on earth), it occurred more than a million years ago. Well, I'm sorry to be a spoil sport. But the change in altitude occurred AFTER the city was built. I would suggest about 4,000 years ago.

And since only a few intermediate surf lines can be detected, the elevation could **not** have proceeded little by little.

The explorer Colonel H.P. Fawcett, who travelled this region early last century, was persuaded by the evidence that Tiahuanaco had been destroyed by the terrible seismic upheavals which accompanied the raising of the Andes to their present height.[5] And I believe he got that right.

Work interrupted

Perhaps the Tiahuanaco we see remains of was built later - and its unnamed predecessor is the city we should be talking about here.

There is some evidence that the monoliths of the city were not entirely finished when the catastrophe struck and suddenly raised the whole city and lake 12,500 feet. What a staggering thought!

Cast-down builders' tools were found in the ruins when the Spaniards came upon the place in the 16th century. The heaps of blocks of masoned stone bear evidence of sudden abandonment... men fleeing for their lives, taken by surprise.

After the disaster, the populace lay buried in gullies that had become mass graves, covered by silt.

Fragments of skeletons, both of animals and men, lay scattered among the ruins. Jewels, pottery and tools were found mixed in utmost confusion.

Can you imagine hundreds, if not thousands, of cubic miles of the body of the earth almost instantly heaved upward? From such an event, violent earthquakes must have spread throughout the entire globe.

This massive uplifting exposed a continental shelf which is now the desert lowlands of Peru and northern Chile.

Witnessed by survivors

In the traditions of the Ugha Mongulala tribe of the western Amazon jungle, the South American continent was "... still flat and soft like a lamb's back, ... the Great River still flowed on either side." But then came a cataclysm: "The Great River was rent by a new mountain range and now it flowed swiftly toward the East. Enormous forests grew on its banks... In the West, where giant mountains had surged up, people froze in the bitter cold of the high altitudes."[6]

Upswellings of other mountains may have been as violent. These were never forgotten by the inhabitants.

For example, the Washo Indians of California say their ancestors witnessed the uplifting of the North American sierras from the plains.

Various other tribes of the Americas likewise recall in their oral history the memory of new mountains being raised and others flattened.[7]

RELIEF FROM STRESS CONTINUES

It took the earth's crust millennia to settle down. During the adjustment, lava continued to flow. Isolated areas of land were submerged or raised thousands of feet.

Today these effects are being felt only to a comparatively minor degree.

Still, it should be mentioned that even in modern times, the ocean has been known to raise or lower its islands or its depths, as much as thousands of feet. No need to invoke long evolutionary periods. THE EARTH'S SURFACE CAN CHANGE RAPIDLY.

RECENT EXAMPLES OF
RAPID UP OR DOWN THRUSTS

- Did you know that a recent Chilean earthquake elevated parts of the coastline 1,000 feet?
- Alaska's Good Friday earthquake of March, 1964, lowered the floor of Seward harbour by 315 feet.
- During the 1755 Lisbon earthquake, a new marble quay upon which crowds of people had collected for safety, suddenly sank. The water now covers it by 600 feet.
- Tuanaki Island in the Cook group sank into the Pacific Ocean with 13,000 inhabitants in 1843. One morning, fishermen left the island in their boats. When they returned home at night, the island was gone.
- In 1923, technicians of a Western Telegraph ship searching for a lost cable in the Atlantic Ocean detected that the cable had been thrown up by the rising ocean bed 2¼ miles in only 25 years. That's right. A 12,000 foot rise in one spot!
- Again, in 1929, the Great Banks seaquake resulted in the cutting of the northern series of transatlantic cables. When the cables were repaired, measurements of the sea floor indicated that certain areas had suddenly risen almost 5,000 feet.
- In May, 1973, part of the Banin Trench near Japan rose 6,000 feet.
- The 1960 earthquake which wiped out the Moroccan city of Agadir, uplifted the land from about 90 feet (close to the shore) to around 3,300 feet (several miles from the shore). This occurred in only 45 seconds!
- In Japan, a few years later, a two-minute quake sank the bottom of

the sea around Izu Peninsula well over 1,000 feet. It also sank many houses in the new subdivisions along the coast right into the shale bedrock, which liquified. This led to comprehensive research in Japan to determine how long and of what strength a quake need be to cause rock liquefaction. The result was startling. It was found that medium strength metamorphic rock can liquefy within minutes.

Canoes 4,000 feet up on cliffs

On January 26, 1700 the coastal area of British Columbia and north western U.S.A. was hit by a massive earthquake. A tsunami surged across the Pacific Ocean to Japan. People there recorded the date.

Astonishingly, archaeologists have found remains of canoes on the edges of almost vertical cliffs, as high up as 4,000 feet above sea level!

Today's native elders relate that their ancestors had to run for high mountains... how raging sea carried some of them in their canoes high up the cliffs, where they survived. Heroic deeds of survivors are still recited.

Here, then, is evidence of either a sudden, violent uplifting of the coast to a height of 4,000 feet, or, as the local people claim, a strong earthquake which created a tsunami up to 4,000 feet in height. This quake occurred between Vancouver Island and the mainland, which has a variable distance of plus/minus only 16 miles (25 kilometres) of open sea. This tsunami rushed into a narrow inlet where the town of Bella Coola is today.

Land rises 4,000 feet

During an earthquake off the northern tip of Sumatra on December 26, 2004, the sea bottom in the Straits of Malacca uplifted almost 4,000 in only about 3 minutes.

The US-based National Geospatial-Intelligence Agency, which analyses spy satellite imagery and produces maps and charts for the Defence Department, was reported to have received information that one area of the Straits of Malacca, which separates Malaysia from the Indonesian island of Sumatra had its depth cut from 4,060 feet to 105 feet.

In another affected area, a merchant marine ship logged that the depth was cut from 3,855 feet to just 92 feet.[8] The US Navy reportedly sent two ships to re-chart the waters. Sonar images from British navy ship *HMS Scott* showed the massive uplift of a large area 10 kilometres wide and up to 1.5 kilometres high (4,800 feet plus).

Strange, but true!

The date was March, 1882; the location, some 200 miles west of Madeira and about the same distance south of the Azores. An uncharted island was encountered in heavily travelled sea lanes. It disappeared just as suddenly. This strange event was recorded in a ship's log as well as in the press.

The British merchant ship, *S.S. Jesmond*, en route from Messina, Sicily, to New Orleans, and captained by David Robson, suddenly found itself passing through muddy water and enormous shoals of dead fish. The next day they encountered more of the same.

Smoke was seen rising from mountains of an island which should not exist. Where charts indicated a depth of **several thousand fathoms,** the anchor now hit bottom at **only seven fathoms.**

A landing party found itself on an enormous island with no trees, no vegetation, not even a sandy beach. It was totally bare, as though it had just risen from the sea. Volcanic debris covered it.

Miles away, beyond a plateau broken with deep chasms, rose high mountains which would have taken days to reach.

The men returned to their landing point, where a shattered gravel cliff showed signs of having been subjected to giant force.

The mummy comes back

When one of the sailors stumbled upon an unusual looking arrowhead, the captain ordered picks and shovels brought ashore from the ship.

For two days they excavated. Crumbling remains of walls were uncovered. And the walls were massive. And bronze swords, rings and mallets were found. There were carvings of heads and figures of birds and animals. Two vases or jars contained fragments of bone and an almost entire cranium.

But most startling of all was what appeared to be a mummy enclosed in a stone case. The corpse had done some travelling - thousands of feet down - and back up again!

A scene similar to that on the uncharted island

In the United States, reporters who examined the relics were told by Captain Robson that he intended to donate them to the British Museum. And they probably still lie there in some attic or basement.

About the same time, Captain James Newdick of the *Westbourne*, en route from Marseilles to New York, reported having seen a mystery island at 25° 30' N and 24° W. Coordinates supplied by both captains indicated the island was 20 by 30 miles in area.

The miles of dead fish, probably killed by an underwater explosion which heated the ocean, were the subject of comment by a number of other ship captains at the time. Their reports appeared in various newspapers, such as the *New York Times*.

The volcanic and tectonic activity which *raised* this large area of land **thousands of feet** so suddenly, apparently drowned it once more. The island was never seen again.

Indeed, land CAN rise or sink quickly... even in our day. It does NOT require millions of years.

CLIMATE

Now we turn to climate changes.

The volcanic and seismic upheavals following the Great Flood were accompanied by oscillations and instability of the climate. At times, snowfall continued through winter and summer alike, uninterrupted for years. Our forefathers knew the discomforts of weather that was cold and wet.

Storms were intense. The changed geography and changing temperature gradients were the cause. Oceanic and atmospheric circulations had to adjust to these.

World climatic and weather patterns would have varied from one decade to the next. It might be added that a few large asteroidal impacts continued through this period.

As the climate altered, the fluctuations in temperature must have been almost unbearable.

Such widespread climatic disruptions continued very late into the pre-Christian era. Sernander and others again identify 1500 BC and 800 BC as periods of strong disturbances in climate.

Brooks, in *Climate Through the Ages*, remarks:

"The beginning of the 'period of unchanging climate' has advanced later and later before the attacks of geologists, and now, in the minds of most of the authors who concern themselves with the subject, it apparently stands only a few centuries before Christ."[9]

EXPONENTIAL CHANGE
AFTER THE DELUGE TRAUMA

We have noted how, in the wake of the Great Flood, numerous violent readjustments were taking place. As the graph on the next page illustrates, the rate of change declined exponentially at first. There has since been a settling down to a comparative stability in each sphere.

In relation to the effects of weather change, the melting of ice had drastic effects in some regions. As the walls of ice separating some inland seas from the lower land thinned, a point was reached where these walls could no longer contain the surging tides of the inland seas. As these walls ruptured, the waters and "slime" of the inland seas spewed forth, invading and inundating some low-lying nations. Eastern Asia was one such area devastated by on-rushing waters making their way to the ocean.

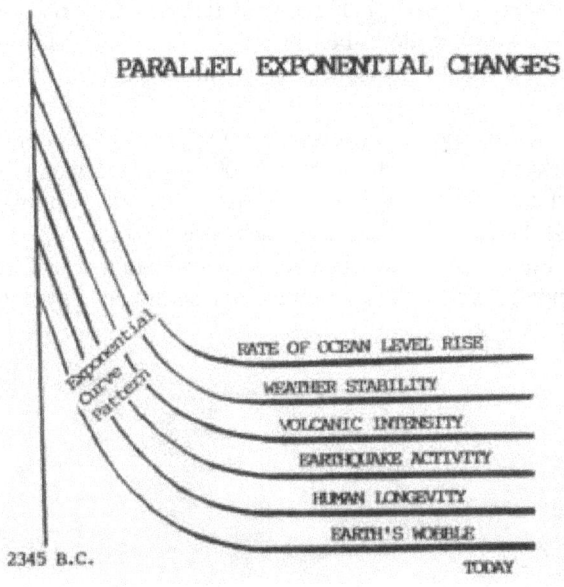

There is evidence of other post-Flood disasters, such as in Europe.

We could mention the *in situ* fossil remains of a sponge reef which stretches 1,800 miles (2,900 kilometres) across Europe from Spain to Romania and as far north as Germany. Its size and depth indicates that some time was taken for it to grow.[10]

This is definitely post-Flood, since it stands above strata containing fossils, including coal.[11]

Some remains which have been attributed to the Flood, are, rather, evidence of significant but lesser catastrophes since the Flood.

For example, the Siberian mammoths. Because Flood-laid deposits underlie their remains, we must regard their sudden freezing as a post-Flood disaster. Agencies involved in this event are described in Book 2, *Surprise Witness*. One likely catalyst was the sudden wrenching apart of the continents some two centuries after the Great Flood.

On this planet, we shall find plenty of mysteries to exercise our minds. We may never explain every single one. But you can be sure of this. The scenario described in this book makes the most sense, with the least unsolved problems, when you consider the evidence as a whole.

Granted, there will be questions to face. For example, if the whole world was wiped out around 4,400 years ago, then what about the Egyptians, who are said to have had a continuous and uninterrupted civilisation before and after this period?"

Good question, Percy. And we'll investigate that in Chapter 23. But right now, suppose start with the initial settling of Egypt.

Hold on tight...

20

The Flood "puddles" left behind -

TRAPPED!

At first, the new, straggling population kept to the hills. The low areas were still very much under water.

Texts of Sumer recorded that cultivation was possible by keeping the Flood waters at bay, but that this was ultimately extended to the lowlands.

The same condition still prevailed when settlers got over to China. One ancient legend says that after the great World Flood, a man named Yu surveyed the land of China and divided it into sections. He "built channels to drain the water off the sea" and helped make the land liveable again. Many snakes and "dragons" were driven from the marshlands when Yu created the new farmlands.

When Egypt's first historical king, Menes (the biblical Mizraim, grandson of the legendary Noah) formed a settlement in Egypt, Egypt was not a country, but rather one great "sea". The whole of Egypt was an extended marsh, due to the unrestrained flowing of the Nile which, after the Deluge, washed the foot of the sandy Libyan mountains.

Before Egypt could become fit for human abode, it was necessary to set bounds to the overflowings of the "Sea", or the "Ocean", as the Nile was then called.

So when Mizraim led a colony into lower Egypt, he found it necessary to raise great embankments to confine the Nile waters. The name *Mizraim* (or *Metzrim*) means "the encloser, or embanker, of the sea." What better name could have been given him for his great achievement? Even today, Egypt is sometimes referred to as "the land of *Mizr (Muzr)*", an abbreviation for "land of the embanker".

The ancient name of Egypt was *Khem* - from *Ham*, the biblical son of Noah and father of Mizraim.[1]

This embanking of the sea was the "making" of it as a river, as far as Lower Egypt is concerned.

The city of Memphis was later constructed in the bed of the previous wide channel.[2]

For centuries Egypt was a land with heavy rainfall.

Author John Anthony West delivered a seismic shock to archaeology in the early 1990s when he and Boston University geologist Robert Schach revealed that the Great Sphinx of Giza, Egypt, showed evidence of rainfall erosion.

Such erosion could only mean that the Sphinx was carved during or before the rains that marked the transition of northern Africa from wet to dry.

By our scenario, the Sphinx was carved during this heavy rain period.

The extent of land originally under water is defined by the Greek historian Herodotus: "No part of that which is now situate beyond the Lake Moeris was to be seen, the distance between the lake and the sea is a journey of seven days."[3]

Thus all of Lower Egypt was under water!

ONCE WELL WATERED

Old legends confirm that well-watered lands extended for hundreds of miles west of the Nile, into Sudan and Libya (now desert).

In 1954, Theodore Monod traversed a region represented on the maps as a huge blank area. For 1,050 miles across the southwest Sahara, he was by day lashed by fiery sandstorms, at night exposed to biting cold. Frequently Monod and his companions walked all day in order to spare their riding camels. At times they were so exhausted that they held on to the tails of the camels and let themselves be dragged along. The march lasted 1½ months.

En route, Monod made some sensational discoveries. He found vast dried lakes in the interior of the Sahara, with the remains of ancient fishing villages along their shores. Thousands of bone harpoons lay strewn about in the desert sand. The dried lake bottoms were covered with the bones of hippopotamuses, fish and crocodiles.

In November, 1981, enhanced radar photographs from the space shuttle *Columbia* revealed under that desert, the beds of buried rivers and tributaries (some as large as today's Nile), which once flowed south and west into a basin that may have been as large as today's Caspian Sea.

That was the situation for centuries after the Great Flood. Rainfall was heavy.

Even 2,000 years ago, the Roman geographer Strabo described the land west of Alexandria as "this lovely land of Mareotis, full of villages and splendid churches; so abundant is the soil that the vine is produced and is of such quantity that it is racked and kept that it may grow old." The region is now a barren wasteland.

AFRICA

The Sahara was at first part of the ocean. Later it comprised a group of fertile regions around a vast inland sea, which, as it diminished, remained a green area.

At the beginning of Egyptian history, there was an immense marsh. The present Lake Chad is probably a vestige of it.

The Piri Re'is map (below), originally drawn thousands of years ago, shows lakes, rivers and cities there.

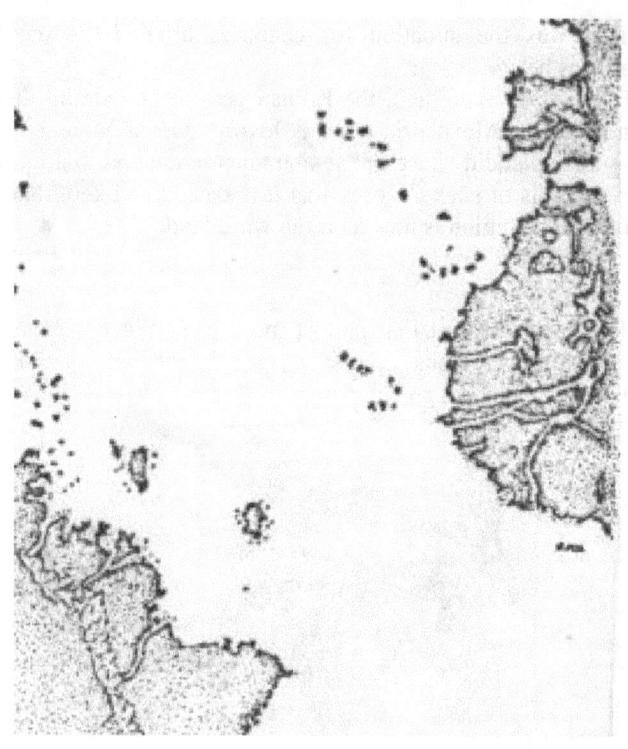

Even 2,000 years after the Flood, North Africa was the granary of Europe, a well-watered fertile land. Vast wheat fields and dozens of Roman towns and cities sat in this region. The ruins of these cities lie buried under shifting desert sands today.

At that time, the drying out was already under way. The old Spanish geographer, Pomponius Mela, around 45 AD, wrote that "here, far inland in Numidia, was once sea where now are barren and sandy plains." He also spoke of old anchors fixed in rocks.[4]

Modern expeditions in the Sahara have found drawings of numerous types of animals, as well as an abundance of ancient man-made implements.

Sophisticated cave paintings in Algeria's Tassili Mountains depict men and animals in a land of lakes, rivers and trees. (This advanced art is often defaced or drawn over by later, more primitive artists.)

At one spot between Sebha, the modern capital of the Fezzon, and the oasis of Ghat on the Algerian border, are 700 miles of tunnels (in places less than 20 feet apart). Considering the 100,000 graves found in the wadi, the region must have been populous.

L. Taylor Hansen mentions the remains of massive port cities existing in the Sahara![5]

She also says: "During the Middle Ages a ship was found not too far from the Draa Depression [the present border of Algeria and Morocco, just east of the Atlas Mountains] in which skeletons of the rowers were lying with the chains still around their bones. The Arabs, I understand, charge a very high fee to take you there. It still must be in existence."[6]

In the late 1950s or early 1960s, a wealthy American couple, the Johnsons, were in the Siwa Oasis in the Libyan desert near the border of Egypt and Libya. In passageways running underground from the temple of Agourmi for some two miles to Djebel Muta, they came upon an ancient picture gallery.

In this now parched region, everywhere was pictured water and ferny forests. There were paintings of buffalo, an elephant pulling fruit from a tree, crocodiles in the water, birds nestling in trees, and some other strange animals peeping through the shrubbery. Also, there were paintings of a city on the shore of a sea, with many square-sailed ships about. The quays were wide and well-made, apparently of stone.

Mrs Johnson related that their Arab guide, for a high fee, took them to "ancient stone quays stretching way out into the desert sand."[7]

Fertile lands dry out

Analysis of excavated pollen shows that initially cedars, lime trees, oaks, maples, pines and elders thrived there. As the climate dried, cypresses, olives and junipers joined the pines and oaks. Eventually, however, acacias and grasses struggled to survive.

People deserted the area as the Sahara dried out into desert.

The Sahara region is now as barren as the surface of the moon.

Where the street-like canyons of the Tassili plateau open into plazas filled with quaint rock pillars, you will still find a few gnarled trees clinging to life. A mere 50 or 60 of them. Their seeds will not grow in the present climate of the desert. But these mighty cypresses still live on, perhaps 3,000 or 4,000 years old – dating to that remote period when the region was fertile.

Along with California's sequoias, these are among the oldest living organisms on earth. In the depths of the canyons they have survived the change of climate.

Also, high in the mountains of the desert, are a few fish, living in waterholes where once a river flowed south. As the desert advanced, the river dried out, trapping the fish. Isolated for thousands of years, they are comparable to the fish trapped in the North American deserts.[8]

Over the past 80 years, an area as large as Britain, France and Germany has been lost to this creeping desert. This desert expands southward into Africa at a rate of 4½ miles (7 kilometers) per year. And a great sea of sand is moving eastward toward the fertile Nile delta at about 8 miles (13 kilometers) a year. As late as 1955, acacias were flourishing around Khartoum. Today these popular dry-zone trees, which can survive on only a few inches of water a year, are found no closer than 54 miles south of the Sudanese capital.

Across the African continent are found dry lakes and shrunken lakes.

Lake Victoria was 300 feet higher than it is today. Lake Chad possesses neither tributaries nor outlets. It is just a huge puddle of trapped water, left behind by the Flood.

An area now known as the Kalahari Desert was likewise once well watered.

MIDDLE EAST

For a short interval after the Flood, the Dead Sea shoreline was 1,400 feet higher.

In 1450 BC the land of Canaan (Israel and Jordan) was described as "flowing with milk and honey".

The huge civilisations of Sumeria, Assyria and Babylonia thrived in fertile country that now lies under desert sand, their sophisticated cities lost.

RUSSIA

The Russian Steppes show evidence of the same type of former Flood "puddles".

The Caspian Sea (between Iran and southern Russia) has shrunk from shore levels 250 feet higher. It was apparently confluent with the Aral and Black Seas. Today within its waters live ocean seals, stranded when the waters withdrew.

The Sea of Azov likewise has shrunk considerably over those 4,000 years.

ASIA

Lake Baikal in Siberia, 1,500 feet above sea level, is proof that all Siberia was once under sea. Seals of the same variety as those found in the Arctic Sea, the Caspian Sea and the Aral Sea, are also trapped in Lake Baikal.

The Gobi Desert was a great inland lake as large as the Mediterranean Sea! Chinese history calls it "The Interior Sea". Russian archaeologists have discovered immense foundations rising from the sand in various places.

Mongolia and Turkestan, now semi-arid wastes of sand and gravel, were once lush lake country.

The Theytis Ocean covered large areas of Central Asia.

Shor Kul, a salt lake in Sinkiang province, China, stood 350 feet above its present level.

In 1730 a Swedish explorer wrote that in or about 1720, he saw "the whole lower hull of an ancient ship with a keel at Barabinsk, in Tartary, where is no ocean and 700 miles from the sea."[9]

Only about 700 years ago, on his travels through parts of Mongolia, Marco Polo reported that the fertility of the soil and the abundance of cattle rendered the people independent of trading. But today, this same area is a sea of sandhills.

In 1935, Swedish explorer Henning Haslund wrote:

"Once we came upon an abandoned Sart village, where newly thrown up dams and uncompleted excavations bore witness to the departed population's desperate struggle to retain the vanishing water. When the river ran dry the fields had not been able to produce crops, and the people had had to subsist on the rapidly diminishing herds of cattle in the patient hope that the river would soon again be filled with water.

"But a day had come when there was no more water to be had."[10]

Russian pilots flying over the Gobi desert have photographed the ruins of quite large cities, which are recognisable from their foundations. And local people, Uigers and Mongols, have told stories of lost cities surfacing after fierce sandstorms.

Many Central Asian and Indian legends recall the time when much of Central Asia, and in particular the Gobi, was once an inland sea.

In 1280, Marco Polo mapped salt lakes which today have dried up to become salt basins.

The Tibetan Tablelands (the highest tablelands in the world, averaging 16,000 feet above sea level) are today dotted with numerous salt lakes. Marine terraces prove that it was submerged under a great sea.

Only the Flood on a global scale, leaving behind its massive "flood puddles", can account for phenomena such as this.

And look at India. India has a well-marked inland basin. There is clear evidence that this was filled with water. As it dried up, the climate became more arid. Relics in this northwestern region (now known as the Thar Desert) prove that great rivers, luxuriant vegetation and cities once existed.

India's desert area continues to expand. In one part of the Rajasthan region, the area of sand cover has spread by 8 percent in 18 years.

AUSTRALIA

Australia, a very flat continent, is now mostly dry. Traces of salt pans and rivers that dried up thousands of years ago indicate that it was once green, its climate mild.

The Australian aborigines speak of an ancient city hidden in the remote hinterlands of northern Australia.

According to the *Australian Weekend News*, three white men made it through the remote outback to visit the ruins of this alleged city, known as Burrungu. They reported ruined walls, stone houses, wide courtyards, and stately arches that look down upon statues set along tree-shaded streets.

Legends of the aborigines tell of white men living in the city many thousands of years ago. "They were so tall they needed very big buildings," the natives claimed. "The city is taboo. It was once a place of much activity."[11]

From a plane I have gazed down upon the sand dunes of this wasteland. Satellite pictures of sand dune patterns indicate that a sea larger than America's Lake Superior existed in Central Australia. Today's salt lakes were once part of this sea.

The dunes were formed as it progressively shrank and the climate became arid.

In December, 2003, Australian researcher Gilbert Deem wrote to me: "We have sites to investigate around the perimeter of the old inland sea in central Australia. We have some amazing stuff from there."

He noted the many references to the inland sea in the early history of Australia.

About 3,000 years ago, the Phoenicians were mining in central Australia, accessing via two entrances: one near Broome and the other in the Gulf of Carpentaria. There was once a strait called "the north-south passage", which ran from the Gulf of Carpentaria in the north to the vicinity of Spencer's Gulf in South Australia.

"This was the one that [the British explorer] Flinders and the Frenchman Baudin went looking for when they met at Encounter Bay," said Gilbert. "Flinders had secret orders to find the passage, as the British East India Company was looking for the old strait mentioned on the Phoenician charts which were used by Columbus, Cook and the early Australian navigators. They knew exactly where they were going.

"The Spanish, Dutch, Portuguese and French (all expanding their empires) had the same maps.

"It is also on record that a Captain Williamson, an American whaler, sailed through the passage - and that was only 'recently.' The British East India Company was interested in it, as it was a much more viable alternative (than to navigate through the Great Barrier Reef) to access the Spice Islands, Timor Sea, etc.

"The early Australian explorers went searching for the inland sea as well. Charles Sturt's journals are a brilliant read. He concludes that the inland sea must have only recently dried up and had been the subject of a great cataclysm as the top section of vegetable matter still stank. He found a bank of sea shells - there are drawings in his books - that was 300 feet thick.

"Also there are many Phoenician petroglyphs in central Australia which are high above the land line now. They trace back to the inland sea levels when they were much higher."

Even today, when the monsoons come in central Australia, the old basin is exposed and it is possible to navigate from north to south within the continent.

"There are many maps of Australia which show the inland basin and the outlines of the passage," said Gilbert. "It's all there."

In Western Australia, the east-west road from Esperance to Ravensthorpe dips down periodically to traverse numerous wide, dry watercourse beds, carved out as the inland sea drained to the Southern Ocean.

Australia's giant animals suddenly became extinct as the freshwater lakes quickly dried and the surrounding grazing lands became arid.

SOUTH AMERICA

A favourite continent. What romance, what mystery, lies concealed here!

In 1799, while wandering in Guinea and the upper Orinoco, the explorer Humboldt came across rock pictures and hieroglyphic signs high up on the mountains.

The natives told him that their ancestors, in the time of the great waters, came to the tops of these mountains in canoes, and that the rocks were still so soft that a man could trace marks on them with his bare fingers.[12]

Do you see the significance? It tallies precisely with conditions that prevailed after the global Deluge. Great inland seas on all continents, with water often trapped at high levels, and not draining back into the ocean for centuries.

The Deluge, as it reshaped continental areas, thrust sedimentary rubble mountains high. This would have remained soft and impressionable for a considerable time.

So it is that along the Orinoco and the Amazon river gorges, as well as in the sierras of Mexico, man-made signs are often found on cliffs that are today inaccessible. "In Siberia, near Krasnoyarski, and in old Tartary, the glyphs [are] cut in the rocks... which, in some regions, are smooth, steep and unscalable."[13]

When the trapped inland waters were higher, these high cliff locations were apparently more accessible.

The Amazon Sea

How different a history is this from that peddled to us in some popular books! My enjoyment of that fine publication *The Amazon* was abruptly cut short when up from page 26 popped these words: "The Amazon jungle is 100 million years old."

Rubbish!

When man first settled South America, the whole Amazon basin was a shallow inland sea. Into the great inland Amazon Sea, many rivers flowed which are now the arms and feeders of the great Amazon River.

According to Indians of the Matto Grosso region, on the shores of the Maranon-Amazon basin were located great cities of shining white stone, ruled over by powerful white chiefs. They insist that remains of some of these cities still exist in the jungle. A great cataclysm forced the cities to be abandoned.[14]

Indian racial memory has it that the sea, called *O Xarayes*, washed the slopes of the old Brazilian highlands and extended a good way southward to what is now Argentina.

There was at that time no mountain range between the Amazon and the Pacific Ocean. The Amazon Sea connected naturally with the Atlantic Ocean in the east and with the Pacific in the west, by canals. These canals remained intact until the Andes mountains were raised.

The shore lines of this inland sea are distinctly visible today:
1. The northern shores: Along the foothills of the Venezuelan highlands are beautiful white quartz beaches.
2. The western shores: Along the eastern foothills of the Andes, these shorelines can also be seen.

In the midst of the Amazon basin there are vast tracks of sand "islands" not too far from the rivers' edges. These sandy strips in the midst of savannah or even forest seem to be ancient beaches where the sea surf once broke; yet they cannot be so very ancient because continental vegetation has not yet deposited more than the thinnest green veneer on most of them.

Some Brazilian scientists claim they have evidence that the Amazon Sea was still there about the year 1200 BC.[15]

In the nineteenth century, James Churchward was travelling through Tibet. At one of the western monasteries he found some large tablets, which on examination proved to contain maps of various parts of the

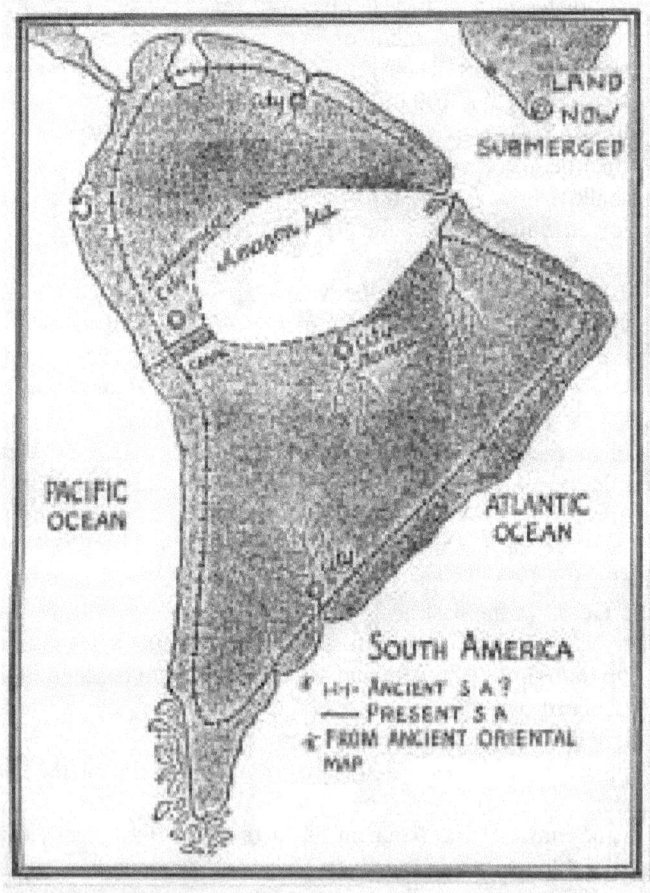

earth. These were very ancient. Among these maps was one of South America.[16]

This South American map (opposite) shows the Amazon Sea. It also shows a city at the exact spot where the ruins of Tiahuanaco are today. And it shows a canal nearby.

If you go to that ruined city today, you can find nearby the remains of ancient stone-lined canals, which are broken up and out of alignment, up and down, like the swells of the sea.

That whole area has risen thousands of feet. And there are clues that it happened suddenly.

But back to the big dry-out.

The now arid regions of the coastal strip of Peru and Chile must once have been very different. Deserts could not have supported the extensive cities with great urban populations whose ruins have been uncovered there. I've flown over the great Peruvian Desert. It is the driest in the world.

Even in our time, Chile's Coquimbo region was used for cattle grazing. It is now so depleted that only hardy cacti and goats seem able to survive.

CENTRAL AMERICA

Mayan legends describe the Yucatan as the land of the "honey and the deer", yet much of the interior of the Yucatan today is uninhabited and uninhabitable.

In Mexico, the Zuni and Acoma tribes lament that "over the Chihuahua Valley, which once was a garden, with commerce, now only Tamesha, the fire god dances in wild dust storms, hurling the hot sand all around him." Seeing that desert today, one could be skeptical of such legends of ancient glory. Until you see it from the air.

Since aircraft have been flying over some of this now barren part of northern Mexico, they have been able to confirm an amazing irrigation system running hundreds of miles, which can be traced from the air.

Some of the ancient terracing can be seen. Hillsides of what is now the most stark wasteland must formerly have bloomed like a garden, bearing out ancient legends of the fertility of the land and the tribes' own wealth in the long-forgotten past.

NORTH AMERICA

There is evidence that for some time the sea covered the region of the Great Plains from Alaska to Mexico, before draining off.

The Great Lakes lie in the heart of the continent, a thousand miles from an ocean. The upper Great Lakes are what is left of the ancient Lake Algonquin which covered about 100,000 square miles. Its ancient beach in the southern parts is almost as distinct as the shores of the modern lakes. The gravel bars are often used as roads. The ancient southern shore stands about 26 feet above the present lakes. On the north shore of Lake Superior, at Peninsula and Jackfish Bay, its splendid beaches rise terrace after terrace for hundreds of feet.

Lake Bonneville was once much larger, covering parts of Utah, Nevada and Idaho. Surrounding its former site are four terraces 50, 300, 650 and 1,000 feet above the present lake level. These were progressive shorelines, before the lake drained and dropped in level. The present Great Salt Lake is one of its small remnants.

Concerning territory south of Cheyenne, Wyoming, geologist George McCready Price says:

"Throughout all this region one cannot fail to be impressed with the visible evidence almost everywhere of a vast mass of water as it stood here for a short time forming real sea beaches, still so clearly marked, and was gradually drained from off these lands, and this vast mass of water must have been here at no very remote period; otherwise the many visible signs of the retreat of the water would long ago have been obliterated. These marks are as fresh looking as if the water had been here only a few centuries ago. The marks of the Romans over much of the Island of Great Britain are less distinct than the handwriting of the ocean in its retreat from off the great plains region at the foot of the Rockies."[17]

The Grand Canyon
not formed by water erosion

Volumes of water, laden with rocks, gravel and debris, running over newly-deposited, still unconsolidated soft ground, could easily scoop out a Grand Canyon in a short time.

Concerning the Grand Canyon, however, it is more likely that it started as a crack in the earth during the latter part of the Flood.

It is believed by some that the canyon was originally cut by an electrical discharge from a passing heavenly body – that is, by a huge lightning bolt. They hold that the cracks perpendicular to the canyon are those resulting from an electrical arc. They are not water-caused rills.

Of course, you will hear it said that the Colorado River formed the Grand Canyon.

But did you know that the Grand Canyon humps in the middle, and that it stretches HIGHER than the upstream Colorado River? This means that to **start** cutting the Grand Canyon, the Colorado River would need to flow uphill!

Also, there is little downstream detritus, which gives no support for the erosion theory.

No – the Colorado River did NOT cut the Grand Canyon.

Grand Canyon seems to be part of a crack in the earth's crust. It starts in Mexico and runs underground all the way up to Yellowstone Park.

It seems likely that the retreating Flood waters poured down into the crack from all directions in great abundance.

The canyon water level much higher in 2000 BC?

Could the river now flowing through this crack have been at a much higher level when explorers first discovered it? Now that's a staggering thought!

On the front page of The Phoenix Gazette, on April 5, 1909, there appeared a most intriguing news report.

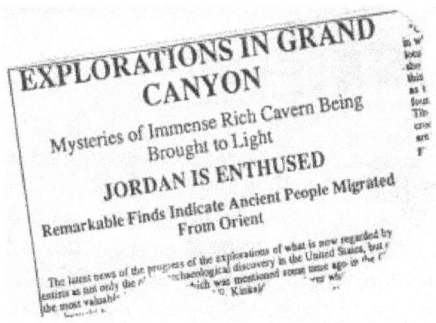

G.A. Kinkaid, an explorer working with Professor S.A. Jordan of the Smithsonian Institution, allegedly discovered a network of caverns, artificially hewn into the side of the Grand Canyon.

His report began as follows:

"First, I would impress that the cavern is nearly inaccessible. The entrance is 1,486 feet down the sheer canyon wall.... I was journeying down the Colorado river in a boat, alone, looking for mineral. Some forty-two miles up the river from the El Tovar Crystal canyon, I saw on the east wall, stains in the sedimentary formation about 2,000 feet above the river bed. There was no trail to this point, but I finally reached it with great difficulty. Above a shelf which hid it from view from the river, was the mouth of the cave. There are steps leading from this entrance some thirty yards to what was, at the time the cavern was inhabited, the level of the river. When I saw the chisel marks on the wall inside the entrance, I became interested."[18]

Following several hundred feet of passage, the explorer found himself in a network of passages and hundreds of rooms radiating from a central point like spokes in a wheel. The relics seen (some of which he photographed by flashlight) were astonishing. There were mummies, images and artefacts of a high technology. And an unknown grey metal resembling platinum. Everywhere he looked, hieroglyphics were to be seen.

It's an intriguing report. But the point to be made is the elevation of this site some 2,000 feet above the present river bed, with steps leading a short distance to what must have been at that time the level of the river.

Of course, the entire story could be an elaborate newspaper hoax. However, the fact that it was on the front page, named the prestigious Smithsonian Institution, and gave a highly detailed story that went on for several pages, lends a great deal to its credibility. It is hard to believe such a story could have come out of thin air.

More recently, two backpackers who entered the Grand Canyon claimed that an elevation of some 800 feet, they saw several cave entrances, just as reported in the newspaper article. But the entrances all seemed to be sealed shut or destroyed, as if to keep everyone out.

(This raises the question, Why would anyone want to deliberately seal off caves in such a remote area, so difficult of access?)

Being expert rock climbers, the two men climbed toward the most promising looking cave entrance. Upon reaching the entrance they discovered that, several feet in, it had likewise been sealed off with native rock. The entrance itself appeared to be man made. A 6 foot circular pattern was clearly hewn into the ceiling.[19]

The question arises, if the newspaper article was a mere hoax, then what did these more recent backpackers stumble upon? And why were the entrances to such extremely remote caves sealed?

And something else. The backpacker's discovery was made at least 40 miles from the location given in the newspaper article. So, if the newspaper report was not a hoax, and the backpackers had found the real location, could the newspaper location have been misinformation to keep people away?

But the point of my mentioning the story, is this.

If the report is genuine, then those early post-Flood, Egyptian-style visitors were in a canyon whose water run-off was still copious, the Flood-laid sediments still relatively soft.

And in the few millennia since that time, the river has dropped anything up to 2,000 feet lower. Or 800 feet lower. It doesn't matter how much. It has not taken millions of years.

Fascinating.

Yes, we're talking about the trapped Flood waters on the continents, their retreat, and the consequent drying out.

Death Valley

Death Valley, now one of the most hellish places on earth, once contained a hundred mile lake. Fossil and skeletal evidence show that this desolate area was once a tropical garden of majestic palm trees where a race of giants lived and enjoyed palatable foods taken from the local lakes and forests.

In that same valley lie the ruins of a city more than a mile in length. The streets are still traceable, running at right angles. There are stone buildings reduced to ruins by the action of some great heat that passed over. All the stones are burnt, some of them almost cindered, others glazed as if melted.

In my book *Dead Men's Secrets*, you will find further mention of ancient cities in this now-desert region.

On file I have reports of five different ships found in dried-up seas of North America, now desert. And I know of others. Indian and Spanish legends likewise speak of such ships – stranded when the inland seas dried up.

As the rainfall decreased, widespread forests gave way to grasslands.

Year by year, the imprisoned Flood remnants dwindled. Finally, the dry-out broke the grass cover, exposing the soil to wind action. Very likely, terrible dust storms arose at this time. Desert conditions gradually crept over this early dominion of man.

In the wild region at the head of the Gulf of California, "a day's march from San Diego", in 1850, were discovered seven lofty pyramids within a mile square, massive granite rings and dwellings, blocks of hieroglyphics and ruins reminiscent of ancient Egypt. This once fertile, bustling land of people has now become an unpeopled, thirst-stricken and heat-crazed land.

Even in our time, so much fertile farmland has had to be abandoned for lack of water along the interstate highway between Tucson and Phoenix, Arizona, that by the latter half of the twentieth century dust storms were frequently sweeping across the road. I heard that the state had to install expensive warning lights to tell motorists of dust storms ahead.

A ONCE FLOODED LAND DRIES OUT

In a nutshell, then, this is the picture.

At the termination of the Deluge year, large amounts of water were stranded in the interior basins. Such bodies of trapped water existed all over the planet. And rain continued to be abundant.

As man spread out to repopulate the globe, cities sprang up where there was water.

But eventually, the rampant volcanism wrought tremendous atmospheric changes. Strong jet-stream winds swept the earth. These gave rise to great wind-blown sand deposits. The climate became generally dry, warm and windy.

And since that time, the interior basins, not maintained by the local precipitation, have been drying up.

Now many of them have become creeping deserts.

Over one third of the globe's land surface is now menaced by perpetual desert. It is estimated that 80 percent of the dry rangelands, 60 percent of the rain-fed croplands and a third of all irrigation lands on earth are already affected by the march of the deserts.

Deserts everywhere are spreading relentlessly and with alarming speed – often emerging in places separate from existing wasteland. Thanks largely to man's own folly, desertification now threatens the fragile existence of over 900 million people.

Worldwide, the area of desert grows by 40 square miles every day.

* * * * * * *

Let's now switch our attention away from deserts… from the progressive drying out of the earth after the Great Flood.

Just as intriguing are civilisations that once thrived in areas that have since reverted to jungle. Again we shall discover physical adjustments going on as a result of the Great Flood.

Get on your tramping boots. You'll enjoy the exercise…

21

City folk become savages -
SECRETS OF A LOST CITY

The trekkers stood breathless. In the afternoon sun, they had come upon it suddenly.

Down in the ravine, it was like a place enchanted; so many towers and buildings grew out of the green jungle, all made of stone, gleaming white.

They were seized with wonder. After a long pause, one of them spoke. "It must be magic! Is this a fairytale? Am I dreaming?"

They were beholding things never heard or even dreamed about before.

* * * * * * *

In 1926 or 1927 an expedition led by a doctor from Hamburg travelled in canoes up a tributary of the Rio Negro, into the unknown border country of northwestern Brazil and southern Venezuela.

They touched the territories of several tribes of wild Indians. Leaving behind the "green hell" of the jungle and the booming drums of natives they never saw, they began to ascend.

It was weeks later, when they reached a gorge from which they followed an ancient road tunnel through the cliff walls. On the other side, the paved way continued high above a tremendous valley, until they looked down into another large ravine.

What they saw took their breath away: a dead city of towering palaces, splendid ruins, temples, carved pillars and pyramids, mostly swallowed in jungle. There were magnificent gardens with broken fountains, which once must have spouted cool water.

Further along the paved way, they ambushed and caught a dwarfish man, about four feet tall. He was almost naked except for a leather belt with buckles of pure gold. Later they met more of these men – all white-skinned. Their women, likewise nude, had long hair and beautiful classic features. They wore gold bracelets and gold necklets.

The party explored a massive pyramid-temple, whose interior fairly blazed with gold. Pillars, roof and walls were sheathed in it. Strange letters were engraved on the gold plates. Numerous utensils and chains of solid gold were marvellously chased and engraved, as by the finest goldsmiths.

On deep, blue-veined marble altars were traces of ancient blood, or rust(?); perhaps of ancient sacrifices of some horrible cult.

Most parts of the dead city were inaccessible. The intruders entered only the suburbs.

The white tribe had become degenerate, living on the outskirts either in tunnels, rooms in the rock, or little stone houses. Each carried a long, curved knife of pure gold. It was not valued here.

The heavy burden of gold carried out by the expedition led to the death at the hands of hostile Indians, of three-quarters of the party.

CITIES LOST

Other huge stone cities, very ancient, with paved streets and tall pyramids choked with forest, have been sighted in the Amazon jungle by several explorers in recent centuries.

Tantalised by the descriptions, many other explorers, including an entire military expedition, have vanished in the jungle without trace.

These mysterious cities were built when the climate in the Amazon basin was more temperate and the rivers drained a fertile area before the jungle took over.

Unfortunately, if much of Amazonia was covered by the Atlantic around 1200 BC (see Chapter 20) we cannot expect to find significant ancient sites conveniently located along the river banks. Such sites will likely be in the "green hell" far from the present river courses.

BEFORE THE JUNGLE GREW

We know something of mankind's early achievements in the Asia-Africa-Europe region. Little is heard about the Americas. On a subject that could fill volumes, I feel somewhat restrained in these few pages. But I'll try.

Literally thousands of inscribed stones have been found in the unknown jungles, some of them giving directions to ancient mines now under virgin forest too thick to penetrate.

In the early days, when South America was still free of jungle, the human race had already settled and built a civilisation.

There were wonderful and elaborate cities. The citizens wallpapered their houses with thin sheets of beaten gold.[1] Nothing was so cheap, so common, so easy to get as gold and silver.

The cities were built by people with classical Greek features. But the people were not Greek. The cities were walled – not against savages, but the mighty gulf, or sea, of the Maranon (the Amazon Sea).

They used gold coinage and operated fleets. Their buildings were of shining white stone. Their cities boasted magnificent plazas, paved streets, ornamented temples, round-topped pyramids, mansions and fountains.

They erected lighthouses and used lenses and reflectors, the elements of the telescope. Some of their ruins have been seen, so this is not fantasy. Many of their alphabetic letters are identical with those of the Phoenicians and Greeks.

According to native traditions, they used a light source akin to our electric bulb.

EVOLUTIONARY "EXPERTS" IN DENIAL

In the 1940s, when researcher Harold Wilkins asked a professor of geography at a Brazilian university about ancient ruins, he replied: "There are none. All we have are primitive Indians in Amazonas and the Matto Grosso, in jungle clearings and on river banks."[2]

"In modern Brazil I did not find any great enthusiasm for mysteries of the past," said Wilkins. About the last persons on earth to know, or even care, about these mysteries are, with rare exception, the Brazilian professors and scientists in Rio, Bahia and Sao Paulo.

One will find such lack of interest or even polite contempt to be common. The freaks who have pushed their noses into the savage interior are usually foreigners – who often as not are visited with sudden death from horrible insects, malignant fevers or unpacifiable Indians.

Recently a scientific "expert" wrote, from his throne in an academic tower, that the Amazon jungle has been there for millions of years, that only primitives have lived there and that writing was unknown in ancient South America.

Experts, I fear me, constitute near tragedy.

Little of what is known has found its way into textbooks. The theory of evolution is at risk if it gets out.

There is overwhelming evidence that South America was well known in antiquity. Before the jungle took over, it was resplendent with great cities. Mighty empires spanned the continent. They knew how to write. And global communication in the distant past equalled that of modern times.[3]

It is abundantly clear that history needs to be rewritten.

DESTRUCTION OF THE CITIES

It was fire from heaven and the earth below that ruined many of the cities. The earth shook and day turned to night. And from yawning crevices in the paved roads, beside their splendid palaces and temples, came volumes of deadly gases.

Blinded, asphyxiated, maddened by the appalling suddenness of the catastrophe, brilliant men and beautiful women, educated and sophisticated, fled out of the shining cities.

Everything was left behind. Bars of gold and silver were thrown to the ground, in panic haste, by men thinking only of how to save their lives.

They fled along paved roads, now cracked, fissured and overwhelmed by great boulders.

An empire of sophisticated people. All gone. We don't even know their name.

SURVIVORS DEGENERATE

When the earthquakes rendered these huge stone cities uninhabitable, the climatic conditions were such that great reptiles, facing extinction in most other parts of the earth, moved in.

Before long, the green forest covered the whole landscape.

Traditions of this ancient race and their continent-wide empire are today crystallised in the oral history of primitive tribes.

Many ancient traditions survive of an advanced culture which flourished thousands of years ago to the north and west of the Brazilian highlands.

Their descendants are now scattered as primitive tribes throughout the jungle.

At this point, may I share with you something that befell Lawrence Griswold. He was, by the way, the American who brought the famous Komodo dragons from the Dutch East Indies to the zoo in New York.

In 1929, somewhere up the Rio Juara, Griswold was captured by Shuara Indians. These are a branch of the savage Jivaro headshrinkers of the Amazon. His captors took him toward the foothills of the Andes.

One day, as he pursued a peccary along a dry streambed, he came upon the foundations of an ancient structure. The stonework was carefully jointed. Following its direction uphill, he found himself gazing upon two pyramids between the arms of a horse-shoe amphitheatre.

The old man of the tribe told him that these were built by their superior ancestors.

PRIMITIVE DESCENDANTS RETAIN LEGACY

The Tapuya, a native Indian race in eastern Brazil, are still skilful workers in precious stones and wear diamonds and jade ornaments.

Spanish missioners found that primitive Aymara Indians of Lake Titicaca could still write with a script identical to that found carved in a dead city (referred to below) in the Bahia region of Brazil.

Books of wonderfully executed paintings and hieroglyphics were found among naked Panos savages of the deep Peruvian forests near the gorge of the Ucayle, in the Amazon headwaters, in the eighteenth century. The Indians explained that the books, handed down, contained a history of events in the days of their ancestors.

The pages of fine cotton, in external appearance resembling modern quarto leaves, were bound with a cover, glued together and fastened by agave threads.

One of these ancient books was acquired by Fray Narcissus Gilbar and sent to Lima to be inspected by P. Cisneros, compiler of a periodical called *El Mercurio Peruano*. A number of people inspected it.

Every page was covered in paintings and organised lines of hieroglyphic style characters.

So here we have modern savages, living in a primitive state, but with a heritage passed down from superior ancestors.[4]

MODERN DISCOVERIES

An amazing document, filed in the archives of the old royal public library of Rio de Janeiro, describes an ancient abandoned city accidentally discovered in 1753 by a party of 300 – led by a Portuguese bandeirista.

These early land-pirates reached places in the interior, 400 years ago, that white men, even today, have not penetrated and returned alive to tell the tale.

The manuscript has been badly mutilated by the copim insect. It recounts a trek in search of the famed silver mines of Moribecu. After almost ten years of wandering, the group came upon a mountain pass, from which they spied in the distance a great city on the plain. Cautiously descending, they found it to be uninhabited.

They entered under colossal arches, to paved streets flanked by statues and buildings of enormous size. There were mysterious inscriptions, which they copied down.

A great part of the city lay completely in ruins, dissected by almost "bottomless" crevices. It appeared to have been overthrown by an earthquake.

Once a metropolis of great wealth and grandeur, it was now home to swallows, bats, rats and foxes, not to mention swarms of hens and geese (descendants of poultry once raised by the citizens?).

This dead city lies in the unexplored hinterland of the Brazilian state of Bahia.

The marks of authenticity to this whole story are found at the end of the bandeiristas' document. All of the men on this expedition were illiterate. And they all attached their signatures to the end of this Document 512, as it is known. Their signatures were nothing more than a sort of fancy "X", such as were used to identify each person, illiterate as they were.

But they had carefully copied the ancient writing they saw in that lost city – four inscriptions.

Harvard professor Dr. Barry Fell was, in the twentieth century, able to identify the script mostly as corrupt Ptolemaic Greek, from around 400 BC. He translated it as follows:

1. *Kuphis* – "Fragrant Perfumes"
2. *Hedysmos* – "Aromatic Herbs and Spices"
3. *Khrys Phlkioun* – "Gold Treasury"
4. *Asem Ephedria* – "Guardhouse for Unstamped Ingots of Silver"

It is these inscriptions that ensure the document's validity. You see, nobody – much less illiterate Portuguese explorers – could ever have forged ancient Ptolemaic Greek in the manner in which we find it in this document.

And here also is evidence that Mediterranean traders were commercially exploiting Brazil's resources as early as about 2,500 years ago.

In fact, in my book *Ark of the Covenant* you will find pages of evidence pointing to South America as both a source for King Solomon's silver and as the location of the fabulous gold mines of Ophir.[5] Interestingly, maps of the Middle ages (with origins going back thousands of years) likewise place the legendary Ophir in Brazil!

On March 23, 1773, the archives of the governor of Sao Paulo record a further accidental discovery of a dead city in the unexplored forest of the Rio Pequery.

Froy Pedro Cieza de Leon, a Spanish soldier-monk, who died in 1560, was one of the first to discover an ancient city with immense buildings in the Brazilian jungle. The local natives called it Guamanaga. It was located on the great Cordillera in Latitude 12°59' S., Longitude 73°59' W.

In 1913, former British Consul-General in Rio, Lieutenant-Colonel O'Sullivan, penetrated to the dead city of the bandeiristas – and survived.

In the following decade, the noted explorer-scientist Colonel P.A. Fawcett, while completing a thorough survey for the Royal Geographical Society of London of a disputed jungle region, entered this lost world. He came out claiming to have sighted such a city in the upper reaches of the Amazon, near the Brazilian border with Bolivia. He attempted a return to it, but vanished.

Peculiar pyramids, rounded at the top, are seen still, today, deep in the jungle. Native traditions speak of a light which was used, akin to our electric bulb.

Then in 1984, Dr. Aurelio Abreu, vice president of the Sao Paulo Archaeology Institute, confirmed the discovery of the legendary lost city of Ingrejil in the northern Ingrejil mountains of Bahia state. The city had been sought for centuries.

Ingrejil was described as a 2 mile by 1½ mile plateau accessible only by mountain paths. The ruins contained precision-cut stones without mortar, in the style of the Inca architecture of Peru, as well as dolmens and stone arches.

Abreu insisted that where there is one lost city, there are usually others. Brazil's deadly jungle may be full of megalithic cities. Much of Brazil's jungle interior is still feared and unexplored.

In May of 1985, South American explorer Gene Savoy and a group of 25 explorers discovered other remains in north eastern Peru's jungle choked mountains. These ruins, which covered 120 square miles, proved to be the largest ancient city complex ever found in South America. Savoy named the ruins Gran Vilaya.

This dead city is located in the remote, largely inaccessible Maranon River region. It looks down on a river gorge 6,000 feet far below. There are calculated to be at least 23,950 structures, built atop terraces that climb the slopes like stairs. Savoy described them as "complex units of circular buildings with doorways, windows, niched walls... that soar up as high as a 15-story building."[6]

Stone highways lead from the city in many directions, into the surrounding jungle.

UNEXPLORED WILDS

When I entered this largely impenetrable "green hell", there was a huge blank space on the map. You literally walked off the map! Certain areas of unexplored swamps and forests are perhaps less known today than they were 500 years ago. These are a lost world, even shunned by the fiercest and most unpacifiable natives, who bar off white explorers from it.

There are areas where no roaming adventurer has ever been and returned alive to tell the tale. And far behind a screen of forest and swamp that lines the still unexplored rivers, are secrets which the jungle keeps dark. You will never get into the forest beyond the river belt, nor will an Indian agree to act as guide, whatever the bribe.

And *Indios bravos* will track down men for days. Moving noiselessly, they keep themselves out of sight. The *whing* of a curare-tipped arrow is the first you hear of their presence. It is also the last.

THOUSANDS OF UNEXPLORED CITIES

From Mexico to Chile, literally thousands of ruined towns and cities, buried under dense jungle or desert sands, have never been explored.

In Mexico's Yucatan region, I ascended a mound in the jungle and was able to make out several more – Mayan ruins overgrown with jungle – where a small hill covered with forest was in fact an ancient pyramid!

In 1976, Dr. David Zink and a team journeyed to Honduras in search of a particular lost city. In the region of the Rio Klaura, they discovered half buried in the jungle the fragments of a beautifully carved stone bench with a trough in it for grinding grain. But what awed them was its gigantic size. It was two metres long with large stone legs to support it - weighing, they estimated, about 20 tons!

These graceful remains speak of a sophisticated culture that was able to carve grinding stones with big legs from hard rock weighing at least 20 tons.

The present day descendants of what was once the greatest empire in the Americas are mere jungle savages, unable to read or write their ancestors' hieroglyphics; unable to construct large buildings, much less whole cities.

One thing seems crystal clear. In an area that is now swamp and jungle, a mighty civilisation once thrived.

There are estimates of more than 10,000 undiscovered pyramids in Guatemala's Peten region alone![7] That's not a mis-print. I'll repeat it... ten thousand.

NORTH AMERICA

Settlers came to North America on the first migration wave after the Flood. Surprisingly (?), what is now the United States once swarmed with populous cities. They were spread out from Florida, through the Mississippi and over into Arizona and New Mexico. There are traces still to be found if one knows where to look.

The Indians of Florida said a white civilisation was there when they arrived. (Examples of surviving white Indian tribes in North America are the Zuni of New Mexico and the Menominees.)

And there were the Mound Builders – who lived in cities and were agricultural. They enjoyed an enlightened system of government. No idols, known to be such, have been found. All traces of their architecture (wooden, thus impermanent) have disappeared.

Not so well known is an ancient complex in Francis County, Arkansas, across the Mississippi from Memphis, Tennessee. It is a complex of pyramids, artificial lakes with paved bottoms, and canals and mounds, There is evidence of a large, sophisticated civilisation here in the distant past.

According to Mexican and North American oral history, some of the North American cities were wiped out through fiery aerial warfare.[8]

Traces of a buried city appear to lie below 4 square miles of Rockwall County, Texas. Great stone walls, in places up to 49 feet high, are constructed in the manner a modern fine mason would build a wall. The walls are totally regular in appearance. In the 1920s Count Byron Kuhn de Porok, an archaeologist of some fame, noted that the walls resembled those of buried cities he had excavated in the Middle East and North Africa.

The stones, apparently bevelled around their edges, are joined by a mortarlike substance. Four large stones extracted from this underground wall appear to have been inscribed with some form of writing.[9]

L. Taylor Hanson spent considerable time with Red Indian tribes. Dark Thunder, chief of the O'Chippewa people of Michigan, revealed to her:

"Once we had books, but those were times long distant in the past. Books are of such stuff which can be swept into oblivion. Since then we have placed our stories in the chants of our people."[10]

Certain Red Indian tribes chant the stories of long ago when they lived in cities, always near mighty rivers, avenues of ancient commerce. When war came, the people abandoned the cities and took to the forest.[11]

However, in the global post-Flood changes, the climate gradually became drier.

I am tempted to ask, if man evolved from beasts, then why is it that there existed among all of the peoples of all continents a long tradition of a Golden Age, instead of that of a savage past?

Surely it's time the truth was out. Here is evidence of men conscious of their civilised background, compelled to use all their technical skill in a savage and hostile environment; men able to make contact with other civilised people once, but afterwards isolated and forced to make use of crude implements for survival.

Speaking of primitive tribes people whose ancestors once lived in shining cities, Colonel Fawcett wrote in his notes:

"I have good reason to know that these original people still remain in a degenerate state... They use script."

AFRICA

In 1932, a South African farmer-prospector named van Graan persuaded an African to show him a way to the top of a small table mountain known as Mapungubwe. It was precipitous on every side. To local natives this was a "place of fear", sacred to the Great Ones among their ancestors. And they believed it would mean death to climb it.

Graan and four others took the concealed way up and found the flat top to be littered with broken pottery. Later probes turned up bits of iron and copper, pieces of beautifully worked gold plating, over 12,000 gold beads and buried with just one of the skeletons there, over 70 ounces of gold.

But here was the most surprising discovery of all: the skeletons were of non-Negroid Hottentots. This proved that the Hottentots (who lived an essentially "stone age" existence at the time Europeans arrived) had once enjoyed a highly technical, metal-using civilisation![12]

Here again, as in the Americas, was evidence of a regression of culture.

It is a worldwide phenomenon.

THE TIME FACTOR

If my guess is right, you may still have a lingering question or two about TIME.

So, before continuing, let's review what we have covered on this question so far.

In Book 1 of this series[13], we addressed apparent problems in regard to my dating timeline. These included the "long" Sumerian king list, radiometric dating, the time required to form stalactites, sandy beaches, fossil coral reefs, canyons and so on.

In Book 2 of this series, *Surprise Witness*,[14] we addressed the time required to form such things as coal, oil, "multiple" petrified forests, rock strata and fossils, as well as evidence on the age of dinosaurs and even of our solar system.

And we asked, Was there time for all the human races and numerous animal varieties to develop? And enough time for them to migrate to the ends of the earth? Enough time for continental splitting, mountain building, creation of deserts, and so on.

Now I shall let you examine ten clocks which all shout to us that something very big happened to this earth just over 4,000 years ago – and from which an adjustment process has been going on ever since.

You should find this fascinating.

22

The nature "clocks" say 4,000+ years -

THE LOST SQUADRON

"You're kidding!" laughed the lab worker. "Only 4,400 years ago!"

"Yes," repeated Kent. "The surface of this whole planet was remodelled by the Flood only 4,400 years ago."

"No way! In case you don't know, Dr. Hovind, I work at the Denver National Ice Core Laboratory here in Colorado. And we've been taking cores of ice from Greenland and Antarctica. It's dry… very cold…the glaciers are MILES THICK… but their annual growth rings are very THIN."

He paused to observe Kent's reaction. Then he thrust home. "We've measured the ice… and I tell you, man, it's 135,000 years old! Your 4,000 years is a joke."

"I'd like to see your lab," said Kent, calmly.

The next day my friend Dr. Kent Hovind met the worker at the lab.

The employee ushered him into the giant freezer which stored the long cores from ice drilling.

"See this core from Greenland?" said the worker. "We drilled down and brought it up from 10,000 feet. See the rings? This core takes us back 135,000 years. You'll notice the rings along its length… dark – light – dark – light.

"Well, these represent annual rings, because in summer the top layer of snow melts and then re-freezes as clear ice, which shows up dark here. In winter, the snow doesn't get a chance to melt, so it packs – and shows up as a white layer. These layers of dark – light – dark – light, indicate 135,000 summers and winters."

Hovind looked him in the eye. "Aren't you *assuming* those are *annual* rings?"

Let's step back a few years… to the famous lost squadron.

THE LOST SQUADRON

In 1942, during World War II, some war planes landed in Greenland. When the war ended, those planes were left there and forgotten.

In 1990, an aircraft enthusiast came up with the bright idea to find them and fly them off again.

He organised a group and they went searching. As it turned out, they had to use radar, because the planes were under the ice... in fact, so deep under the ice, the men had a hard job finding them. Do you know, that lost squadron had got covered by 263 feet of ice in 48 years!

Let's do some arithmetic.
- 263 feet divided by 48 years... that's an ice growth of about 5.5 feet per year.
- Now divide 10,000 feet by 5.5. And you get 1,824 years for ALL of the ice to build up.

We should allow longer for the fact that the deeper ice is pressed into finer layers.

So 4,400 years is no problem!

Note: those planes did *not* sink into the ice, due to pressure on the ice. The ice had grown OVER them.

In April, 1999, Kent visited Bob Cardin at his museum in Middleboro, Kentucky.[1] Cardin had dug out and was restoring the P-38.

You may be wondering, how did they get that plane out? Ingenious. They had melted a hole down to the airplane, broken it apart and brought up the pieces through the hole.

"When you dug it out," asked Kent, "did you see any layers of ice... dark – light – dark – light, above the airplane?"

"Yeah, I did, as a matter of fact."

"How many layers of ice were there?"

"Many hundreds of them."

Hundreds of annual rings in just 48 years?

"How could there be many hundreds of annual rings in only 48 years?"

"THOSE ARE NOT ANNUAL RINGS. That's not summer and winter," replied Cardin. " It's warm – cold – warm – cold – warm – cold. You can get ten of those in one day."

And that's a fact!

Yet, the scientific elite was still calling them *annual rings* in 1998.[2]

Somebody's either ignorant... or lying.

I'm worried. The textbooks you read today are textbooks not only about science, but about evolution. They're trying to sneak evolution in with the science.

Sneaking beer ads in with football matches doesn't mean beer is football. Sneaking evolution in with the science, doesn't make it science.

So let's take a fresh look at the facts.

Is it possible that a Great Flood completely re-fashioned the surface of our planet only 4,350 years ago... really?

GLACIERS – c.4,000 YEARS

Field work in the European Alps on the speed of glacier growth and retreat has revealed the fact (surprising to evolutionists) that numerous glaciers there are no older than 4,000 years.[3]

The eminent French geologist A. Cochen de Lapparent noted the expansion rate of today's larger glaciers. For example, Mer de Glace, on Mont Blanc, moves 50 centimetres a day. The Rhone Glacier would at this rate have taken 2,475 years to expand to its maximum from Valais to Lyons.

De Lapparent then compared the terminal moraines (debris) of several modern glaciers with those left by the Rhone Glacier when it retreated from its maximum expansion. The Rhone Glacier had taken 2,400 years to retreat.

Thus the *total period of advance and retreat* was 4,875 years.

One could expect that conditions soon after the Flood would hasten the ice build-up and thus *reduce the above time span.*

"He also concluded that the entire Ice Age was of very short duration."[4]

Researchers Suess and Rubin concluded that in the mountains of the western United States ice advanced only 3,000 years ago.

According to the latest evidence, glaciers may **NOT** even need thousands of years to build up, nor to disintegrate.

New Zealand's Tasman Glacier, for example, is dying within our life time.

Brent Shears runs his Glacier Explorers cruise on a lake which didn't even exist when he was born. Lake Tasman, the result of the melting of the Tasman Glacier, is not much more than 20 years old. As the glacier recedes, at an ever-increasing rate, it is leaving in its wake the body of water now known as Lake Tasman.

Visiting the site, Stephen Lacey writes of "the creaks and groans of melting and movement. It strikes me that what I can hear is the death throes of the glacier as it drags its body back up the valley... its long claws ripping and tearing at the ground like a great wounded beast. Suddenly I hear a sound like an express train, roaring through a tunnel.

"All heads turn towards the direction of the noise, just in time to see a huge chunk of ice break away from the glacial wall and plunge 10 metres into the lake. The splash sends a shock wave through the water and the boat rocks steadily. I realise that the crippled glacier is a whole lot more dynamic than the cold white photos in our high school geography books.

"'That was a serac fall,' Brent says. 'It was only a small one... I've seen them the size of houses.'"[5]

The Tasman Glacier is retreating at an estimated 80 metres every year. Lake Tasman is already six kilometres long and growing.

Over the years, on the glaciers around Mount Cook (including Tasman), one hundred people have vanished into crevasses and other spots. Now, as the glaciers retreat, bodies are appearing in the terminals.

In 1998, research by a team at the University of Colorado, in Boulder, revealed that mountain glaciers all over the world are in retreat.

The European Alps have lost about 50 percent of their ice in the past century, while 14 of 27 glaciers that existed in Spain in 1980 have disappeared. In Africa, the largest glacier on Mount Kenya has shrunk by 8 percent in the past 100 years, while those on Mount Kilimanjaro are only 25 percent as big.[6]

INLAND LAKES - c.4,000 YEARS

We saw in Chapter 20 that present desert areas show evidence of recent water bodies.

Studies of salt and mineral deposits in numerous glacial lakes that have no outlet to the ocean suggest that none of them is older than 4,000 years. This is based on concentration, area, water composition and evaporation rate.[7]

A study by Claude Jones of the lakes of the Great Basin (from larger glacial lakes) showed that these lakes have existed only about 3,500 years. Van Winkle obtained the same result on Albert and Summer lakes in Oregon, and also Gales on Owen Lake in California.

The end of the Ice Age, therefore, as well as the remains of prehistoric animals found in the lake deposits, apparently goes back no more than 40 centuries ago.

Lake Agassiz, the largest glacial lake in North America, was formed when the ice of North America melted. Study of its sediments shows that its total life span was only a few hundred years.

The American glaciologist Warren Upham expressed surprise at the "geological suddenness of the final melting of the ice-sheet, proved by the brevity of existence of its attendant glacial lakes."[8]

Erosion on the shores of Lake Agassiz and the condition of residue indicate that this great change took place no longer than "a few thousand years at the most."[9]

RIVER DELTAS - 3,600 to 5,000 YEARS

The deltas of the Nile, the Volga and the Mississippi are all essentially alike and could be of about the same age.

The beginnings of these deltas were made by the enormous rivers whose old high terraces we see far above the present channels.

The Mississippi River brings down mud at the rate of 80,000 tons an hour. From an evaluation of the debris borne to the Mississippi delta as sediment, two scientists, Humphries and Abbot, in 1861, calculated the delta to be 5,000 years old.

Of course, excessive water flow during the early post-Flood centuries would *reduce this time span*.

On the Alaska -British Columbia border is the Bear River, a stream still fed by a melting glacier that enters the Portland Canal.

Concerning the Bear River delta, Immanuel Velikovsky notes:

"On the basis of three earlier accurate surveys made between the years 1909 and 1927, G. Hanson in 1934 calculated with great exactness the annual growth of the delta through deposited sediment. At the present rate of sedimentation the delta is estimated to be 'only 3600 years old.'"[10]

WATERFALLS - c.4,000 YEARS

Rarely has a waterfall either deepened its bed at the top of the falls or shown more than slight erosion into the cliffs. This is evidence of "newness".

We stand in awe before the mighty Niagara, deafened by the roar of its spectacular plunge. And we say, "What power!"

The rate at which the Niagara Falls are moving upstream indicates that they are no more than a few thousand years old. The rim of the falls has been wearing back from its original precipice to form a gorge.

Examination of records shows that since 1764, the falls cut the gorge from Lake Ontario toward Lake Erie at the rate of 5 feet per year. If this wearing down of the rock has continued always at the same rate, 7,000 years would have been sufficient to do the work.

However, closer to the Flood, erosion was much more rapid. Therefore the age of the gorge must be **considerably younger**.

G.F. Flint of Yale, noting "the present rate of recession of the Horseshoe Falls to be, not five feet, but rather 3.8 feet, per year," calculated the age of the Upper Great Gorge, the uppermost segment of the whole gorge, to be "somewhat more than four thousand years."[11]

Careful investigation by another scientist, W.A. Johnston, of the Niagara River bed, disclosed that the present channel was cut by the falls less than 4,000 years ago.[12]

CORAL REEFS - c.4,000 YEARS

Drill samples have confirmed coral reefs to be growing like tree rings.

The Pandora Reef in Queensland, Australia, has grown 15.3 mm (c. ½ inch) per year in 118 years. This was discovered by scientists from the Australian Institute of Marine Science at Cape Ferguson, south of Townsville.[13] On this basis the whole 10 metre (32½ foot) thickness of coral that makes up this reef would have taken only about 660 years to grow!

Previously measured growth rates for massive coral colonies elsewhere on the Great Barrier Reef are from 5 mm to 25 mm per year. At their thickest part (at the edge of the continental shelf) the outer 'barrier' reefs are about 55 metres (180 feet) thick.

On the basis of an average growth rate of ½ inch per year, the Great Barrier Reef can be no older than 4,320 years. (At 15 mm per year it would be less than 3,700 years old - which fits the sea rise scenario described in another chapter.)

TREES - c.4,000 YEARS

Today's oldest living things date to the post-Flood times.

Sequoia: Some believe that these monsters may enjoy perpetual life, since they seem to be immune to disease and pest attack. Many are over 3,000 years old. A remarkable fact is that these still-living trees seem to be the original trees in their present stands.

Edmund Schulmann, writing in *Science*, asks:

"Does this mean that shortly preceding 3275 years ago (or 4000 years ago, if John Muir's somewhat doubtful count was correct) **all** the then living giant sequoias were wiped out by some catastrophe?"[14]

Kauri: Late in the 19th century, on New Zealand's Coromandel Peninsula, a giant kauri was felled.

This lordly tree, measuring 76 feet (23.4 metres) in girth and 80 feet (24.6 metres) to the first limb, was discovered in the Mill Creek area, north-east of Thames. It was thousands of years old and still alive - when ruthlessly felled. Legend is that the stump thereafter supported a dance band and a goodly group of dancers.

If reports at the time were true, this would be the oldest of all living kauris. Its age was given as 4,000 years.

Bristlecone pine: The oldest bristlecone pine "began growing more than 4,600 years ago," according to Schulmann.[15]

Whitcomb and Morris comment:

"Since these, as well as the sequoias and other ancient trees, are still living, it is pertinent to ask why these oldest living things apparently have had time to develop only one generation since they acquired their present stands at some time after the Deluge. There is no record of a tree, or any other living thing, being older than any reasonable date for the Deluge."[16]

In regard to the 4,600 year figure for the oldest bristlecone pine, it should be stated that tree-ring measurement is not entirely satisfactory. In irregular years there can be two rainy seasons, and this would produce two rings instead of one.

Dr. Clifford Wilson summarises the position rather well:

In fact, under certain conditions a tree may demonstrate more than two rings in a year. Three is not uncommon, as with a tree that grows on a slope. If the water supply runs off rapidly it sometimes gives an artificial wet and dry period three or more times in a year. There are even cases where the opposite sides of a tree have exhibited different numbers of rings."[17]

Taking this into account, the oldest bristlecone pines reflect fairly closely the date of the Great Flood, after which trees began once more to take root around the planet.

OLDEST DESERT - c.4,000 YEARS

The Sahara Desert has what's called a prevailing wind pattern (meaning, the wind usually blows the same way). And this creates a problem. The hot air blowing off the desert "cooks" the trees at the edge and they die. Then that area also becomes desert. (The process is called desertification.)

In 1999 it was announced that the Sahara Desert is about 4,000 years old. This figure was based on desert growth patterns, rate of growth, and so on.[18]

Now, this does raise a question. If the earth is billions of years old, shouldn't there be a bigger desert some place? Why is the biggest desert on earth only 4,000 years old?

As we've noticed, there was a worldwide Flood some 4,350 years ago. It's pretty hard to have a desert under a flood, right? So the biggest desert *should be* – and is – less than 4,350 years old!

AXIS RECOVERY - c.4,340 YEARS

We dealt with this in *Surprise Witness*. But it can bear repeating. South Australian government astronomer George P. Dodwell investigated what astronomers call "the secular variation of the obliquity of the ecliptic". Put simply, he studied measurements of the sun's shadow-length by ancient astronomers from five continents. Available records of the position of the sun at observed solstices showed that an exponential curve of recovery had taken place in relation to the earth's axis.

He concluded that the earth's axis had once been upright, but it had suddenly changed to a 26½ degrees tilt, from which it had been wobbling back to its present mean tilt of 23½ degrees.

Dodwell realised that such a sudden change would result in massive, worldwide flooding and catastrophic effects. The date of this event, from his curve of observations, is 2345 BC - about 4,340 years ago. That is also, as we have seen, the traditional date for Noah's Flood.

If you've heard anyone say that the earth has tipped over several times since then, don't believe it. They haven't heard of Dodwell's findings. The evidence shows a tipping of the axis in 2345 BC, followed by a measurable corrective wobble. There is a clear a pattern of recovery since 2345 BC that has not been disrupted.

THE EGYPT "PROBLEM"

"But a global wipe-out in 2345 BC?" I hear someone say. "How can that be? If the Flood really occurred only 4,350 years ago, then how on earth do you explain that the Egyptians have had a continuous and uninterrupted civilization before and after this period?"

A good question. And here's the straight answer...

23

The human "clocks" say 4,000+ years -

PUBLISH – IF YOU DARE

I am going to let you know about a boycott threat… as well as the sabotage of ancient documents… all in the name of "science".

You can stake your life on it. There is a WAR under way. A battle to the death between the TRUTH and an entrenched FAIRYTALE.

The evidence for a global Deluge about 4,350 years ago is overwhelming. Yet, the established line is that this cannot be. The Egyptians, we are told, have had a continuous and uninterrupted civilization before and after this period. So throw out the worldwide Flood. It simply never happened. Or, not in 2345 BC.

EGYPTIAN DATES *BEFORE* THE FLOOD?

All right, brace yourself for a shock. Our conjectured history of Egypt is probably 600 to 800 years too long!

Some six to eight supposed "dynasties" never existed!

In case you didn't know, inscriptions we dig up don't carry a date, nor a ruler's sequence number. It means we can easily get our dates wrong, even by hundreds of years.

The problem began in the early days of Egyptology. Until recent years modern archaeologists were giving highly exaggerated datings for the Egyptian dynasties. Dates like 6000 BC… 4000 BC.

Scholars built up a system of Egyptian dating that went back thousands of years earlier than is possible if one accepts the Genesis chronology. Clearly one party was wrong – either the modern scholars (with their longer system), or the Bible (with its shorter dating system).

So why were the longer dates for Egypt accepted?

Simply because all the listed kings were placed one after another, in succession. This added thousands of extra years to Egyptian history.

5 WAYS WE WERE MISLED

Here are some facts of which early Egyptologists were not aware:

Problem 1:

Rulers were known by a title, as well as by a personal name. For example, it has now been discovered that Rameses II was not Rameses II, at all! He was most probably Rameses XLII – that is, the 42nd ruler called Rameses, which was rather a title, like Pharaoh.[1]

So where a ruler's title and name both appeared, Egyptologists had listed them separately, as though they were different pharaohs. Correcting this would shorten the list.

Problem 2:

Then it was discovered that pharaohs regularly had as many as five, and even more, names. The Egyptologists had taken these and listed them one after another.

So, again, the chronology had to be shortened.

Problem 3:

It was also discovered that other listed pharaohs ruled at the same time over different parts of Egypt.[2] Rulers sometimes appointed others as co-regent during their lifetime. This means that two "names" ruled concurrently.

Egyptologists have been adding many of these names on to a long list of what they thought were "consecutive" reigns.

What a mix-up! The dating was thrown into chaos. More shortening!

With such discoveries, the span of Egyptian history had to be progressively reduced. So that today it is commonly believed that Egyptian civilisation began about 3000 BC.

But as it turns out, even that is too long!

Problem 4:

To add fuel to the fire, here's another shocker.

Linguistic expert and university lecturer Edo Nyland of Canada has recently decoded and translated some 120 of the pharaohs' names.

These appear in his book *Linguistic Archaeology*. In a personal communication to the author, Ed reported:

"In doing my research I came upon some disturbing mistranslations by the 'specialists'. I found two early pharaohs whose names could not possibly be correct, because instead of names, they were curses aimed at intruders to the tomb. When I pointed this out to an archaeologist, I was brushed off with: 'All pharaohs' names have been properly translated, the book is closed on that subject'".

Do you see? If some pharaohs were **not** really pharaohs at all, but merely curses...
More shortening of the chronology? Oh, boy!
But that's not all!

Problem 5:
Comparing documents on a generation-by-generation basis, Immanuel Velikovsky matched the history of Egypt with those of Babylon, Assyria, Israel, Greece and Persia, from roughly 1400 BC to about 330 BC.

His conclusion was startling: events of Egyptian history are described twice - and 600 years later they are repeated exactly, to the detail.

Boycott threat
Velikovsky's findings evoked an uproar.

His original publisher was threatened by professors and universities. They warned that if his books were published, there would be a boycott of the publisher's standard textbooks!

Popular history is too long
The mistake lies not with history, but with the historians. This has led to a mistaken increase in the total year count.

As a result, dates are commonly accepted which ante-date the Flood. For example, the Great Pyramid construction is usually put at 2650 BC.

"Scholars" sabotage ancient documents

And at this point the *Turin Papyrus* enters the picture. This ancient document was prepared during the late 18th Dynasty of the Pharaohs and included lists of all the kings of every dynasty of ancient Egypt through to the 18th Dynasty.

This papyrus was found during a temple excavation in the 19th century. The King of Sardinia carefully preserved it and entrusted it to some "scholars" at Turin for translation.

It arrived in perfect condition, but then something went wrong. The "scholars" destroyed or hid most of it. Why would scholars do that? Horror of horrors, it proved the "LONG dynastic" history of Egypt to be UNTRUE!

So to "explain" the "changed condition" of the papyrus, they accused the King of Sardinia of sending it "unwrapped".

The *Palermo Stone* contained a similar list. And while many "scholars" quote from "missing parts" of the stone, "unapproved researchers" can have access to only a few fragments. It is obvious that the stone was broken recently, since all inner edges of the fragments show recent fracture conditions.

Dating of early world history in chaos

Okay, here is confession time. Until recently, the "experts" had me believing that Egypt sprang up around 3000 BC (and likewise all the other civilisations of great antiquity).

And since these all emerged after the Flood, then the dating for the Flood just had to be earlier.

Not so. It now turns out that a mistaken chronology is the framework of the scientific structure of Egyptian history. And since Egyptian chronology is the rule and the standard for the entire world history, consequently the history of the entire ancient world is now in a most chaotic state.

Our Egyptian knowledge mostly guesswork

W.B. Emery is one of the rare few who admit how limited our knowledge of ancient Egypt really is. He says:

"Unfortunately our knowledge of the archaic hieroglyphs is so limited that reliable translation of these invaluable texts is at present beyond our power and we can only pick out odd words and groups which give us only the vaguest interpretations."[3]

Yet, in the majority of books, translations and conclusions are never stated as being theory; they are stated as firm fact.

WRITTEN RECORDS

So here are the facts. We have no incontestable proof of the existence of human beings on earth more than a few thousand years ago. Dates given to man before about 3000 BC are purely arbitrary.

History, in the sense of written records, supports the Bible chronology.

Shortened history re-aligns increasingly with despised biblical history

Adjustments and revisions of Egyptian history will tend to considerably shorten human history in general.

A pertinent observation here. Place the Bible side by side with the confused accounts of other nations and you'll be struck by the incomparable distinction which lifts it out of the class and category of all other writings, and proclaims it of another origin, and of another kind. The palpable difference is its objective, historical character. Martin Anstey puts it this way:

"The chronology of the Old Testament is in the strongest contrast with that of all other nations. From the Creation of Adam to the death of Joseph, the Chronology is defined with the utmost precision... With all other Chronologies the case is exactly the reverse. They have no beginning. They emerge from the unknown, and their earliest dates are the haziest and the most uncertain."[4]

A date for Egypt

Unfortunately, Egypt's monuments themselves do not begin their records before the 19th dynasty. As Anstey notes:

"There was an older Egyptian Empire which may have come to an end about 1750 BC, and to it the pyramids belonged. But its duration can only be guessed. Canon Rawlinson thinks it may have lasted 500 years or so. This would bring us to 2250 BC, as the date of the establishment of civilization in the form of a settled government in Egypt."[5]

All authorities are agreed on this: however far we go back in the history of Egypt, there is no indication of any early period of savagery or barbarism there. Menes (Mizraim) came, dammed the waters and started building.

Some scientists contend that the Great Pyramid tells the date of its construction (foundation). Its tubular entrance passage pointed to the north polar star in 2144 BC. at the same time that the pyramid apex pointed to Alcyone, the "pivot of the solar system", known anciently as the "Foundation star".[6]

VAST AGES FROM ASTRONOMY NOT VIABLE
However, attempts to establish vast ages for some civilizations on the basis of astronomical data are not valid, because of the disruptions to the earth's orbit since the Deluge.

Immanuel Velikovsky produces evidence for such disruptions in his book *Worlds in Collision*, in which he states:

"Previous efforts to build chronological tables on the basis of astronomical calculations – new moon, eclipses, heliacal rising or culmination of certain stars – cannot be correct, because the order of nature has changed since ancient times."[7]

Attempts to date the Sphinx and pyramids of Giza by astronomical alignments to, say 10,500 BC, are futile for the same reason.

A date for China
The credible, self-consistent history of ancient China dates from no earlier than 781 BC. The period prior to that is unverifiable.

Chinese literary records do, however, give dynastic epochs that are identical with dynastic epochs of the book of Genesis.[8]

There is nothing in the high antiquity of China to conflict with the conclusion that 200 years after the Deluge, Noah's descendants arrived in northwest China.[9]

A date for Sumeria
Anstey points out, regarding the Mesopotamian region:

"The Era of the Chaldean dynasty of Berosus, the earliest which has any claim to be regarded as historical, is placed somewhere about the year B.C. 2234."[10]

This is close to the Tower of Babel date, soon after the Great Flood.

WRITTEN HISTORY - c.4,000 YEARS
No verifiable dates for written records go back earlier than about 4,000 years. Any earlier dates are based on questionable assumptions and are highly speculative.

If one is determined to push everything back further, one has to speculate, without evidence. Keep in mind that our goal is to discover the FACTS. We want *verified* information.

POPULATION INCREASE - c.4,000+ YEARS
We might also cite world population growth statistics. These likewise converge on the date of the Great Flood.

It can be demonstrated, by taking the rate of population increase, per century, and working back from our present world population (6,400,000,000), that mankind could have started with 8 people not very long ago.

Statisticians agree that 150 years is a reasonable average to assume for population to double itself, having made allowance for wars, famines, etcetera. Today's global population, if counted back to an original 8 persons, would require slightly less than 30 doublings. By a doubling process every 150 years, this would require about 4,400 years.

Or to calculate by a different method, world population increases at about 2 percent per year. Let's be conservative and halve it to an increase of 1 percent per year.

On average, every 82 years (through wars, diseases and natural disasters), half the population is wiped out.

Using this formula, over 4,350 years, how many people should we have now? - 7.3 billion. How many people do we have? - 6.4 billion.

Using the same formula, the population after 41,000 years would be 2×10^{89} (That's two times ten with 89 zeroes after it!)

It can be argued that exceptional events, such as Hitler's massacres, plagues and natural disasters could have decimated populations. But even if HALF THE TOTAL WORLD POPULATION were wiped out, it would extend the historical span by only 150 years.

There have been periods of slow down and of rapid growth, but a continuous increase is evident throughout history.

If mankind has been around for as much as one million years, the population would have doubled only once in every 32,258 years, which is absurd.

All considered, the evidence is a pointer toward recency of the type the Bible suggests. It is entirely reasonable and scientific to trace the entire human race back to eight people some 4,350 years ago.

The data is consistent with the proposition that Noah and his family were the only humans alive after a general wipe-out of the human race.

If man was **not** virtually wiped out, there should be a very much greater population across the earth's surface.

SOMETHING BIG HAPPENED 4,000+ YEARS AGO

We have the same approximate dating from all parts of the planet.

More importantly, it comes from all types of clocks, calculations and approaches.

A coincidence? Think again. It is compelling evidence that the biblical dating is correct.

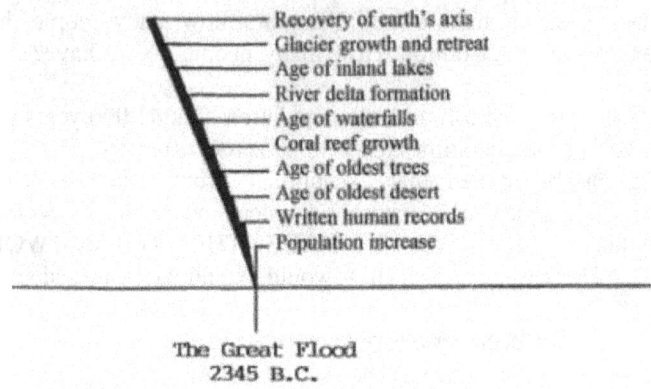

The Great Flood
2345 B.C.

* * * * * * *

...But now let me tell you about the drunken princess – and how she altered the geography of her home town...

24

Why the sea is rising -
A DEADLY PRACTICAL JOKE

A high-spirited filly, was the princess. She could down alcohol with the best of them. The binge had gone on all afternoon.

I don't know what triggered the idea. It may have been a dare. Or just plain and simple curiosity. In any case, what I shall relate to you shortly is almost beyond belief...

* * * * * * *

That brings me to a most fascinating phenomenon. (and in the course of explaining it, I shall tell you what that high-spirited princess of Caer Ys did).

GRADUALLY RISING SEAS

For 4,000 years, the world's sea level has been inching up.

This has been caused by
(a)   the melting of the post-Flood ice and
(b)   the gradual evaporation or outflow of post-Flood inland basins to the sea.

The gradual rise of the oceans is thus another clear relic of the Deluge.

Flood waters left behind on the land, in the form of ice or inland lakes, have been gradually returning to the oceans. The result has been not only a drying out of the land, but a corresponding rise in sea level.

The Hadji Ahmed map of 1559, whose original source dates back thousands of years, shows a landbridge between Siberia and Alaska, which existed when the original map was drawn. If the ocean between these two land masses were lowered 100 feet today, there would be a dry-land path between them.

According to some oceanographers and geologists, the ocean level may have been as much as 500 feet lower than today.

Ireland was connected with England; the North Sea was a great plain; Italy was joined to Africa, and exposed land cut the Mediterranean into two lakes.

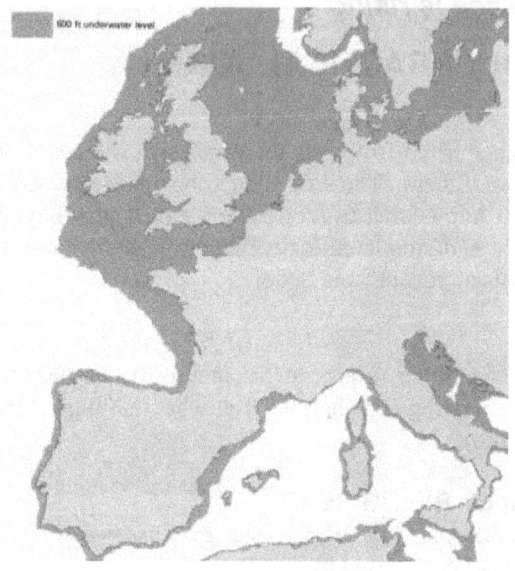

Grey area: 600 foot underwater level. (Map: Francis Hitching)

Since then, the rising seas have engulfed coastal land and islands, turning isthmuses into straits and large islands into underwater plateaus.

Along many of the world's shorelines are lost islands, now deep below the sea, with remains of cities, palaces and temples.

THE CONTINENTAL SHELF

In fact, most of the continental shelf, which marks the true boundaries between the ocean basins and the continental areas, now lies under a mean depth of 430 feet of water. (It ranges from 300 feet to about 1,500 feet.)

The present continental shelf probably defines the edge of the oceans as they developed during the post-Flood glacial peak. With the ice melt and the draining or evaporation of inland basins, the seas rose, with minor fluctuations, to their present level.

"The ocean basins can thus be characterized as overfull – water not only fills the ocean basins proper, but extends out over the low margins of the continents." So concludes a panel of geologists.[1]

Oceanographers and geologists generally agree that a dramatic, rapid rise of water occurred several thousand years ago. This has slowed to about 1.5 feet per century.

UNDERSEA CANYONS

Around the world's coastlines are undersea river canyons, which were once above the ocean. Such canyons cannot be cut underwater.

* The submerged Hudson Canyon, one hundred miles long and hundreds of feet deep, could only have been formed above water when this extension of the Hudson River was dry land.
* Off the coast of Europe are the Loire, Rhone, Seine and Tagus canyons. The drowned Rhine Valley runs under the North Sea to disappear between Norway and Scotland – showing that the North Sea was dry land.
* Numerous other canyons were cut at the edge of the former ocean basin (now submerged) : La Plata in Argentina, the Delaware and St. Lawrence in North America, the Congo in West Africa. Off the African west coast are submerged river canyons whose rivers no longer exist in the now-arid land.

All these canyons were cut out above water. Now they are submerged.

ANCIENT MAPS SHOW
NOW-DROWNED ISLANDS

The curious Buache map was copied from sources whose origins are lost in antiquity. This ancient "treasure map" portrays correctly the location of the Canary Islands and the correct outline of an underwater plateau which formed their extended shape before the oceans rose.

Anciently, the Greek islands would have been larger and more numerous, as well. The Ibn Ben Zara map of 1487 (likewise copied from charts apparently thousands of years old) does in fact show many islands which are now under water.

OCEAN POURED INTO MEDITERRANEAN AND BLACK SEA

In fact, there is evidence suggesting that as the ocean level rose, it back-filled the Mediterranean. And as the Mediterranean rose, it back-filled the Black Sea. Consequently, a number of post-Flood roads and settlements became permanently submerged.

This explains the drowned remains found in the Black Sea by Russian scientists in the 1950s and later by Robert Ballard.

During an exploration of the seabed, Soviet archaeologists discovered the legendary town of Diosuria at the bottom of the Black sea, off Sukhumi.

Then, in September, 2000, at 311 feet beneath the surface of the Black sea, Ballard's team, with a submersible, discovered a collapsed man-made building with planks and beams.

Ballard said, "If you drained it back, it would be rolling countryside with meandering streams. We located the countryside and located the river systems." The media saw this as evidence of a local flood that may have inspired the biblical story of Noah.

How little do they know! What Ballard found was a post-Flood regional catastrophe that occurred several hundred years **after** the world-wide Flood – when melting glaciers raised sea level until the waters of the Mediterranean breached the natural dam of the Bosphorus.

Sea water which had first come in from the Atlantic to fill the Mediterranean, now from the Mediterranean poured into the Black Sea basin. It poured in at 200 times the volume of Niagara Falls. The heavier salt water plunged to the bottom of the existing fresh water lake and began to fill the basin like a bathtub. This rising lake-sea inundated and submerged thousands of square miles of land, destroying local communities, killing people and wiping out plants and animals.

But that was NOT Noah's Flood.

DROWNED CITIES

In the Mediterranean, silting – as well as uplifting – of land has occurred - so that some ancient ports, such as Ephesus, Priene and Miletus are now miles from the sea. And the remains of the former ancient harbour city of Phalassarna, in Crete, lie 20 feet above sea level, on the cliffs!

Conversely, other ruins, such as a temple at Pozzuoli on the Adriatic Sea's Gulf of Venice have sunk... then come back up again. This temple now shows the distinct holes left by underwater borers from its prolonged immersion 20 feet under the sea!

In the Mediterranean, earth movements resulting from earthquakes and volcanoes account for most of the submerged cities, but not all.

Because of the general rising of the water level of the Mediterranean, large sections of cities well known to history are now under water. Among these are Baise (a sort of ancient Las Vegas), numerous points along Italy's western coast, cities along the Adriatic coast of Yugoslavia, parts of Syracuse in Sicily, Lepis Magna in Libya, as well as the ancient harbours of Tyre and Caesarea.

There are more than 250 known drowned cities in the Mediterranean.

Helike is believed to lie on the sea bottom near Corinth. In ancient times this sunken city was a tourist attraction for Roman visitors to Greece. They used to pass over it in boats, admiring the ruins visible through the clear water. The statue of Zeus, still standing, was clearly visible on the bottom.

The small island of Malta, with its giant megaliths, gives evidence of having once been part of a larger, now drowned, land.

ROADS DISAPPEAR INTO THE DEEP

A thousand feet offshore from the island of Melos are the ruins of an ancient city at a depth extending to 400 feet. From it there branch out roads, descending even deeper – to unknown destinations.

Jacques Costeau found on the sea bottom another paved road far out in the Mediterranean.

Sicily was once joined to Italy by land over which ships now sail.

DROWNED MINES

Five miles directly offshore from Marseilles, on the French Riviera, at a depth of 80 feet, divers have found horizontal and vertical mining tunnels, smelting facilities and slag heaps lying outside the shafts.

HANNIBAL'S DROWNED CAMP

The camps that Hannibal used as a staging area prior to his invasion of Rome lie under shallow water off Peniscola, on the eastern coast of Spain.

GIGANTIC SUBMERGED RELICS

Off Morocco, on the Mediterranean side of Gibraltar, marine archaeologist Dr. J. Thorne has investigated an undersea wall. The wall extends for 9 miles atop a submerged mountain 120 feet below the surface. Some of its stones are each larger than 2-story houses (about as large as those used in the gigantic foundation of the Baalbek temple of Lebanon). Dr. Thorne observed roads going down the mountain further into unknown depths.

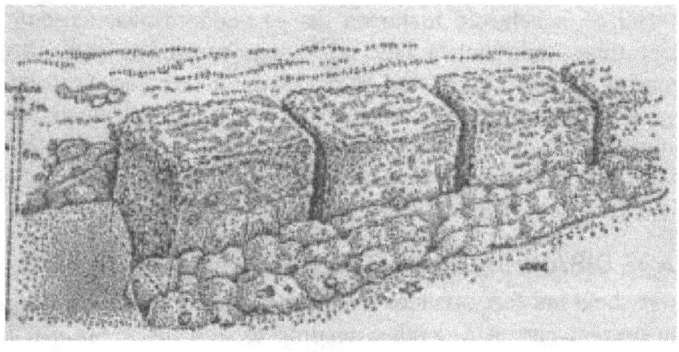

Picture: Charles Berlitz

ATLANTIC OCEAN RUINS

Off Spain's Atlantic coast, 2½ miles out to sea from Cadiz, in 95 feet of water, sunken walls and pavements have been photographed on several occasions. Eleven miles offshore are evidences of roads and large columns, some with concentric spiral motifs.

Late in 1942, a pilot engaged on military flights between Recife, Brazil, and Dakar, Senegal, reported sighting a city beneath the waves of the mid-Atlantic. The crew saw what appeared to be clusters of buildings just below the ocean, on the western slope of a submarine mountain near the St. Peter and St. Paul Rocks (1°N, 30°W). It was in the late afternoon sun, when the water was still and clear. The rays of the sun struck the water at such an angle that they penetrated diagonally to a considerable distance. This clarity would occur only once in a thousand flights or more.

Others flying the same route have since noticed what appear to be shallow underwater stone walls and ruins at about 6°N, 20°W, near the Sierra Leone Rise.

The Piri Reis map (another map with ancient origins) traces an island no longer indicated on modern maps. This large island appears exactly where the tiny St. Peter and St. Paul Rocks are now located – about 700 miles east of Recife.

Here are some other discoveries:
* Off the Cape Verde Islands, a drowned city and market place;
* Off the Canary Islands, on the 50 foot deep sea bottom, wide engraved stone steps and a central pavement;
* Off Madeira, at a depth of about 600 feet, a wall containing large stone slabs, as well as a stone staircase cut into the cliff;
* Off Greenland, submerged forests, as well as buildings on former low islands.

In 1985, several hundred miles east of the Azores, a Russian submarine under the command of Nikolai Seleznev, was filming the ocean floor with a special deep-diving camera, when, at a depth of 120 feet, they noticed a string of stone columns and then a massive dome-topped building.

"We couldn't believe our eyes," he said. "We were viewing an entire city with magnificent boulevards and avenues and they were lined with what looked like temples and halls, government buildings and homes."

Suddenly their power flickered. The engines shut down on their own and then the needles on the instruments, including clocks, began to quiver and run backward. Many of the crew began to hallucinate. The terrifying experience ended as suddenly as it began, after about 15 minutes.[2]

Other explorers have reported a mysterious energy field in the area.

EUROPE

Today one of France's most celebrated tourist sites is Mont Saint-Michel. Now almost a mile offshore, the 237 foot high cone shaped islet is crowned by a medieval abbey church, which supplanted a much older building.

It is not generally known that the whole Saint-Michel mound is artificial. That's right. Thousands of years ago a pyramid was built here. Much later the pyramid was partially covered with earth to make it into a mound. Then a building was erected upon it. When you push aside the gorse growing on the slopes, the stone steps of the original pyramid can be seen. The fine masonry interior includes a long circular wall and crypts.

Now for the point I wish to make. Originally this structure stood on an inland plain, surrounded by forest. By the tenth century, the rising sea had encroached on and obliterated the forest. Today it is surrounded by a great expanse of sand. And twice daily the high tide comes racing over the sands. You would need to run at the speed of a galloping horse to avoid being caught in it.

In Brittany, ancient avenues of huge upright stones go down to the Atlantic shore, then continue on under the sea.

An exceptional neap tide in 1970 exposed what looked like piles of dripping stone ruins. These were so far from shore that observers could not visit them before the tide returned.

All these sites are in France.

THE PRANK THAT KILLED A CITY

The sunken city of Caer Ys is placed traditionally close to the French coast. Here was played out an intriguing story of juvenile delinquency. It is reputed that Dahut, the daughter of Gradlon, king of Ys, during a drinking bout with her lover, opened the city floodgates with a stolen key, to see what would happen....

(In case you haven't guessed, the sea rushed in and the whole city went under, forever!)

* * * * * * *

There is evidence that there were forests where now the North Sea extends. On the Dogger Bank in the middle of the sea are stumps of trees with their roots still in the ground. Divers have brought up stone axes and mastodon bones, from the time when the North Sea was land.

German archaeologist Jurgen Spanuth, in 1954 described a sunken walled city he had found on the floor of the North Sea, five miles north of the isle of Heligoland. The city's rock walls were constructed of black, white and red rocks. He claimed that its streets were paved with molded slabs of firestone and that there was ample evidence that its inhabitants knew how to smelt ore.[3]

Pollen analysis of the sea bottom suggests that this sea, in its present shape, originated within "recent" times. The date of 1500 BC is often selected.

THE DAY THE SEA BROKE THROUGH

England was once part of the European mainland, with a land bridge between present-day Dover and Calais. During this initial early period, settlers probably trekked across the intervening valley unimpeded. But soon the rising sea level became noticeable.

I can imagine a grandfather standing one day on a hilltop with his grandson. They look down on the valley below. The old man points and says, "The sea comes further up that inlet now, than when I was a boy."

Perhaps that grandson lived to see that first, historic high tide go roaring all the way through the valley, scouring out its sides, joining the North Sea with the Channel.

In locations all around England and Wales are submerged forests. Trawlers have brought up fragments of oak trees in their nets. The oaks grew where now are 60 fathoms of stormy water.

The isles of Scilly which lie 28 miles (45 kilometres) off England's Land End today consist of 100 islands. But in 240 AD it was all one large island, according to the Roman historian Solinus. He called it Siluram Insulam – the Scilly Isle. If the sea level were lowered by 60 feet, it would again be one island.

Three Welsh kingdoms have been submerged by the sea, according to Manuscript Number 3514 in the library of Exeter Cathedral, dated at about 1280. All along the coast of Wales are submerged forests, walls - and roads that disappear into the sea.

RUINS UNDER LOCH NESS

Under the waters of Scotland's Loch Ness, sonor photography has traced ancient stone ruins. Unlike most lakes, Loch Ness connects underground to the sea. These ruins were evidently submerged as the sea level rose to form the lake.

STAIRCASE

More ruins lie on the ocean bed off the Irish coast; also a mammoth staircase descends 5 miles into the deep sea.

INDIAN OCEAN

Off Mahabalipuram, Madras, India, lies another sunken city.

Southward from the River Indus, there extends under the Indian Ocean a large oval of shallow water. Often, when water and sky conditions are favourable, fishermen report sighting submerged structures. The ruins commence at about $21°N$ and extend almost to the equator.

Shri Lanka has traditions that the rising waters of the Indian Ocean cut it off from the Indian mainland.

PACIFIC OCEAN

Pohnpei Island (formerly named Panope) lies about 1,000 miles (1,600 kilometres) north east of Papua New Guinea. On this small volcanic island sits Nan Modal, a mysterious dead city covering 11 square miles (28 square kilometres).

The hauling up of immense blocks, some of them 25 tons in weight, to such a height as 60 feet (as high as a 6-story building) was done either with advanced technology or with a population of tens of thousands, all of whom would have to be housed and fed.

Today, there is just not enough land there for so many people.

Its structures continue off the land into the sea and eventually disappear in the depths of the Pacific.

In fact, there is evidence of yet another large city nearby, drowned in the sea.

Japanese pearl divers claim to have seen buildings, streets and sunken columns encrusted with coral in the deep waters.

In recent years, the Universities of Ohio and Oregon and the Pacific Studies Institute (Honolulu) have undertaken expeditions.

Giant stone columns were discovered submerged, as well as a system of tunnels through the coral reef.

Swimming along the underwater streets among sharks, author and adventurer David Childers found columns up to four stories high in 60 to 100 feet of water. There was evidence of ruins descending to depths of over 200 feet. His team discovered underwater inscriptions – "geometric designs such as crosses and rectangles."

Aerial photographs reveal straight lines running hundreds of metres and turning at right angles in the coral reef, forming what appear to be city blocks encrusted with coral.

Divers have been able to walk on the bottom on well-preserved streets, which are overgrown with coral and mussels. They report carved stone tablets hung on the remains of clearly recognisable houses. There are also pillars and stone vaults. Japanese pearl divers with modern equipment reported finding watertight platinum coffins. They brought up bits of platinum day after day, as well as pearls and bars of silver.

Degeneration

The stones for ancient Nan Madol were transported by sea. But when this island was discovered in modern times, natives were not known to have had ocean-going canoes. Something else. Pottery shards have been found in the ruins of the old city. But pottery was not used by the natives at the time of European discovery. Moreover, the natives now living in grass huts could no longer build structures out of rocks weighing 20 to 50 tons.

Here is evidence of cultural regression.

John MacMillan Brown of the University of New Zealand collected evidence on the island of Loeai in Western Micronesia of a former written language. This had since vanished. More evidence of cultural regression.[4]

In 1773, Captain James Cook visited Easter Island. He wrote compassionately about the people, who were as poor as the arid earth on which they lived.

Expressing astonishment, he contrasted this with the superior civilisation that had made the enormous statues. Someone long ago had fashioned megalithic stone blocks of incredible perfection (as witnessed at Vinapu).

But the natives now lived in reed huts.

Other island evidences

In the same Micronesian group as Pohnpei, the small island of Palau has its "sunken city", off the northern coast.

And west of Okinawa, off the islands of Aguni, Kerama and Yonaguni, Japanese divers in 1995 discovered stone carved pyramids and terraces that go down to depths of 80 feet or more.

On low, barren and uninhabited Malden Island in Kiribati are pyramids, platforms and megaliths, as well as roads that disappear into the ocean. On this remote island, the remnants of 40 stone temples show off the same architecture as on Pohnpei, 3,400 miles away.

The Marquesas Islands, like Easter Island, are full of gigantic platforms. Some of the smooth-sided, oblong shaped stones are up to 15 feet long and 5 to 6 feet thick... single stones! Some of the platforms are so big that whole villages once stood on them, with each individual house likewise constructed of massive stones.[5]

"Land that is gone"

Easter Island legends recall that "King Hout-Matua... saw that the land was slowly sinking in the sea."[6]

Easter Island was once much larger. And a tradition has it that Motu Motiro Hiva, an islet about 100 miles away, was once part of it.

The land "slowly sinking" means that the sea level was slowly rising.

Evidence of rising sea is seen in drowned roads. For example, divers have followed a road that leads off Easter island into the ocean.

A former Pacific empire?

The Easter Islanders claimed that Hiva was the name of the original Pacific continent. "Hiva is a land that is gone. Now it is below the Pacific Ocean."[7]

The evidence does suggest that:
1. there was either a large continent, or groups of small "continents" throughout the Pacific, before the sea level slowly rose to drown it.
2. there was once an extremely sophisticated nation which covered the Pacific.

Tongatapu is thought to have been its capital. It sent huge ships to trade with other nations – and built gigantic pyramids, monuments and roads. Colleges were operated for instruction in astronomy, climatology, navigation and theological history. And there are clues that this great trading empire spanned the entire Pacific from India and China to the great civilisations of Peru and Mexico.[8]

For several hundred years the people lived an idyllic existence, and then the Polynesian culture fell into decline.

On most islands of Polynesia and Micronesia are remains of cities, temples, harbours and statues, whose size and elaborate architecture indicate a civilisation incomparably more advanced than exists there today.

Pacific sea level rise

We noted that according to some oceanographers and geologists, the ocean level may have been as much as 500 feet lower than today. This would have allowed a large section of the Pacific to be above water.

New Zealand's continental shelf shows evidence that it was once dry land with forests and rivers.

And on the opposite side of the Pacific, places like the Cobb Seamount would have been habitable. In fact, students from the University of Washington, have made this location a special project. The Cobb Seamount is a flat-topped mountain 120 feet below the surface of the ocean, just off-shore from Washington state. Dives to the "drowned city" on its summit have produced pottery and evidence of a culture that mummified animals.

I am told that several years ago, some divers found a number of buildings off the west coast of Vancouver Island, submerged in about 80 feet of water, close to the town of Uculet.

NORTH AMERICA

The story is naturally the same on the Atlantic side.

Off the Nova Scotia and New England coasts, stumps of trees stand in the sea, where country once forested now lies drowned.

On the ocean floor off Georgia, is a roadway of unknown length; off the Delaware coast a ten mile wall; and off Rhode Island a round tower and walls in sea 40 to 50 feet deep.

LATIN AMERICA

Among discoveries off South and Central America are these:
* Off Guayaquil, Ecuador, a drowned city from which statues, lenses and other artefacts have been brought up;
* Off Venezuela, a 30 foot wall running straight for at least 100 miles;

* Off Haiti, an entire submerged city;
* Off Cuba's north coast, submerged streets and buildings white like marble;
* From Belize, ancient roads on land continue to destinations now under the sea;
* Off Hispaniola, Mexico, sunken buildings (one of them 240 by 80 feet);
* At 165 feet underwater, Costeau's "Calypso" expedition discovered a huge grotto with stalactites and stalagmites, which can form only on land.

Cosmul is a jungle island. Once part of Mexico's Yucatan mainland, it is now 12 miles from the shoreline. Yet there is a great highway with its lifted line of trees streaking across the jungle to Cosmul. The roadway, with its huge 9 foot sandstone flagging and hard cement cover, dips down under the waves at the coastline and again reappears on the dry land of Cosmul.

More in the Caribbean

A fairly shallow stretch of clear water between Florida and Haiti is scattered with 700 sunlit islands. This Bahama Banks area was once above water. An extensive cedar forest once grew here.

Under the sea, numerous giant stone constructions extend for miles among the coral and swaying seaweed. When the water is clear and unruffled, successions of architectural patterns are often observed on the seabed by pilots of commercial and private aircraft. There are pyramidal formations, straight and intersecting lines and large rectangular forms; long stone walls or roads, pillars, archways, stone circles and stepped terraces on the ocean floor.

In 1979, a 3,000 foot wide three-ringed circular structure resembling a stadium was discovered near Andros Island. There are also circular walls around freshwater springs – possibly ancient reservoirs. Composition analysis of pillars comprising one structure a mile long near Bimini indicated they were of pink marble, quite foreign to the area.

Near the north end of Andros, covered by sea plants, are the submerged remains of a temple-like building approximately 100 feet by 75 feet in size.

An underwater road or wall runs along the top of an underwater cliff near Cay Lobos. It is possible that the ancient road ran along the cliff when both were above sea level.

Divers who had just discovered a sunken anchor from a Spanish galleon and were scratching the bottom around it found that it was lying on top of a mosaic floor or terrace!

In another location a 1982 expedition found a sunken quarry, complete with shaped blocks of stone still inside it. Heavy surface waves and strong underwater surges foiled attempts to photograph the quarry.

The area of this submerged plateau covered in remains is extensive. Off Bimini and Andros, submerged buildings extend over 38 square miles! Constructions run along the seabed to the drop-off of the continental shelf, up to 100 miles out to sea. They are all encrusted with fossilised shells and petrified mangrove roots.

In 1964, off the coast of Puerto Rico, the French submarine "Archimede", descending from the continental shelf to lower levels, accidentally bumped against a flight of giant stone steps, cut into the steep sides of the shelf 1,400 feet below the surface. Apparently the stairway once ascended from the sea coast to a high plateau – the present low-lying island of Andros.

The flooding was probably very gradual; many of the submerged walls appear to be dykes, built to protect areas from the rising ocean. But they were not enough. The sea ultimately rolled over the land and a civilisation was lost.

Pyramid under the sea

Southwest of the Cay Sal Bank, a 1978 expedition organised by Ari Marshall, a Greek industrialist, captured a pyramidal shape on videotape. As they neared the area, all the compasses spun wildly. The pyramid rose from a depth of 650 feet to 150 feet from the surface. Marshall recounts:

"We lowered the camera and high intensity lights down the side of the mass and suddenly came to an opening. Light flashes or shiny white objects were being swept into the opening by turbulence. They may have been gas or energy crystals. Further down, the same thing happened in reverse. They were coming out again at a lower level. It was surprising that the water in this deep area was green instead of black near the pyramid."[9]

Mysterious crystal

In 1970, Dr. Ray Brown of Mesa, Arizona, and four other divers, were off the Berry Islands of the Bahamas when their compasses went berserk and their magnometers failed.

Suddenly they saw the outlines of buildings under the water. They dived down for a look. Dr. Brown recalls:

"I turned to look toward the sun through the murky water and saw a pyramid shape shining like a mirror. About thirty-five to forty feet from the top was an opening. I was reluctant to go inside... but I swam in anyway. The opening was like a shaft debouching into an inner room. I saw something shining. It was a crystal, held by two metallic hands. I had on my gloves and I tried to loosen it. It became loose. As soon as I grabbed it I felt this was the time to get out and not come back."[10]

In the years following, Dr. Brown has sometimes shown the round crystal to lecture audiences. Inside it, a series of pyramidal forms are visible. A throbbing sensation is felt in the hand when it is held, according to reports.

This underwater pyramid is reportedly surrounded by buildings. The total complex is estimated at 5 miles wide, and even longer.

MORE RECENT INUNDATIONS

Denmark: Off the coast is the small island of Nordstrand. It is the last trace of a large tract of rich farmland that, as recently as 300 years ago, was covered by an inrush of the sea. Six thousand people and their homes were swept away.

Holland: In the thirteenth century, the slowly rising North Sea suddenly rushed inland over parts of low lying Holland and formed the big inlet called the Zuider Zee, destroying 30 villages and 80,000 people. Last century, the Dutch reclaimed this rich land with dykes.

England: During the reign of Henry II, one of the most important seaports of England was Shipden in Norfolk on the east coast. It had a large and beautiful church famous all over England.

Five hundred years ago, Shipden was swallowed up by the sea – church, dock and all.

BELLS THAT RING UNDER THE SEA

Have you heard about that great city Dunwich? In the days of King Alfred (remember, the "cake-burner"?), Dunwich in East Anglia was a bustling town. And in the reign of Henry II, it had a royal palace and more than 200 churches.

Among sailors and merchants its market was known all over Europe. Dunwich was so important, it used to return TWO members of parliament.

Imagine this great city being slowly but surely swallowed up by the greedy sea. In 1347, more than 400 houses and as many shops and windmills were engulfed. When Drake was fighting the Spaniards, scarcely a quarter of the fine old city was left. At last, all that remained of Dunwich were the cracked and battered walls of the Church of All Saints, which for years hung poised on the very edge of the cliff – and then one day crashed into the sea beneath.

The low cliffs are still crumbling away by five to six feet annually.

It is reported that during storms the bells of lost churches have been heard pealing as the sea currents surge through the bell towers.

Coastal erosion along a strip of the Yorkshire coast of England has resulted in the loss of 35 towns since Roman times.

Perhaps you have been following with your atlas? On a map showing the narrowest part of the England Channel, namely the Strait of Dover, close to the English coast you may see marked the Goodwin Sands, a line of sandbanks just beneath the water. These sandbanks are all that is left of the vast estate of Earl Godwin, father of King Harold. All this land, with its park, cattle, sheep and deer, sank beneath the waves 900 years ago.

The Dover Strait is still widening by about one foot a year.

There are, of course, places where land has been built up with earth eroded from other sites. But the overall result has been loss of land.

Again, not all underwater ruins resulted from the rising sea level. In some cases the land actually sank under. Nevertheless the rising ocean is still slowly but steadily wearing away the coastlines of the world. Generally the erosion is scarcely noticed. At times, however, the waves suddenly gulp down wide stretches of land without warning.

In fact, I was recently invited to conduct a seminar series in the Solomon Islands in the south west Pacific. The news was given me of a low-lying island in the Solomons which was recently abandoned by its inhabitants, due to a rising sea level.

Currently the sea level is rising at the rate of 1.5 feet (45 centimetres) per century. It's a pity... some of our most exotic low-lying tropical islands seem next in line to be swallowed up.

Want to see some special place before it disappears? There's probably no need to rush your travel agent... not yet.

* * * * * * *

But there are some big times ahead...

25

Prophecies -

A "SECRET" REPORT ON OUR FUTURE

On February 22, 2004, an alleged "secret report", suppressed by U.S. defence chiefs, was published by *The Observer* in Britain.

It predicted that very soon widespread flooding by a rise in sea levels would create major upheaval for millions.

Nuclear conflict, mega-droughts, famine and widespread rioting would erupt across the world.

RAGING SEA

The "Pentagon report", as it was called, predicted that major European cities will be sunk beneath rising seas.

It forecasted that by 2007 violent storms will smash coastal barriers, rendering large parts of the Netherlands uninhabitable. Cities such as the Hague will be abandoned. Bangladesh will become nearly uninhabitable due to rising sea level contaminating the inland water supplies. Parts of low lying areas in the United Kingdom and coastal areas of the United States will also become uninhabitable.

Before scanning this report, I had been reading a 2,000 year old prophecy concerning our 21st century which says: "There shall be… upon the earth distress of nations, with no way out; the *sea and the waves roaring*; Men's hearts failing them for fear, and for looking after those things which are coming on the earth."[1]

How spot on!

Did you know that a study by the Federal Emergency Management Agency (FEMA), says one-fourth of the buildings within 500 feet of America's coastlines are threatened by erosion in the next 60 years?

The study concluded that close to 87,000 homes and other buildings stand on land likely to wash away into the oceans or the Great Lakes.

"The findings are sobering," the director of the agency, James Lee Witt, said in a statement. "If coastal development continues unabated, and if the sea levels rise as some scientists are predicting, the impact will be even worse."

Jesus' 2,000 year old prophecy said that a defining feature of our day would be "the sea and the waves roaring".

The new climatic developments were a focus of the 1994 Yokohama Conference. In 1996, a report was released by the Millennium Group[2] on the findings of the conference.

Titled "The Arrival of New Conditions and Consequences", it drew attention to "the abrupt growth of meteorological/weather catastrophes in recent years."

The paper stated: "The dynamic growth of significant catastrophes shows a major increase in the rate of production since 1973. And in general, the number of catastrophes has grown by 410% between 1963 and 1993. Special attention must be focused on the growing number and variety of catastrophes."

Nine types of "significant catastrophes" were listed: flooding, hurricanes, drought, frost, storms, earthquakes, landslides, epidemics and starvation.

Years	total	Annual	total	annual	total	annual
1963-1967	16	3.2	39	7.8	89	17.8
1968-1972	15	3.0	54	10.8	98	19.6
1973-1977	31	6.2	56	11.2	95	19
1978-1982	55	11.0	99	19.8	138	27.6
1983-1987	58	11.6	116	23.2	153	30.6
1988-1992	66	13.2	139	27.8	205	41.0
	241	8.0	503	16.8	778	25.5

According to Russian academician Kondratyev, "data indicates that we are moving in the direction of climatic chaos."[3]

FAMINE AND WAR

The 2004 Pentagon document predicted that abrupt climate change could bring the planet to the edge of anarchy as countries develop a nuclear threat to defend and secure dwindling food, water and energy supplies. The threat to global stability vastly eclipsed that of terrorism, said the few experts privy to its contents.

Mega-droughts would affect the world's major breadbaskets, including America's Midwest, where strong winds would bring soil loss. Access to water would become a major battleground.

Rich areas like the United States and Europe would become "virtual fortresses" to prevent millions of migrants from entering after being forced from land drowned by sea-level rise or no longer able to grow crops. Waves of boatpeople would pose significant problems.

The report warned of serious trouble. Within ten years global warming would shut down the Gulf Stream, forcing North America, Britain and Northern Europe into what it termed an "ice age". Then these regions also, claimed the report, would no longer be able to grow their own food or breed their own livestock. Nothing grows when the thermometer falls to minus 50C.

Deaths from war and famine would run into millions. Climate change would lead to nuclear war and global catastrophe that would cost millions, perhaps billions of lives. "Disruption and conflict will be endemic features of life," concluded the Pentagon analysis. "Once again, warfare would define human life."

Another 2,000 year prophecy, zeroing in on our day, says it will be characterised by *"wars and rumours of wars... and... famines."*[4]

But here we have someone claiming to be the Creator who says he is not taken by surprise. In predicting these events, he assures us they are signs of the promised Second Coming and the glorious days that will follow.

And that brings us to another amazing prophecy.

EUROPE'S "TOWER OF BABEL"

Earlier in this book, we noted that the Babel builders, for their arrogant behaviour, were forcibly scattered.

But their occult system has survived worldwide. And it presently controls this planet through world leaders under its power. This is a whole big subject on its own. Many books have been written on it.

The upside-down pentagram, often superimposed on a goat's head, is a common symbol in occult and satanic ritual. The circle of upside-down stars in the poster below, ostensibly representing the nations of the European Community, would appear to be a conscious attempt to convey an occultic message.

Is it accidental, that the Council of Europe chose a religious motif for their desired United States of Europe?

They decided to employ the Tower of Babel in the above poster as the central motif to symbolise their efforts to build the European super state. What a telling choice! It would appear to be an open statement of defiance to God the Creator, especially considering that the stars have been intentionally inverted to form occult pentagrams.

And what significance does this have prophetically?

There is a 2,000 year old prophecy which says that as man's control of this planet draws toward its climax:
- The divided nations of Europe will unite to support a new world order, under the control of a world religion.
- America will direct the whole world to accept the rules of this new world order.
- Economic sanctions will be imposed against dissidents.[5]
- The new world order will bring the earth to the brink of ruin.

- The natural environment will be thrown into chaos, as a penalty on a planet that has rebelled against its Maker.
- There will follow total economic and social collapse.[6]
- The rejected, but real Owner of this planet will intervene in time - and all who have ordered their lives in harmony with him will be rescued. That's the Second Coming.

Yes, it's all in that amazing prophecy!

Look around you. Can you see the pieces fitting into place? Okay then, in one sentence... here is the key: watch America, Europe and the Vatican. Astonishing events will soon burst upon us.

Of this you can be sure. The first Babel collapsed in chaos. And the modern imitation Babel will likewise experience a shocking catastrophe.

Just wait and see.

ARE THE MOVES BEING PLANNED?

Is history following a PLAN, then?

Is there a direction, a purpose, even a theme to history, that is not perceived by today's scientific materialism?

Yes, there are PATTERNS in the events of human life and history that mock the idea of mere coincidence. Some events almost shriek out that a Superior Intelligence is behind it all.

To a careful observer, the events of history can be recognised as LINKED together, unfolding one by one, in a complex but inevitable sequence, as though pre-planned.

One may even sense that there is a power at work which is not of this world. And recognise the interplay of natural forces used to accomplish certain aims.

I have a couple of questions for you.

Think back to Chapter 4. We saw that in 2344 BC Noah's survival vessel (its occupants not knowing where they were) fortuitously ran aground in the centre-most point of the world's land mass, for optimum ease of dispersion. Tell me, was that just blind chance, or deliberate design?

Again, we noted that after the forced scattering of the rebels from Babel, that the physical land masses were suddenly divided (pages 117-118). Was this just chance, or was it to reinforce a divine purpose that they remain scattered?

PROPHECY =
HISTORY WRITTEN IN ADVANCE

If this world is carried along of its own accord, without a ruler, like a ship without a pilot, we should not see all things come to pass according to pre-written prophecies. I refer now to prophecies discovered in the Bible.

Researchers have noticed that, as history progresses, various biblical prophecies have been fulfilling – according to a pre-written, timed schedule. Some of them are so specific, they detail names and dates.

In these prophecies, the major events of history, stage by stage, are touched upon... leading up to a final, sudden interruption to human control of this planet.

Then, as you look at history, you see events, step by step, move by move, obediently fulfil those prophecies - often in uncanny detail. They have the hint of intention.

Yes, I know. We have pushed him out of history. It makes some of us uncomfortable to mention him. But could it be that this same Creator is not merely a factor, but THE supreme, controlling factor?

Could it be that while he gives us perfect freedom of choice, always within limits, yet he himself determines what those limits shall be... and how long, how deep and how broad, the stream of time shall flow?

Could it be that he has also revealed to us the central purpose, and the final goal, of human history?

Indeed, we saw in Book 1 of this series, *The Killing of Paradise Planet,* that centuries before the Great Flood struck, a 120-year advance alert was given. And today? There do exist prophecies giving a similar alert now, before a so-called, clearly described Second Coming.

And did you know, those prophecies link both events, urging us to note that the reality of the first event ensures the certainty of the second?

WILL A COMET END ALL LIFE?

Some folk today are predicting the end of all life on earth, from some passing or colliding heavenly body.

But you can take comfort in this. NO accident will totally extinguish human life.

In the full sweep of human history as predicted, there are only two major events scheduled to bring a total world wipeout:
1. The Great Flood
2. The Second Coming

Two. And only two.

In any case, as we approach the countdown... what should we expect? Will there be inter-action with heavenly bodies passing through our solar system?

Some observers see mention of such events in the book of Revelation, when "hail and fire mingled with blood" burn up a third of the earth; and "a great mountain burning with fire" is cast into the sea; and "a great star from heaven, burning as it were a lamp" falls upon a third part of the rivers and waters.[7]

On an average day, about 50 asteroids, measuring at least 30 feet (10 metres) across, pass between the earth and the moon.[8]

It is estimated that up to 4,000 earth crossing asteroids exist that are half a mile (one kilometre) wide or more - plus an equal number of comets.

"The kinetic energy of a mountain-size object travelling at 25 kilometers per second is enormous," writes Roger Lewin. "Such impacts... carry the potential to threaten the survival of civilization."[9]

It cannot be discounted that comets or meteorites may play a role upon earth in the closing scenes. Certainly, increasing disasters can be expected.[10]

The prophecy made by Jesus is worth noting: "For then shall be great trouble, such as was not since the beginning of the world to this time, no, nor ever shall be. And except those days should be shortened, there should no flesh be saved."[11]

"Fearful sights from the sky"

Early in 2004, speculation raged concerning the near approach to Earth of a large celestial body, accompanied by a consortium of asteroids, comets, and smaller planetary bodies. Some, it was feared, might strike the earth.

And if the larger object merely bypassed the earth, yet, its huge size and magnetic field, might cause a "polar shift" – that earth's inner metallic core might "lock" to the magnetic field of this body as it came whizzing past, while the earth's crust and oceans would continue to move. This could cause horrific worldwide surface winds of up to 400 kilometres per hour, massive tidal waves, earthquakes, and volcanic activity.

Already volcanic magma was swelling under America's Yellowstone, below a very thin crust. Wildlife was leaving the area. It was postulated that an eruption under the lake would be 2,500 times as large as the Mount St. Helens eruption and would kill everyone within 600 miles of the Yellowstone Lake.

Interestingly, 80% of the American military was believed to have been transferred out of the country in anticipation of the possibility of MARTIAL LAW being implemented in the U.S. – while a million foreign soldiers (with no emotional empathy for the local population) had taken their place on US soil.

Researcher Cal Steinberger, in his email bulletin advised, "You MUST get your emergency provisions IN HAND IMMEDIATELY! You must also convince your loved ones to GET OUT OF ANY LARGE METROPOLITAN AREA. Further, they must move at least 300 miles inland from ANY COASTLINE. And, STAY AWAY FROM THE FLOOD PLAIN OF THE MISSISSIPPI RIVER. Be further advised, that NO ONE SHOULD BE LIVING ANYWHERE WITHIN 600 MILES OF THE YELLOWSTONE PARK SUPER VOLCANO AREA." (Emphasis his)

This brings to mind the prediction of Jesus that shortly before His return, **"fearful sights and great signs shall there be from heaven**...and upon the earth distress of nations, with perplexity; the sea and the waves roaring; Men's hearts failing them for fear, and for looking after those things which are coming on the earth."[12]

Certainly this prophecy is being fulfilled in the unparalleled fear now seizing the nations.

"The sea and the waves roaring."

A computer model has been designed to show the way a tsunami will build after a volcano in the Canary Islands next erupts. The volcano, called Cumbre Vieja, is on the western island of La Palma.

Most of the volcano's western flank is unstable enough to be dislodged in the next big eruption. A massive slab of rock twice the volume of the Isle of Man would break away from the island of La Palma and smash into the Atlantic Ocean to cause a tsunami – a monster wave.

The computer model compiled by Simon Day, of the Benfield Greg Research Centre at University College, London and Steven Ward of the University of California, Santa Cruz, predicted that the tsunami would have a height of 330 feet (100 metres) when it crashes into the shores of Morocco in nearby north west Africa.

Travelling at speeds of up to 500 miles an hour, the tsunami would hit the South and North American coasts up to 16 stories high, then travel four or five miles inland, flattening everything in its path.[13]

EXPECT RAPID CHANGES

It is generally assumed that earth changes will be slow and the world will find time to discover the solutions to the problems.

But new powerful evidence strongly suggests that this scenario is simply wrong, and we had better prepare for another, more abrupt, possibility.

According to the Pentagon, a satellite photo of the North Polar region in 1970 and again in 2003, reveals that 40% of the North Polar ice had melted in just 33 years. And it was melting faster and faster now.

It's the same story in the South Polar region. In 2002, Larsen A ledge broke off from Antarctica. This surprised many scientists. Still, those studying this event told us it was no big deal.

They also assured us that another ledge behind it, Larsen B ledge, would never melt, since it had "been there for many ice ages." Surprise! In 2003, Larsen's B ledge broke off and went to sea. These same scientists said that, due to its immense size, it would take six months to melt. Wrong again. It melted in a mere 35 days. And more significantly, it raised the entire world's ocean levels by almost an inch.

Now with Larsen's B ledge gone, an incredibly enormous ice shelf called Ross's Shelf is exposed - and the only thing holding Ross's Shelf from sliding into the ocean was Larsen's B ledge.

And Ross's Shelf is cracking. If Ross's Shelf were to slide into the ocean, estimates are that it would raise the world's oceans by 16 to 20 feet. And that if all the polar ice completely melted, the ocean levels of the Earth could raise on the order of 20 meters - 66 feet!

How that would change the world! Almost every coastal city in the world, the country of Holland and many islands, would be underwater.

Perhaps it will take an event such as this to wake up the world to become serious about those matters that count.

The threat was considered so real that in March 2004, the US Senate appropriated 60 million dollars to the study of abrupt global climate changes.

By the estimate of most scientists, it is too late to alter the course of what is about to happen. All we can do now is PREPARE for the shock.

THE 40-FOOT WALL

The Pentagon report suggested that the United States build a 40-foot wall around the entire country to keep out immigrants, including people trying to escape the coming world weather disasters.

This sounds like something out of a weird movie. But did you know that the United States government is reported to have already begun the construction of this wall between the U.S. and Mexico?

A U.S. military person involved in the construction, when informed of the slowing of the Gulf Stream, the ice melt and the world food problems expected to follow, said, "Oh, now I understand. You see, the wall is straight up and down on the Mexican side, but it has steps and ladders on the US side to get over the wall and into Mexico. I never could understand why the government was doing this."

HOW SHOULD ONE PREPARE?

Really, fear should never rule our lives. However, it could be good insurance to *live as though this were your last day* (i.e. be ready to meet your Maker), *but plan as though you have an eternity before you* (i.e. get your life in shape for the new earth).

In any case, it is wise to be ready for any emergency. Relocating from large cities is a good start. And don't count on essential services, such as electricity, phone and water being readily available in time of crisis.

To be sure, some enormous disasters do lie ahead, in which millions will lose their lives. But in all of recorded history – and linked to reliable prophecies - there are only two total cleansings of this planet: (a) The Great Flood, and (b) The Second Coming.

1. THE FLOOD

In the first book of this series, *The Killing of Paradise Planet*, we touched a little on the causes of the Great Flood.

We noted the claim in very ancient writings that a beneficent and merciful Creator had given us a bountiful world to look after – and laws for our well-being - but that humans had rejected the Maker's instructions and messed everything up.

The Flood (a) punished a world in rebellion, and (b) rescued those in danger from the rebels.

The nations of planet Earth were in chaos. They had reached an impasse.

More than that, man was about to blast himself to extinction. It was time for the Supernatural to intervene.

Even those few who remained loyal to their Creator were in danger of being wiped out. So this destruction became the means of their RESCUE.

A cleansing of the planet would slow down the rebellion and prepare the earth for future generations. For that reason, the surface of the entire earth was now to be disturbed, refitted as a more austere and less bountiful home, where a rebellious race would be better off with less ease and abundance, in an environment not conducive to longevity.

For this new start, those who chose rightly were spared. They were to be rewarded with life in a new world free from the existing human threat.

The destruction of the original earth is portrayed by numerous ancient traditions as a sovereign act of the Creator.

So it happened. Suddenly it struck ... a disaster neither man-made nor ordinary. Created forces already latent in nature were suddenly orchestrated on an unnatural scale. These forces acted according to known laws of hydrostatics and hydrodynamics.

Just a handful of people lived to see both worlds. They were already forewarned WHEN it would occur and had been preparing for 120 years.

And now we come to our day. There also prophecies – about 40 of which I am aware - that indicate when the Second Coming is near. We've already touched on a few of those.

2. THE SECOND COMING

Other biblical prophecies spell out that when the Creator interrupts world history for the second and final time, events such as these will occur:

- The most violent earthquake in history, in which the cities of the nations will fall.[14]
- Islands will sink, mountains will disappear.[15]
- This will be a worldwide event, with no place to hide.[16]
- The rebellion will be totally and finally blotted out.[17]
- There will be survival for all who have made peace with their Maker, through his appointed means of rescue – the promised Deliverer.[18] The prophecies are emphatic about that.

And if you don't know much about these prophecies, you can do worse than investigate them. Especially if it could mean survival for you and your family.

Survival through a Deliverer? An outside Rescuer?

There's good evidence that we are not alone. And the Creator does care about his creation. We are informed that he has a plan of rescue already worked out for us.

Through history, ancient civilisations have known of this coming Deliverer. As the centuries passed, some 300 specific prophecies outlined his life in advance, even to the precise time of his appearance on earth. You are reading this right. These prophecies, written down before the events, actually identified him... even to the precise year of his scheduled appearance.

In my book *Ark of the Covenant*, you'll find good evidence that this Person actually appeared. He did what was he was predicted to do – and he threw out the rescue rope for every human being who would accept it. You could say, he handed us the key. Showed us how to get a reserved seat for life in the coming new world. And also how to enjoy real quality of life HERE AND NOW!

We are assured that this rescue offer is still open... until the Second Coming – when he returns to activate it.

You might liken Planet Earth to a plane ready to crash. The safety parachute is provided. But your survival and mine requires an individual response.

So you see, the situation's far from hopeless. In fact, when you know HOW man's rule of this planet will end, and WHAT you can personally do about it, you have a well-founded reason for HOPE and CONFIDENCE.[19]

THE TIMING

Concerning specifics: here is one particular prophecy that tells us the time is near.

Shortly before the Second Coming, said Jesus, the old city of Jerusalem will return to Jewish control. (And as you and I both know, after a 2,000 year span, that unlikely prophecy was fulfilled in 1967.) From that time on, said he, natural and man-made disasters will increase. And the coming "time of trouble" will end with his Second Coming – to take over this planet.[20]

"Therefore will we not fear, through the earth be removed, and though the mountains be carried into the midst of the sea."[21]

These will be natural calamities resulting from man's messing up the earth. Physical and spiritual laws set in motion by the Creator for our good have been seriously violated. From the beginning, we were given something precious – freedom to choose. And we can't avoid the consequences of our actions.

However, we have good reason to be certain that this mess – with its pain, hatred and death – is approaching its end. And individuals who choose the appointed way through all this, are to be handed back a new, unspoilt planet. A world in which the lion and lamb will lie down together, and peace, mutual caring and genuine happiness will be restored.

EPILOGUE

You want to know where we're going? Then you have to know where we came from.

To be realistic, what happens next is umbilically attached to where we've been.

That's why this subject is so packed with importance. So how about we do a quick recap of what we have discovered?

THE WORLD *BEFORE* THE FLOOD

In the first book of this series, *The Killing of Paradise Planet*, we explored our amazing planet Earth as it was originally.

Geology testifies to a once mild and uniform climate over the entire globe. There is reason to believe that this paradise world existed within the memory of the human race.

Most of the earth's surface was then land. There were no high mountains forming physical or climatic barriers. Ocean beds were relatively shallow.

There was luxuriance of vegetation, pole to pole. Plant and animal types were of greater variety than today. They were also more widely and evenly distributed – and of greater size and quality – than their modern descendants.

A water envelope surrounding the planet not only precluded winds, storms and rain, but also filtered out life-shortening cosmic rays.

Several factors favoured a much longer human life span. Indeed, while ancient records recall such longevity, modern science admits to its possibility.

Expansion over some two millennia may have produced a population comparable to our own, sufficiently large to cover the earth. With the incredible mental faculties of man at that time, tremendous scientific advances were made, advances that we can't even begin to imagine.

Yet the human race was sliding into spiritual bankruptcy. Corruption was widespread. Violence was exploding out of control. Mankind may have become totally extinct, had not supernatural power intervened.

Population explosion – a proliferation of science and technology – worsening corruption – exploding violence. Does that sound familiar?

Suddenly the great disaster struck. And I submit to you that this Great Flood was neither a man-made accident, nor an ordinary calamity. It appears to have been an intelligently directed event, in which vastly different natural agencies were suddenly orchestrated on a super-natural scale.

THE GREAT FLOOD ITSELF

This was not just a Flood, you see. It was a CATACLYSM!

In the second book of this series, *Surprise Witness,* we saw evidence that the earth's axis **was** tilted –**suddenly** – bringing terrific stresses upon the earth's surface, and total destruction.

Earthquakes tore the crust into gigantic fissures, to pour forth water, steam and molten rock.

As untold amounts of primary water broke free, they rushed out over the earth in a great swell. The sea began to overflow, sweeping inland, tearing away the land.

The breaking of the surface to a depth of several miles produced terrific strains and friction, which developed pent-up heat. Simultaneously, volcanoes burst out in America, Africa, the Pacific and everywhere else. With a roar, thirty thousand fiery columns spouted miles high into the sky. Lava also pushed upward from immense cracks in the crust. The volcanoes gave off vapour in quantities almost beyond comprehension, causing great rain on an unprecedented scale.

The sudden tilting of the planet's axis and the expulsion of jets of boiling water and of volcanic ash high above the atmosphere disrupted the vast amounts of invisible water in the canopy surrounding the planet. This outer canopy began to disintegrate, to collapse upon the earth. It poured down in such volume and force, the result was disastrous.

This was not a calm, monotonous rise of water. Colossal tidal waves surged over the planet. The winds, now of uncontrollable force, whipped them to enormous heights. Boulders of up to 18,000 tons were carried hundreds of miles. Some were hurled to levels 2,000 feet higher.

This was a Flood of global proportions. All the latent forces of nature – volcanoes, earthquakes, waves and hurricanes – were unleashed in a terrible alliance for a universal destruction. For a year, their continued action created power for destruction and transportation that is beyond human calculation. Erosion and sedimentation took place on a gigantic scale.

The Flood can explain many otherwise puzzling geological features of today's earth.

All over the world, the cataclysm uprooted trees and threw sand and rocks over animals which had gathered on mountains. Thousands of feet up, many were washed into crevices and held tight.

We have noted that on every continent, and in numerous places, are vast "fossil graveyards", where masses of creatures have been swept to a sudden death in their millions. These areas are packed with land and sea creatures from different habitats and even from different climatic regions – all **mixed and buried together in a completely unnatural way**.

For months longer, the storm raged. Unceasingly, in repeating 12 hour cycles, the mighty ebb and flow wore down the earth's surface and each wave returned with its debris. Travelling long distances under water, fast moving currents of suspended mud and sand spread out over thousands of square miles. The ebb and flow laid down successive strata, alternately burying land organisms and water creatures, to ultimately fossilise. As well as laying down strata, the Flood sorted debris into piles here and there.

THESE FOSSIL GRAVEYARDS SPEAK NOT OF SLOW EVOLUTIONARY DEVELOPMENT AND BURIAL, BUT OF A VIOLENT GLOBAL FLOOD.

Frequently, remains of whales and other **deep-sea** creatures are found far removed from the sea, mixed in with land animals, plants and trees.

Marine fossils are found on mountain tops hundreds of miles from any sea, or buried under clay, sand, gravel and other debris sometimes a mile deep.

Here is the shocking truth. Fossils in every part of the world testify not of evolution, but of a global Flood.

Only one force known to mankind is capable of accomplishing a sudden, wholesale destruction, followed by an immediate burial. That force is *water*.

In this global Deluge, not one inch of the planet's surface remained untouched. Man, his technology and all forms of life were buried together.

The significance of this is world-shaking!

This simply means that the entire evolutionary hypothesis, which appeals to the fossil record for its foundation evidence, is left stranded – with no evidence for evolution!

Not only that, but the evolutionary dating system is in utter *chaos*! We have provided startling *evidence* of so-called 1-million year old human beings mixed up with so-called 100-million year old dinosaurs and coal beds... and that's just for starters.

OUR WORLD SINCE THE GREAT FLOOD

Finally, in the present work, the third book of this series, we have examined the aftermath of the Great Flood event.

We saw that the Great Flood of 2345 BC was NOT the only cataclysm to occur in history. It was, however, the ONLY global event, in the sense that ALL inhabited land was destroyed and remoulded.

We have followed the re-establishing of human settlements, the sudden explosion of "instant" civilisations, as it were out of nowhere, and the expansion of mankind again over the earth.

And for centuries after the Great Flood, we see a still beautiful, but ruined world labouring to cope with the violent changes which have been introduced by the Great Disaster.

We see how mankind has been affected by these continuing changes.

Many hundreds of years would be required for our planet to settle down to relatively stable conditions following the Flood. Release

and adjustment of new stresses in the earth's crust continued. Results included:
- the final splitting up of the continental mass
- the sudden upthrust of the Andes, Himalayas and the Alps
- the sudden subsidence of some inhabited land masses
- a brief ice age
- the gradual raising of ocean levels and
- the drying out of inland water basins.

We have seen compelling evidence that all this has occurred within the brief time frame of less than 5,000 years.

On a diminished scale, these inter-related activities continue to play their dying notes today – although gradually, more settled conditions have become the norm.

A FINAL TURNING POINT

According to some prophecies to which we referred, for one brief end-time this comparative tranquillity in the forces of nature will be reversed.

Mankind will suddenly become anxious about "the sea and the waves roaring", food shortages, earthquakes, epidemics, global violence, corruption, the economy and "fearful sights in the sky."

Life on earth will, as before the Great Flood, reveal the clear signs of its coming extinction.

No future, UNLESS…

Unless there is again intervention from outside… as occurred at the Great Flood.

Another re-modelling of the whole planet… with this world of ours finally restored to its original, superb, pre-Flood condition, FOREVER!

If you want to know what that new world will be like, just go back to Book 1 of this series, *The Killing of Paradise Planet* – and re-read chapters 2 to 7.

Think it over. What lies ahead should thrill you!

SUMMARY

A DAMAGED PLANET When their survival vessel ran aground in November, 2344 BC, in the mountains of Turkey, the occupants recoiled in horror from the desolation that met their gaze. The world of almost perfect beauty which they had known was no more.

Stones, ledges and jagged rocks covered the ground. There was virtually no vegetation. Hills had disappeared without trace; plains had given way to broken mountain ranges. Gashed and torn, the surface was desolate. All the luxuriant forests were gone. Green meadows and flowering trees were washed away or buried.

Here and there clumps of growth had begun to re-establish, but the rich antediluvian world was largely plowed under, out of sight. The soil that remained was leached and relatively infertile. It would take centuries to rebuild enough soil to carpet large areas.

Later exploration would confirm new, harsh climatic zones.

POST-FLOOD EROSION Before plant cover would become re-established, erosion of unbelievable magnitude would occur on the planet.

As the waters of the global Flood rushed off the continental areas to fill the newly expanded sea basins, violent land movements resulted in massive buckling, folding and tilting of the soft, newly-laid Flood strata.

The enormous run-off of water rapidly eroded great gorges in the soft, exposed sediment.

With the new temperature differentials, violent winds beyond anything known today were whipped up. The soft land suffered incredible erosion during those weeks of continuing, wind-driven waves, while the Flood was abating. Some new mountains with their soft strata, were reduced to mere hogbacks within weeks.

THE CRADLE OF CIVILISATION Ararat, in eastern Turkey, was the stepping-stone between the former world and the new, post-Flood world. Here world civilisation was replanted. Here are found the earliest archaeological sites. And these show advanced technological knowledge.

RAPID MIGRATION   There is evidence that both human and animal migrations to the ends of the earth were undertaken rapidly.

Two early dispersions of people across the world have been identified and recorded:

- (a) from the Ararat region of Turkey: The dispersed population spoke one global language. Included among them were those who re-mapped the post-Flood world and who re-calculated the calendar.
- (b) (b) from the Babel region of Turkey: These spoke many different languages and carried with them the tradition of a tower where their language had become suddenly divided. They migrated with much original knowledge, which enabled the new civilisations of Egypt, Sumeria and Indus Valley to spring up suddenly "out of nowhere".

HIGH CIVILISATIONS AND PRIMITIVES   Among these family groups which dispersed over the earth, some developed into prosperous nations. Others, edged out more and more to the fringes, became more primitive through loss of availability of technology.

Broken communication lanes were later restored through the world trading explorations of the Phoenicians and others.

TRACING THEIR ANCESTRY   While many societies lost all trace and memory of their beginnings, and thus resorted to a mythical history, there were others who kept accurate and independent records of their descent from Noah and his three sons.

RAPID RACIAL VARIATIONS   Genetic evidence shows that all races, with their different features, could have descended in a very brief time from one family. There has been no evolution of genes that did not previously exist. All that has occurred is the recombination and degeneration of pre-existing genetic information. And the differences did not take countless ages to produce.

This is likewise true of animal species variation.

THE ICE AGE   In the aftermath of the Deluge, continuing volcanic activity, warm oceans and massive evaporation resulted in thickening clouds of dust, which blocked out the sun's heat. Atmospheric temperature dropped. Copious and rapid condensation of the vapours, instead of falling as rain, descended as snow.

Large quantities of stranded water filled all continental areas. Volcanic activity evaporated enormous quantities of water into steam clouds. It also provided dust, which blocked solar heat and lowered temperatures. The warm oceans and cold air caused heavy precipitation of snow and ice. Ice rapidly piled up on the land. This brought on the "Ice Age".

The evidence points to just one Ice Age, which lasted for several centuries.

GEOLOGICAL READJUSTMENTS   Many hundreds of years would be required for the planet to settle down to relatively stable conditions following the Deluge.

The new layers of rock and mountain, as well as rearranged land and sea, produced tensions. These needed to find release and adjustment. The result was continuing earthquakes and volcanic lava flows. There were some massive local catastrophes.

One short, violent burst of tectonic activity occurred soon after the Ice Age had begun. It was this violent upheaval that finally wrenched the continents apart and triggered sudden, violent mountain raising. The splitting of the continental mass also isolated various groups who had already migrated into the extremities.

In the post-Flood adjustments, changes in ocean levels, volcanism, earthquake activity, weather, the earth's wobble, and the human life span, were at first exponentially great. All of these eventually settled down to a more stable condition.

INLAND WATERS DRY OUT   At the termination of the Deluge, large inland bodies of water lay trapped as inland areas. In time, vegetation took hold and people moved in. Cities sprang up in these well watered areas.

But as these huge "Flood puddles" evaporated and the climate dried out, many of these regions became creeping deserts. This trend continues today. Civilisations also once thrived in areas that later reverted to jungle.

SEA LEVEL RISE For 4,000 years, the world's sea level has been inching up. This has been caused by (a) an influx of water into the sea from the melting of the post-Flood ice; and (b) the gradual evaporation or outflow of water from post-Flood basins to the sea.

DATING THE GREAT FLOOD There are ten "clocks" all of which indicate to us that something very big happened to this planet just over 4,000 years ago – and from which an adjustment process has been going on ever since.
- Recovery of the earth's axis
- Glacier growth and retreat
- Age of inland lakes
- River delta formation
- Age of waterfalls
- Coral reef growth
- Age of oldest trees
- Age of oldest desert
- Written human records
- Population increase

PROPHECIES Ancient prophecies warn that, as the Great Flood was a divine judgment on a world gone mad, so a second and final cleansing of Planet Earth is imminent, this time by fire. There will emerge a renewed planet in many respects similar to the original paradise world that mankind spoiled. But this one will last forever – not to be abused.

NOTES

Chapter 1 – NERVOUS WAIT

1. Genesis 7:18
2. Jonathan Gray, *Dead Men's Secrets, pp.15,16*
3. Ibid, pp. 258-259
4. Rene Noorbergen, *Secrets of the Lost Races*. London: New English Library, 1978, p.67
5. Ibid, pp.70-71
6. *Gilgamesh Epic,* lines 128-137, free translation
7. Genesis 8:4
8. Genesis 8:13
9. Ibid
10. Genesis 6:11
11. A tradition of the Ugha Mongulala tribe of Brazil. Karl Brugger, *The Chronicle of Akakor.* New York: Delacorte Press, 1977, p.42
12. Genesis 8:1
13. Harold T. Wilkins, *Mysteries of Ancient South America.* Secaucus, N.J.: Citadel Press, 1974, p.29
14. Wilkins, *Secret Cities of Old South America.* Kempton, Ill.: Adventurer Unlimited Press, 1998, p.388
15. C.H. Kang and Ethel R. Nelson, *The Discovery of Genesis*, St. Louis: Concordia Publishing House, 1979

Chapter 2 – WHAT HAPPENED TO THE WATER?

1. Genesis 7:24 to 8:1
2. Genesis 8:3
3. Genesis 8:1
4. A. Hallam, "Alfred Wegener and the Hypothesis of Continental Drift", *Continents Adrift and Continents Aground*. San Francisco: W.H. Freeman and Company, 1975, pp.8-17
5. S. Uyeda, *The New View of the Earth*. San Francisco: W.H. Freeman and Company, 1979
6. S. Carey, *The Expanding Earth*. Amsterdam: Elsevier, 1976, p.9
7. S. Carey, "The Necessity for Earth Expansion", in Carey, ed., *Expanding Earth Symposium*, University of Tasmania, 1983, pp.375-393
8. Ibid, p.383
9. David W. Unfred, "Flood and Post-Flood Geodynamics: An Expanded Earth Model", *Creation Research Society Quarterly*, Vol. 22, March 1986, pp.171-179
10. R. Brunnschweiler, "Evolution of Geotectonic Concepts in the Past Century", in Carey, ed., *Expanding Earth Symposium*, University of Tasmania, 1983, pp.9-15
11. International Series of Monographs in Natural Philosophy, vol.37, *The Expanding Earth: Some Consequences of Dirac's Gravitational Hypothesis*. Edited by G. Ter Haar and translated by A. Beer. Pergamon Press, 1971
12. V. Oppenheim, "Critique of Hypothesis of Continental Drift", *Bulletin of the American Association of Petroleum Geologists*, vol.56, pp.1354-1360, 1967
13. Carey, 1976, p.24
14. Ibid
15. G. Morton, "Creationism and Continental Drift", *Creation*

Research Society Quarterly, vol.18, pp.42-45

16 H. Owen, "Ocean Floor Spreading Evidence of Global Expansion", 1983. In Carey, S., ed., *Expanding Earth Symposium*, University of Tasmania, pp.31-58

17 J. Stocklin, "Himalayan Orogeny and Earth Expansion:, in Carey, ed., *Expanding Earth Symposium*, University of Tasmania, 1983, pp.119-130

18 p.43

19 G. Morton, "Creationism and Continental Drift", *Creation Research Society Quarterly*, vol.18, pp.42-45

20 Carey, 1976, pp.42-43

21 Ibid. p.43

22 M. Rickard, "The Polygonal Tesselations of the Earth's Crust and their Bearing on Continental Reconstructions", third *Gondwana Symposium*, Montevideo, 1967, pp.1-7

23 Carey, 1983, pp.375-393

24 D. Dailey and A. Stewart, *Problems of Ocean Water Accumulation On a Rapidly Expanding Earth*. In Carey, S. (ed.), *Expanding Earth Symposium*, University of Tasmania, pp.67-69

25 R. Morton, *Prolegomena to the Study of the Sediments*, Creation Research Society Quarterly, 1980, 17: 162-167

26 Morton, "Mountain Synthesis on an Expanding Earth", *Creation Research Society Quarterly*, vol.24, September, 1987, pp.53-61

27 "The Miracle of the Sea", *Reader's Digest*. Undated in my files

28 Kenneth K. Landes, "Illogical Geology", *Geotimes*, vol.III, no.6, March, 1959, p.19

29 Psalm 104:6

30 v.7

31 v.8

32 v.9

Chapter 3 – HURRICANE

1. *Evening Post*, Wellington, New Zealand
2. See Book 1 of this series, *The Killing of Paradise Planet*, Chapter 1
3. Immanuel Velikovsky, *Stargazers and Gravediggers*. New York: William Morrow and Company, Inc., 1983, p.93

Chapter 4 – MOUNTAINS OF SURPRISE

1. Moses Chorenensis, 1.4, sec.9-11
2. Charles Burney and David Lang, *The People of the Hills*, Weidenfeld & Nicolson, London, 1971, p.110
3. Burney and Lang, *The People of the Hills*, p.67
4. *Anatolian Studies* – Yearly Journal – The British Institute of Archaeology at Ankara
5. *The People of the Hills, p.54*
6. 2 Kings 25:13-17
7. Charles Burney and David Lang, *The People of the Hills*, Weidenfeld & Nicolson, London, 1971, p.44
8. *Prehistoric Investigations in Iraqi Kurdistan*
9. Zecharia Hitchen, *The Twelfth Planet*. Avon, New York, 1978, pp.6-7. Emphasis mine
10. Sitchen, Ibid
11. *The People of the Hills*, p.35
12. Gen. 6:21
13. Charles Burney and David Lang, *The People of the Hills*, Weidenfeld & Nicolson, London, 1971, p.4

14 *Ibid.,* p.10
15 Sitchen, p.414
16 Burney and Lang, *The People of the Hills*, pp.9,10
17 Gen.9:20
18 Gen.8:4

Chapter 5 – A SHOCKING DISCOVERY

1 M. Heun et al., "Site of Einkorn Wheat Domestication Identified by DNA Fingerprinting", *Science*, 278 (November 1997), pp.1212-14

2 Lugi Luca Cavalli-Sforza and Francesco Cavalli-Sforza, *The Great Human Diasporas: The History of Diversity and Evolution*, trans. Sarah Thorne, Reading (Mass.), Addison-Wesley, 1995, p.135

3 James Mellaart, *The Neolithic of the Near East*, London, Thames & Hudson, 1975, p.71

4 Ian Wilson, *Before the Flood*, p.93

5 Colin Renfrew, *Archaeology and Language*, London, Jonathan Cape, 1987, p.168

6 James Mellaart, *The Neolithic of the Near East*, London, Thames & Hudson, 1975, p.78

7 Ryan and Pitman, *Noah's Flood*, op.cit., p.180, after ibid.; also U. Esin, *"Asikli, Ten thousand Years Ago: A Habitation Model from Central Anatolia"* in *Housing and Settlement in Anatolia - a Historical Perspective*, Istanbul, Tarih Vakfi, 1996, pp.31-42

8 http://www.auckland.ac.nz/cir_newsevents/index.cfm?action=display_news&news_id=3393

9 Genesis 8:4

Chapter 6 – THE MARSUPIAL MYSTERY

1. Jonathan Gray, private files
2. *The Reader's Digest Great World Atlas*, p.125
3. *Maggies Farm,* No. 28, p.2
4. *Science*, vol 302, p.1934, December 12, 2003
5. *Surprise Witness*, pp. 186,187
6. A. Franklin Shull, *Evolution,* 2nd ed. New York: McGraw-Hill Book Company, Inc., 1951, p.60. One might note that Shull was an evolutionist
7. *The Weekend Australian*, January 23-24, 1993, p.10. *Sydney Morning Herald*, January 21, 1993, p.5
8. S.L. Pimm, "Rapid morphological change in an introduced bird," *Trends in Evolution and Ecology*, vol. 3, pp.290-291, 1988
9. P.R. Grant, "Natural Selection and Darwin's Finches", *Scientific American*, October, 1991, pp.60-65
10. Research paper emailed to Jonathan Gray, *"Rapid Adaptive Changes in Organisms After the Flood – Evidence of Creation"*
11. Ibid

Chapter 7 – INTO THE UNKNOWN

1. 2 yrs inclusive – Genesis 11:10
2. Book 1 of this series, *The Killing of Paradise Planet*, pp. 33,55-56
3. A.R.M. Lower, *Canadians in the Making, 1958, p.113*
4. Jonathan Gray, *Dead Men's Secrets*, chs.2,5
5. Genesis 11:1

6   Genesis 11:9
7   Nelson Glueck, *The River Jordan.* McGraw-Hill, 1968, pp.16,17
8   John Philip Cohane, *The Key.* New York: Crown Publishers, Inc., 1970
9   Ibid

Chapter 8 – ONE GLOBAL LANGUAGE

1   Jonathan Gray, *Dead Men's Secrets*, pp.34-41
2   Paul White, "Journey to Australia's Central Vortex", *Nexus* magazine, April-May 1993, p.34
3   see Chapter 17
4   Serge Hutin, *Alien Races and Fantastic Civilisations.* New York: Berkley Publishing corporation, 1970, pp.38-39
5   Genesis 11:1
6   Hugh A. Moran and David H. Kelley, "The Alphabet and the Ancient Calendar Signs", *Daily Press*, Palo Alto, 1969, pp.4-11
7   Gustavus Seyffarth, *The Literary Life of Gustavus Seyffarth.* New York: E. Steiger and Co., 1886, pp.53,54
8   Moran and Kelley, pp.xiv-xviii
9   *Encyclopaedia Britannica*, 11th ed., vol.28, pp.995-997
10 Moran and Kelley, pp.xi-xii

Chapter 9 – PYRAMID AND STONEHENGE MYSTERIES SOLVED

1   Isa.13:13
2   Gerald Hawkins, *Stonehenge Decoded.* Souvenir Press, 1966

Chapter 10 – THE NIMROD CONSPIRACY

1. Ex.23:29
2. Gen.10:8,9
3. Gen.11:2
4. Dan.1:2
5. Genesis 11:1-4
6. Gen.11:3
7. Gen.11:4
8. Gen.9:1
9. Gen.11:6
10. See our book, *Dead Men's Secrets*
11. Gen.11:7-9

Chapter 11 – LANGUAGES AND THE DISPERSION

1. "*Legends of the World*", edited by Richard Cavendish, 1989, p.137
2. *The New Learned History Encyclopaedia*, 1922, col VIII, p.6,743
3. "*The Tree of Culture*", Ralph Linton, 1955, p.314
4. Genesis.10:31
5. Henry Hiebert, *Evolution: Its Collapse in View?* Beaverlodge, Alberta: Horizon House Publishers, 1979, p.63
6. "*Encyclopaedia Brittanica*", 15th ed., Macrop., vol.19, p.1033
7. Suzette H. Elgin, *What is Linguistics*. Englewood Cliffs, NJ: Prentice-Hall Inc., 1973
8. Robert T. Boyd, *Tells, Tombs and Treasures. A Pictorial Guide to Biblical Archaeology*. Grand Rapids, MI: Baker Book House, 1969
9. "*The Sumerians*", S.N. Kramer, 1970, pp.284-5

10   *Larousse World Mythology,* 1965, p.58
11   *"The Pentateuch in its Cultural Environment"*, G.H. Livingstone, 1974, p.144
12   v.11,12
13   http://www.archaeologyanswers.com/egyptgods.html
14   Donovan Courville, *The Exodus Problem.* Loma Linda, Ca.: Challenge Books, 1971
15   Norman Hammond, *Ancient Maya Civilization.* Cambridge, U.K.: Cambridge University Press, 1982, pp.92,93

Chapter 12 – THE MIGRATION BEGINS

1   Raci Temizer, *"Museum of Anatolian Civilizations"*, 1969, p.52
2   Burney & Lang, *The People of the Hills*, Weidenfeld and Nicolson, London, 1971, p.21
3   Raci Temizer, *"Museum of Anatolian Civilizations"*, 1969, p.18
4   W. F. Albright, *Recent Discoveries in Bible Lands.* New York: Funk and Wagnalls Co., 1955, p.4
5   Genesis 9:19
6   chapter 10
7   ch. 10:32

Chapter 13 – THE MAJOR CIVILISATIONS AFTER BABEL

1   Marcel Brion, *The World of Archaeology*, 2 Vols. MacMillan Co., 1959, Vol. 1, pp.97-98
2   Brion, Vol 1, p.113
3   James Mellaart, *Earliest Civilizations of the Near East.* Thames and Hudson, London, 1965, p.107

4 Jean-Philippe Lauer, *Saqqara*, p.99

5 Zecharia Sitchen, *The Twelfth Planet*, p.49

Chapter 14 – SKYSCRAPER TO "STONE AGE"

1 See what the fossil evidence reveals in Book 2 of this series, *Surprise Witness*, chapters 11 to 18

2 Henry Field, "The Cradle of Homo Sapiens," *American Journal of Archaeology*, Oct-Dec, 1932, p.427

3 Griffith Taylor, *Environment, Race and Migration. University of Toronto*, 1945, p.8

4 Ibid., pp. 120,121

5 Kenneth Macgowan, *Early Man in the New World*. Macmillan, 1950, p.3 and map on p.4

6 Alfred Kidder, *Appraisal of Anthropology Today*. University of Chicago Press, 1953, p.46

7 *Dead Men's Secrets*, pp.278-304

8 Ibid., pp.10,11

9 H.A. Bancroft, *The Works of Hubert Howe Bancroft; The Native Races.* San Francisco: A.L. Bancroft and Company, 1883, vol.III, pp.451-453, vol V, pp.27,28

10 Pierre Honore, *In Quest of the White God.* London: Hutchinson and Co. Ltd., 1963, p.165 (trans. from the German by Oliver Coburn and Ursula Lehrburter

Chapter 15 – AN ASTONISHING PROPHECY COMES TRUE

1. Genesis 10:24-27

Chapter 16 - ROYAL FAMILIES TRACE BACK TO NOAH'S SON

1. Flavius Josephus, *Against Apion*. From *Josephus's Complete Works*. Tr. William Whiston. Pickering and Inglis, 1981, pp.607-636
2. *Institutes of Menu*, 1280 BC; J.H. Titcomb, "Ethnic Testimonies to the Pentateuch", *Trans. Victorian Institute*, 6, 1872:249-253
3. Aristophanes, *The Clouds*. Roger's Trans., line 998); John Skinner, *A Critical and Exegetical Commentary on Genesis*. Edinburgh: T. and T. Clark, 1930, p.196
4. Transl. by Edgar Truax of the oral traditions of the Miautso. Bill Cooper, *After the Flood*. Chichester, UK.: New Wine Press, 1995, pp.243-246
5. Bill Cooper, *After the Flood*. Chichester: New Wine Press, 1995
6. *Reliq. Antiq.*, p.173
7. Genesis 10:1,2
8. M.F. Cusack, *The Illustrated History of Ireland*. 1868. Published in facsimile by Bracken Books, London, 1987
9. John Mackay, *Ex Nihilo*, vol.6, no.4, May, 1984. Emphasis added
10. William C. Boyd (Professor of Immunochemistry at Boston School of Medicine), *Genetics and the Races of Men*. Blackwell's Scientific Publications, 1950, p.200 ff
11. Jonathan Gray, *Dead Men's Secrets*, pp.16-19. http:www.archaeologyanswers.com

Chapter 17 – SHIVER ALL SUMMER

1. R.W. Williamson, *Religious and Cosmic Beliefs of Central Polynesia*, 1933, Vol.1, p.41
2. Roman Black, "The Story of the Boomerang," *Old and New*

Australian Aboriginal Art

3   Velikovsky, *Worlds in Collision*, p.131
4   R.A. Daly, *The Changing World of the Ice Age*. 1934, p.16
5   Charles H. Hapgood. "The Earth's Shifting Crust", *Saturday Evening Post*, Jan. 10, 1959
6   John Tyndall, *Heat Considered as a Mode of Motion*. 1883, pp.191-192
7   D. Manzel, *Our Sun*. 1950, p.248
8   Tyndall, pp.188-189
9   Immanuel Velikovsky, *Earth in Upheaval*. London: Sphere Books Ltd., 1978, p.121
10 L. Don Leet, *Encyclopedia Americana*, vol.28, art. "Volcano", 1983 ed.
11 *Dead Men's Secrets*, pp.24-27
12 Francis Maziere, *Mysteries of Easter Island*. New York: Tower Publications, Inc., 1965
13 J.F. Lindsay, "Carboniferous Subaqueous Mass-movement in the Manning-Macleay Basin, Kempsey, New South Wales", *Journal of Sedimentary Petrology*, vol.36, pp.719-732, 1966
14 John C. Whitcomb and Henry M. Morris, *The Genesis Flood*. Phillipsburg, New Jersey: Presbyterian and Reformed Publishing Co., 1961, pp.247-249,292-310
15 Willard F. Libby, *Radiocarbon Dating*. 1955, p.148
16 "Evidence for an Abrupt Change in Climate Close to 11,000 Years Ago", *American Journal of Science,* vol.258, June 1960, pp.441,429
17 Velikovsky, *Worlds in Collision*. London: Sphere Books Ltd., 1978, pp.40-41 (emphasis added)
18 C.H. Hapsgood, in an article in *Saturday Evening Post*, 1959. Cited by Richard Mooney, *Colony: Earth*. London: Souvenir Press Ltd., 1974, p.91
19 Jonathan Gray, *Dead Men's Secrets*, pp.24-30

20 Velikovsky, *Earth in Upheaval*. Chapter entitled *"Thirty-five Centuries Ago"*
21 *Miracle in Stone*, pp.203-206
22 Job 38:29,30
23 The Irish *Annals of Clonmacnoise*, tr. into English in 1627 by Connell Mageoghagan. Dublin: University Press, 1896, Murphy ed., pp.13,15

Chapter 18 – HUMAN LIFE-SPAN SLASHED

1 Genesis 10:25
2 Josh.10:13; 2 Sam.1:18
3 *The Book of Jasher*. New York: M.M. Noah and A.S. Gould, 1840. Transl. c.1830, ch.7 v.19 (emphasis supplied)
4 L. Hissink, 1993. "Euhemerism and aboriginal myths." Letter to the Editor, *The Australian Geologist*, No. 86, pp.6-7
5 Other such chronicles appear in *The Myths of the American Indians*, by L. Spence, 1916. G.G. Hurrup Co., London
6 David Fasold, *The Rediscovery of Noah's Ark*. U.K.: Sidgwick and Jackson, 1990, p.54
7 http://www.archaeologyanswers.com/giants.html
8 Eduard Suess, *The Face of the Earth*. 1904, I, pp.17-18
9 Immanual Velikovsky, *Earth in Upheaval*. London: Sphere Books, Ltd., 1978, p.172
10 Ibid., p.156
11 Suess, pp.17ff

Chapter 19 – THE MUMMY ROSE FROM THE SEA

1   Bailey Willis, *Research in Asia*. II, p.24
2   J.S. Lee, *The Geology of China*. London: 1939, p.207 (Emphasis supplied)
3   Arnold Heim and August Gousser, *The Throne of the Gods, An Account of the First Swiss Expedition to the Himalayas*. 1939, p.218
4   Velikovsky, *Earth in Upheaval*, p.76 (Emphasis supplied)
5   Fawcett, *Exploration Fawcett: The Travel Diaries and Notes of Colonel H.P. Fawcett*. Edited by B. Fawcett, London, 1953
6   Karl Brugger, *The Chronicle of Akakor*. NYC: Delacourte Press, 1977
7   Velikovsky, *Worlds in Collision*. London: Sphere Books, Ltd., 1978, p.102
8   *Star* newspaper, Kuala Lumpur, January. 13, 2005, quoting a report in the shipping journal *Portsworld*
9   Brooks, *Climate Through the Ages* (9th ed.) p.28
10. J. Ghiold, "The Sponges that spanned Europe", *New Scientist*, February 2, 1991, p.38
11 H.H. Read and J. Watson, *Earth History – Part II*. McMillan, 1985, p.38

Chapter 20 – TRAPPED

1   Genesis 10:1,6
2   Wilkinson, *Egyptians*, vol.1, p.89
3   *Herodotus, lib.ii, cap.4*
4   Harold T. Wilkins, *Secret Cities of Old South America*. Kempton, Ill.: Adventures Unlimited Press, 1998, p.427
5   Hansen, *The Ancient Atlantic*. Amherst, Wi.: Amherst Press, 1969
6   Ibid
7   Ibid

8 Uwe George, *In the Deserts of This Earth.* Trans. From the German by Richard and Clara Winston. London: Hamish Hamilton Ltd., 1978, pp.29-30

9 Strahlenberg, *Das Nord und Ostliche Theil von Europa und Asien.* Stockholm, 1730

10 Henning Haslund, *Men and Gods in Mongolia.* London: Kegan Paul, 1935, p.176

11 Eric Norman, *Gods, Demons and UFOs.* New York: Lancer Books

12 Baron Friedrich Alexander Humboldt, *Views of Nature,* Bd. 1

13 Harold T. Wilkins, *Mysteries of Ancient South America.* Kempton, Ill.: Adventures Unlimited Press, 1947, p.139

14 Harold T. Wilkins, *Secret Cities of Old South America.* Kempton, Ill.: Adventures Unlimited Press, 1998, p.25

15 Ivan T. Sanderson, *Abominable Snowmen: legend come to life, the story of subhumans on five continents from the early ice age until today.* Radnor: Chilton Book Company, 1961

16 James Churchward, *The Children of Mu.* New York: Ives Washburn, 1956, p.80

17 George McCready Price, *Geological Ages Hoax.* Chicago: Fleming H. Revell Co., 1931, pp.28ff

18 David Hatcher Childress, *"Archaeological Cover-Ups?", Nexus Magazine,* April-May 1993, pp.36-39

19 *Ancient Secret of The Flower of Life*, Vol. II, p. 302

Chapter 21 – SECRETS OF A LOST CITY

1 See my book *Dead Men's Secrets,* pp.130,131,178

2 Harold T. Wilkins, *Mysteries of Ancient South America.* Secaucus, N.J.: Citadel press, 1974

3 See my book, *Dead Men's Secrets,* pp.77-98

4   Harold T. Wilkins, *Mysteries of Ancient South America*. Kempton, Ill.: Adventures Unlimited Press, 1947, pp.144-148

5   Jonathan Gray, *Ark of the Covenant*, pp.98-109

6   Associated Press, July 7, 1985

7   David Hatcher Childress, *Lost Cities of North and Central America*. Stele, Ill.: Adventures Unlimited Press, 1993, p.102

8   See *Dead Men's Secrets,* pp.336,337,342

9   Brad Steiger, *Mysteries of Time and Space*. Englewood Cliffs, N.J.: Prentice-Hall, Inc., 1974, pp.52,53

10 L.Taylor Hanson, *He Walked The Americas*. Amherst, Wisconsin: Amherst Press, 1964, p.70

11 *Ibid.,* 48,69,78,82

12 Basil Davidson, *The Lost Cities of Africa*. Boston: Atlantic-Little, Brown Co., 1959

13 *The Killing of Paradise Planet,* Chapter 14 – "Dating Shock" and Chapter 15 – "The Cover Up"

14 *Surprise Witness*, Chapters 9 to 18

Chapter 22 – THE LOST SQUADRON

1   www.thelostsquadron.com Phone 606 248 1149

2   See *Scientific American*, February 1998, p.82

3   R.F. Flint, *Glacial Geology and the Pleistocene Epoch*, p.491

4   Immanual Velikovsky, *Earth in Upheaval*. London: Sphere Books, Ltd., 1978, p.143

5   "The Big Thaw", *Panorama Inflight Magazine*

6   Charles Arthur, in an article in *The Independent*, U.K., June 8, 1999

7   Velikovsky, pp.148-150

8   Warren Upham, *The Glacial Lake Agassiz*. 1895, p.240

9   Ibid., p.239
10 Velikovsky, p.145
11 Flint, p.382
12 Velikovsky, p.176
13 Scientist Peter Isdale of A.I.M.S. reported his findings in *Nature*, vol.310, 16 August, 1984, pp.578-579. Also reported in *Creation Ex Nihilo*, November, 1985, pp.6-9
14 Edmund Schulmann, "Longevity Under Adversity in Conifers", *Science*, vol.119, March 26, 1934, p.399
15 Schulmann, "Bristlecone Pine, Oldest Living Thing", *National Geographic*, vol.113, March, 1958, p.355
16 John C. Whitcomb and Henry M. Morris, *The Genesis Flood*. Phillipsburg, New Jersey: Presbyterian and Reformed Publishing Co., 1986, p.393
17 Clifford Wilson, *The Chariots Still Crash*. Old Tappan, N.J.: Fleming H. Revell and Co., 1976, pp.53,54
18 (Potsdam Institute for Climate Research, in Germany, July 15, 1999. *Geophysical Research Letters*)

Chapter 23 – PUBLISH – IF YOU DARE

1   Charles V. Taylor, *Creation Ex Nihilo*, September-November, 1987, p.9
2   Ibid
3   W.B. Emery, *Archaic Egypt*. Penguin Books Reprint, 1984, p.59
4   Martin Anstey, *The Romance of Bible Chronology*. London: Marshall Brothers Ltd., 1913, p.107
5   Ibid, p.95
6   D. Davidson and H. Aldersmith, *The Great Pyramid: Its Divine Message*. London: Williams and Norgate, Ltd., vol. I, 1936, p.215.

Joseph H. Seiss, *The Great Pyramid: A Miracle in Stone.* New York: Harper and Row, 1973, pp. 83-85. Seiss gives the year 2170 B.C

7   Immanuel Velikovsky, *Worlds in Collision.* London: Sphere Books, Ltd., 1978, pp. 371-372

8   Davidson and Aldersmith, pp.438,439

9   Anstey, p.103

10   Ibid., p.92

Chapter 24 – A DEADLY PRACTICAL JOKE

1   J.V. Trumbull, John Lyman, J.F. Pepper and E.M. Thompson, *"An Introduction to the Geology and Mineral resources of the Continental Shelves of the Americas", U.S. Geological Survey Bulletin 1067,* 1958, p.11

2   *Australasian Post,* January 30, 1986

3   Jurgen Spanuth, *Atlantis of the North.* New York: Van Nostrand Reinhold Co., 1979

4   Brown, *The Riddle of the Pacific.* Auckland, 1924

5   Robert Suggs, *The Hidden Worlds of Polynesia.* NYC.: Harcourt Brace, 1962

6   Francis Maziere, *Mysteries of Easter Island.* NYC.: W.W. Norton, 1968

7   David Hatcher Childress, *Lost Cities of Ancient Lumeria and the Pacific.* Stelle, Ill.: Adventures Unlimited Press, 1988, p.293

8   David Hatcher Childress, *Ancient Tonga and the Lost City of Mu'a.* Stelle, Ill.: Adventures Unlimited Press, 1996

9   Charles Berlitz, *Atlantis.* Glasgow:William Collins Sons & Co. Ltd., 1984, p.101

10   Ibid., pp.104ff

Chapter 25 – A "SECRET" REPORT ON OUR FUTURE

1. Luke 21:25,26
2. http://www.tmgnow.com
3. Ibid
4. Matthew 24:6,7
5. Revelation chapters 13 and 17
6. Revelation 18
7. Revelation 8:7-10
8. Simon Mitton, "House-sized asteroids home in on the Earth", *New Scientist*, October 31, 1992, p. 16
9. ***New Scientist*, June 6, 1992, pp.12-13**
10. Matthew 24:7; Luke 21:25,26; Daniel 12:1
11. Matthew 24:21-22
12. Luke 21:11,25,26
13. Associated Newspapers Ltd
14. Revelation 16:18,19
15. v.20; also Jeremiah 4:23-26
16. Revelation 1:7; 6:14-17
17. Jeremiah 25:33; Isaiah 26:21
18. Isaiah 26:20,21; 25:9; Acts 4:12
19. Daniel 12:1; Matthew 24:21,22; Isaiah 33:16
20. Luke 21:24-36
21. Psalm 91

INDEX

Aborigines 80,109,154,162,168,175,202
Africa 43,136-139,176,197-199,224,246,247

Age span of:
- Antarctic ice 167-168,170-171,226-228
- Amazon jungle 204-205
- Axis recovery 235
- Babel dispersion 112-113,152
- China 242
- Coral reefs 232
- Deltas 231
- Deserts 37,234
- Egypt 73,236-241
- Glaciers 228-230
- Grand Canyon 208-211
- Great Flood 111
- History, pegged to Egypt 239
- Ice age 80,161-172,228-229
- Inland lakes 230-231
- Languages 111-112
- Migration, time taken for 140
- Mississippi delta 231
- Mountain chains 183-188
- Nations, pegged to Egypt 239
- Niagara Falls 232
- Population growth 242-243
- Recorded history 236-242
- Sahara desert 234
- Sumeria 242
- Trees (oldest) 233-234
- Waterfalls 232
- World history, pegged to Egypt 239

Agriculture, began in mountains 51-52,54-55
Alaska 35,166,231,245
Alphabet 82-83
Amazon 204-206,214-221
America 81, 139
- Central 207,221-222,258-261
- North 38-41,189-190,207-213,222-223,230-231,258,264,266,267,272
- South 43,140,161-162,184,204-207,214-221,258

Andes mountains 184-185,205-206
Animal distribution 64-69
Antarctic 29,80-81,168,170-171,270
Antedeluvian world 277-278
Ararat region
- inscriptions, ruins 45
- cradle of civilisation 46-55,73

Araxes valley 48,50,51,95,104
Ark
- amenities 10-11
- grounded 12-14,52,268
- site findings 47,50

Art 118,129-132
Asia 138-139,194
Asikli 58,93
Asteroids 269-270
Astronomy, dating by 241-242
Atlantic 43,189-192,215,250-251,272-273
Australia 43,64-65,77,79-80,139,203-204,232
Axis tilted 88,235,278
Axis recovery 235

Babel, tower of 98-102,112,147,266,268
Babylonian tablets, not older than Genesis 119-123
Biblical version of history
- antiquity of 119-123
- reliable 61,106,119,123,128,132,150-152,154,175,240
- superiority of 132

Black Sea 248-249
Boats
- in deserts 198,212

Book of Genesis
- antiquity of 119-123
- reliable 61,106,119,123,128,132,150-152,154,175,240
- superiority of 132

Books, ancient 11-12,218

Calendar 84-90

Canyons 36,39,41,42,208-211
- undersea 247
Caribbean Sea 259-261
Caucasoids, see Indo-Europeans
Cave men, see Primitive men
Central America, see America, Central
China 84,90,150-151,178,184,185,195,200,242,257
Circle, degrees in 84,90
Cities
- ancient ruins 214-224
- drowned 245-263
Civilisations
- origin of 61-62
- earliest post-Flood 10,46,124-133
- later, how destroyed 10,29,128,217
Civilised origins 49
Climate, pre-Flood 168
Climate change 168,192-194,265-266
Comets 269-270
Continental shelf 23,246-247,258
Continents
- once joined 22-24
- separated 24-33,112-113,173-175,273
Coral reefs 234
Cracks in earth 208
Cradle of mankind 45-61,136-139

Darwin, Charles 42,68
Dating of:
- Antarctic ice 167-168,170-171,226-228
- Amazon jungle 204-205
- Art and script 61-62
- Axis recovery 235
- Babel dispersion 111-112,152
- Cave art and script 61-62
- China 242
- Coral reefs 232
- Deltas 231

309

- Deserts 37,234
- Egypt 73,236-242
- Glaciers 228-230
- Grand Canyon 208-211
- Great Flood 111
- Ice age 80,161-172,228-229
- Inland lakes 230-231
- Languages 111-112
- Migration, time taken for 140
- Mississippi delta 231
- Mountain chains 183-188
- Nations, pegged to Egypt 239
- Niagara Falls 232
- Polar shift 235
- Population growth 242-243
- Recorded history 236-242
- Sahara desert 234
- Script and cave art 61-62
- Sumeria 242
- Trees (oldest) 233-234
- Waterfalls 232
- World history, pegged to Egypt 239

Dating methods 225,241-242
- assumptions 100
- hopelessly in error 100,115,117-118

Death Valley 211-212
Degeneration 138-141,215,217-218,222,223,224,255
Deliverer prophesied 118,146,275
Deltas 231
Deserts 37,42-43,197-202,207,211-213,234
Diary of Flood 11,12,14

Dispersals, two 74-75
- first from Ararat 73,75-91,96
- second from Babel 74,92-143
- animal 64-69

DNA (see also Genetics) 57,69
Domestication

- of animals 58
- of plants 52-54,57

Drowned land 245-250,257-263
Drowned cities 245-263

Earth expansion, see Expansion
Earth movements, vertical 183-192
Earthquakes 179-181,188-189,265,275,279
Egypt 10,73,84-86,98,109-110,128-130,180,195-197,231,236-241
Eight Flood survivors 18-19,95
Erosion 35-42
Europe 121,139,151-154,172,180,230,247,252,266-267
Evolution
- not compatible with worldwide Flood 163,280
- no evolution of civilisation 114-115
- language disproves 107

Expansion of earth 26-33,176
"Experts", skepticism of, see Skepticism

Famines 264-266
Finches 68-69
First Tongue 76-82
Flood:
- and Egypt 195-196,236-241
- traditions of 12,15,16-19
- events of 278-280
- chronology of 14
- human interest description 9-10,12-15
- aftermath (human interest description) 20,45,71
- water of Flood, source of 31
- water recedes 20-33
- water of Flood, where it went 20-33
- not an accident 268,273-274
- evidence for 278-280
- reason for 16,273-274
- the world before, See Antedeluvian world
- events since, summarised 280-281

Fossils, post-Flood 64-67

Galapagos Islands 68
Genesis book , antiquity of 119-123
Genesis Flood record
- superior to others 149
Genetics 57,67-69,136-137,154-160
Giants 179
Glaciers 167,228-230
Gods, pagan origin of 94-96,110,118
Grand Canyon 39,208-211
Great Pyramid 85-86,238,241
Greenland 226-228,250

Ham 94,142,144,148,150-151,195
Himalayan mountains 28,184
Historical records confirm Genesis 150-154
History
- foretold, see Prophecies
- a plan to 267-268,274

Ice Age 80,161-172,229
Ice growth rings 226-228
Ice versus water action 16
India 150,201-202,253,257
Indian Ocean 43,253-254
Indians
    - Central American 222
    - North American 142,175,222-223
    - South American 205,216-218,221,224
Indo-Europeans 144
Indus valley 125-128
Inland seas 195-213

Japheth 143,144,146-148,150-154
Jasher, book of 53,111,174-175
Jerusalem 123,276

Kangaroos 64-65

Lakes, see Seas, inland
Languages
- dating of 111-112
- originally one 76-82,98,146-148
- not evolved 106-107
- origin of 59-61,146-148
- divided 101,104-106,108-109

Legends
- the Flood 12,15-19
- eight survivors 18-19
- rainbow 16-18
- name Noah 19
- three sons of Noah 150-151
- tower of Babel 108-109,142
- language confusion 108-109,142
- continental splitting 174-175
- sky hanging low 161-162
- Antarctic ice cover 80
- mountains uplifted 187-188

Life span, see Longevity
Longevity, loss of 72
Lost cities, see Cities

Magnetic reversals, see book 1, pp.163-164
Mammoths 194
Maps, ancient 80,171,197,206,245,247-248
Marsupials 64-66
Mediterranean 121,180-181,248-250
Medzamor 48-50,59
Menes 195,241
Mesas 39
Messiah, see Deliverer
Metallurgy 47-51,59,61
Meteorites 270
Migration, see Dispersals
Missing links 136

Mississippi 167,231
Mizraim 195,241
Mongoloids 144
Moon 87-90
Mountains
- covered by the Flood 31
- cradle of culture 51-52,54-55
- uplifting of 183-191,205-206

Nakhichevan 50
Nations, origin of 45-61,136-140,144-147,154-160
Nations, Table of 72,105-106,119-123,151
Neanderthals 159-160
Negroids 144
New World Order 266-267
Niagara Falls 34,231-232
Nimrod 92,94,96,101,109,110
Noah
- name in legends 19
- historical records link to his sons 46,150-154
Noah's Ark 10-15,20,47,50
North America, see America, North

Ocean
- age of 21-23
Ocean bed 21-22
Oil 98-99
Ophir 220
Orbit, earth 85-86
Origin location for:
- agriculture 51-52,54-55,57
- alphabet 82-83
- canyons 39,41,42,208-211
- civilisation, first after Flood 46,124-133
- civilisations post-Babel 129-132
- domestication of animals 58
- domestication of plants 57
- languages 59-61,146-148

- metallurgy 47-51,59,61,116
- paganism 94-96,99,118
- pottery 59-60
- primitive cultures 138-141
- races 136-137
- town planning 59
- woven textiles 57,58

Origin of
- Egypt 129-132
- Indus Valley 128,131-132
- Sumeria 130-132

Pacific 43,83,188,205,254-258
Paganism, origin of 94-96,99,118
Peleg 111,123,173-174,177,178
Petrolglyphs 76-80
Phoenicians 142,202-203
Plan to history 267-268,274
Plants
- distribution 63
- domestication 52-54,57

Plate tectonics 25-26,30-31
Polar shift 235 (for alleged magnetic reversals, see book 1, pp.163-164)
Poles, position of 28,88,235,269
Polynesians 143,145,257
Population 71-73,132-133
Post-Flood settling down upheavals 173
Pottery 58-59,129
Primitive men 138-141
Prophecies 144-146,264-276,281
Pyramid, Great 85-86,238,241
Pyramids 214,222,251,255,256

Races, origin of 136-138,154-160
Rainbow 16-18
Religion
- earliest 78,148

- corrupted 94-96,99,118
Reefs 194
Rings, growth
- in ice 226-228
- in trees 234
River terraces 40
River deltas 231

Sahara 36,196-199,234
Scientific prejudice 24-25,28,59,216-217
Sea level
- dropped 43-44,176
- risen 245-265

Seas, inland 195-213
Second Coming 266,269,274-276
Sediments on seabed 21-22
Semites 142-143,146-148
Shelf, continental 23,246-247,258
Shem 142-144,146-148,150-151
Shinar 97-98,109
Shorelines, raised 43,44
Siberia 163,204,245
Skepticism of some "experts" 24-25,28,59,216-217
Sodom and Gomorrah 122
Solomon, King 142,220
South America, see America, South
Species development, speed of 68-69,154-158
Sphinx 196
Stars 88,162,175
St. Helens, Mount 42
Stone Age man, see Stone cultures
Stone cultures 134-141
Stonehenge 84-91
Stone-writers 76-80
Sudden appearance of
- Egypt 129-130
- Indus Valley 128

- Sumeria 130-131
Sudden dropping of ocean bed 183-192
Sumeria 130-133,242
Sumerian writings 55,81,108,195
Sun 16,87-90,96,162,163,175
Survey, global 79-80,96

Table of Nations 72,105-106,119-123,151
Technology, advanced 10,47-50,114,116-117,126-129,142,171,216
Textiles, woven, the first 57,58
Tiahuanaco 161,186-187,206
Tidal wave, see Tsunami
Tower of Babel, see Babel
Traditions, see Legends
Tree rings 234
Tsunami 190
Tunnels 198
Turkey, cradle of man 45-61

Variations within species 68-69,154-158
Vatican 267
Volcanism 164-167,181-182
- caused ice age 164-167
Votan 142

War 266
Water
- power of (see also Waves) 41,42
- where to after Flood 20-33

Waterfalls (see also Niagara Falls)
- dry 41
- undersea 34
Waves, height of 190
Wind
- erosion by 35-37
- power of 37-38
Writing 74-83,105,107,218-219,223

Writings, see Books

Year length changed 84-90
Yellowstone 270-271

Zodiac 83

FRAME NOT INCLUDED

"The Invitation" – A fine art print by Elfred Lee

THOUSANDS OF YEARS AGO OUR ANCESTORS MADE ONE LAST DECISION...

WHO WOULD ACCEPT THE INVITATION?

"ON AN EXPEDITION IN 1969, ON A TREELESS MOUNTAIN THE BIBLE NAMES AS THE RESTING PLACE OF NOAH'S ARK, WE UNEARTHED 5,000-YEAR-OLD WOOD, MAKING ME REALIZE THE STORY WAS TRUE. THIS ALMOST MYSTICAL EXPERIENCE COMPELLED ME TO PAINT 'THE INVITATION'."
– ELFRED LEE

SAVE UP TO $320
USE PROMO CODE
BCB005
LITHOGRAPHS
STARTING AT $99
WWW.LOSTWORLDMUSEUM.COM

FINE ART PRINT   **CANVAS LITHO**

Limited edition – Order yours today.

LOST WORLD MUSEUM

WWW.LOSTWORLDMUSEUM.COM
ORDER TOLL FREE: 1-866-593-3010

We invite you to view the complete
selection of titles we publish at:

www.TEACHServices.com

or write or email us your praises,
reactions, or thoughts about this
or any other book we publish at:

TEACH Services, Inc.
P.O. Box 954
Ringgold, GA 30736

info@TEACHServices.com

Finally, if you are interested in seeing
your own book in print, please contact us at

publishing@teachservices.com.

We would be happy to review your manuscript for free.

www.ingramcontent.com/pod-product-compliance
Lightning Source LLC
Chambersburg PA
CBHW071654160426
43195CB00012B/1464